"The People's Book of Human Sexuality: Ex [...] compelling narrative and strategy for [...] and engaging in inclusive conversations. This literary collective will be used by sexuality and wellness educators for years to come."

—**James C. Wadley, PhD, CST-S**, *Director of Sex Therapy Program*
Council for Relationships (Philadelphia, USA)

"Astounding and comprehensive, *The People's Book of Human Sexuality: Expanding the Sexology Archive* explores human sexuality deeply rooted in justice and with stunning range. Centering seasoned and community-driven voices, this text is a stellar composition on humanity and our radical needs as we evolve."

—**Kay Ulanday Barrett**, *Writer; Cultural Strategist;*
Poet of More Than Organs, A 2021 Stonewall Honor Award Book +
2021 Lambda Literary Finalist

"This book is timely & necessary! Centering the voices, experiences and wisdom of folx who do the critical work in community with people every single day is important. We deserve to be seen and heard and this book is a wonderful reflection and resource for those who keep pushing us and our profession forward."

—**Mariotta Gary-Smith, MPH, CSE**, *Co-Foundress, WoCSHN*
(Women of Color Sexual Health Network)

"It's about time there was an inclusive interdisciplinary sexuality textbook! This text will not only serve folks in marginalized populations and identities, but also those who work in sexuality studies and on the front lines. As we seek to build a just future for all, this text will help shift the culture."

—**Aiesha Turman, PhD**, *Interdisciplinary Scholar and*
Founder, The Black Girl Project

"As a Black queer person who came into the field of sexuality education over 10 years ago, there has always been a gap in information on sexuality and the lives of BIPOC folks, at minimum our lives are seen as an afterthought. This book continues to pave new ways for sexuality practitioners and all people, to see themselves through an affirming lens for healing and growth."

—**Dr. Shanéa Thomas, LICSW** (he/she/Dr.), LGBTQ+ Training
Specialist and Assistant Clinical Research; Professor at University of
Maryland (College Park)/School of Public Health/Prevention Research Center

"As a Latina working in Reproductive Health, Rights and Justice for almost 20 years, I am ecstatic about The People's Book of Human Sexuality: Expanding the Sexology Archive! For far too long the lived experiences and brilliance of BIPOC folks in the field of sexuality education have been set aside, erased, or appropriated by others. I cannot wait to share it."

—**Aimee R. Thorne-Thomsen, MPA**, Founder,
Guerrera Strategies; Board Member, Collective Power for Reproductive Justice

"Like a baobab tree, this collection is an anchor, a shelter, and will provide deep nourishment for sexologists and practitioners alike."

—**Jamila M. Dawson, LMFT**, sex therapist and author of With Pleasure:
Managing Trauma Triggers for More Vibrant Sex and Relationships
and Essential Clinical Care for Sex Workers: A Sex-Positive
Handbook for Mental Health Practitioners

"This book provides inclusive content and diverse authorship that centers the most impacted on both sides of the work. This holistic textbook is a practice of intersectionality and helps create a multi-dimensional analysis that instigates deep yet practical change at the ideological, institutional, interpersonal, and internalized levels."

—**Aisha Chaudhri**, Co-Director of ICAH (Illinois Caucus for
Adolescent Health); Steering Committee member of ASEC
(American Society for Emergency Contraception)

"Essential reading not only for sexuality professionals, but for anyone seeking body autonomy and sexual liberation! In our efforts to end rape culture and endemic child sexual abuse, the wisdom and expertise of Black, Indigenous and of color folks (especially those who are queer and trans) must be at the foundation of the new world we co-create. I'm hopeful for the ways this book will bring us closer to the world we need and deserve."

—**Amita Y. Swadhin, MPA**, Founding Co-Director, Mirror Memoirs

"Growing up, all my sexual health educators in both media and in person, were white. Here is a book that provides space for voices often overlooked and ignored. This book will create a necessary space where we see ourselves and others in this field as well as a chance to learn, heal and grow as individuals and scholars."

—**Danielle Cole**, Creator of UKnowTheAnswer.com
and Qualitative Sociology Scholar

"It is so important that sexuality be taught and shared from a variety of sources, people, and cultures. This book will equip the reader with a broader depth of knowledge around sexuality."

—**Erin Tillman,** CSE Certified Intimacy Coordinator & Sex Educator

THE PEOPLE'S BOOK OF HUMAN SEXUALITY

This collection aims to fill in the deep gaps of vital contributions that have been erased from the sexuality field, illuminating the historical and current work, strategies, solutions, and thoughts from sexologists that have been excluded until now.

Historically, the US sexuality field has not included the experiences and wisdom of racialized sexologists, educators, therapists, or professionals. Instead, sexuality professionals have been trained using a color-free narrative that does an injustice by excluding their work as well as failing to offer a fuller examination of how they have expanded the field and held it accountable. The result of this wholesale erasure is that today many sexuality professionals understand these contributions as extra or tangential, and not part of the full vision and history of the field of sexology. Highlighting the voices and experiences of those who have been racialized and thus excluded, isolated, erased, and yet have still emerged as vital contributors to the North American sexuality field, this text offers a significant shift in the way we learn and understand sexuality, one that is expansive and committed to liberation, healing, equity, and justice. Divided into three sections addressing safety, movement, and oral narratives, the contributors offer insightful and provoking chapters that discuss reproductive justice, LGBTQ themes, racial and social justice, and gender and disability justice, demonstrating how these sexologists have been leaders, past and present, in change and progression.

This futuristic textbook includes correction, engaged reading, and lesson plans which offers community workers and trainers an opportunity to use the text in their non-traditional learning environments. Creating a path forward that many believed was impossible, this accessible book is for all who work in and around sexuality. It welcomes inquiry and celebrates our humanity for the worlds we are building now and for the future.

Bianca I. Laureano is an award-winning educator, curriculum writer, and sexologist with over 20 years of experience. She is the foundress of ANTE UP! Professional Development, a virtual freedom school.

THE PEOPLE'S BOOK OF HUMAN SEXUALITY

Expanding the Sexology Archive

Edited by Bianca I. Laureano

Routledge
Taylor & Francis Group

NEW YORK AND LONDON

Designed cover image: © Getty Images

First published 2024
by Routledge
605 Third Avenue, New York, NY 10158

and by Routledge
4 Park Square, Milton Park, Abingdon, Oxon, OX14 4RN

Routledge is an imprint of the Taylor & Francis Group, an informa business

© 2024 selection and editorial matter, Bianca I. Laureano; individual chapters, the contributors

ISBN: 9781032008882 (hbk)
ISBN: 9781032021126 (pbk)
ISBN: 9781003181927 (ebk)

DOI: 10.4324/9781003181927

Typeset in Joanna
by codeMantra

For the archives and the future sexuality professional.

CONTENTS

ACKNOWLEDGMENTS

This book is an accumulation guided by love, liberation, and healing. The shapeshifting love that was extended across borders, time zones, and space led us here. This book exists because of community care. There are so many people who made this collaboration possible and this is a short version of an expansive list. Thank you Cory for helping through every part of the process and being my accountability partner. Jessica M Johnson for teaching me how to build an archive and was available to text through sexuality topics from a historical lens. The ANTE UP! Certificate participants and supervisee's who were along for this process; I am always growing and being challenged to do this work better by being in an un/learning space together. Thank you Strug, Aisha, Sen, Kris, Jini, Hilary, James, Emily, Aiesha, Yomi, Erin, Jamila, Kay, Ashley, Mia, Jenny, Amita, Aimee, Daniel, Shane'a, Aaminah, Sofia, Lenée, and Ryan "The Irish Lookout" Shanahan for always being excited for me and us. For RC thank you for showing up for succession planning. To Erika Lopez and whatever rock she is preserving herself under, thank you for being the first person to say to me I can write a book of my own over 15 years ago. To those who could not and wanted to or may never want to, thank you for saying "no" and for caring for your time and attention. Thanks to my youth mentors who keep me curious and accountable. To Heather at Routledge for noticing what was possible. Thank you to each person and contributor who said "yes" and trusted our relationship: Jadelynn, Kalash, Yoseñio, Louie, Mariotta, Juan, Francisco, Serina, Nhakia, Saifa, Jessica, Sara, B.K., Melina, Sucia, Christina, Elliott, Aida, and Bina. Thank you to those who are unnamed and loved through and through. To my G who fills my water glass multiple times every day and makes sure I'm alive and thriving, this book is an example of what your love ignites and produces.

FOREWORD

Relationality and Connection as Key Credentials

From late night cackling in hotels—yelling "GENDER IS A SCAM!" with no elaboration or having lengthy dialogues about cannibalism in history and art—to multi-day facilitation adventures aimed at challenging fellow professionals' preconceived notions about sexuality, from coordinated open-letter writing about white supremacy to designing multi-sensorial workshops about hurricane preparedness and mailing each other cute little gifts, and so much more, my experiences and collaborations with Dr. Bianca Laureano have run the gamut. And that's at the core of what I want to share with you here.

Traditional forewords ask me to kick off by sharing my credentials and explaining why I have authority to comment on a book's content and, sure, I could talk about being an international presenter on a range of issues including mental health & sexuality, about winning awards for my activism and expertise, about critical participation in collectives and coalitions ranging from the "tiny but mighty" grassroots organizations in majority-Latinx neighborhoods to international clinical cohorts developing guidelines around kink and BDSM. (I know all this sounds like a humble-brag or something, but stay with me!) I could tell you about my leadership with groundbreaking data-collection for LGBTQ domestic violence in Rhode Island and building the innovative infrastructure to provide on-site HIV testing, or perhaps my co-authoring peer-reviewed journal articles about the role of social media in sex-ed. I could speak to my work with Ivy League universities and Departments of Health, my immigrant rights' advocacy, or my co-authoring sections for medical pediatric texts on sex-positive approaches to counseling youth up to age 26. I could go on, but I won't.

Why? Because what I most want to lay claim to here are my credentials as Bianca's friend/fam, colleague, and witness. While I bring a depth of content-knowledge around activism and archiving our histories, what truly gives me a well-rounded ability to tell you, dear reader, why the hell this book matters and why Bianca is a perfect person to curate and evolve it is our connection itself and what I know to be true about how she operates in the world. I want this foreword to, itself, challenge what you may expect from it and stay in alignment with this book's purpose: to showcase a variety of brilliances and how people of color carve out spaces for joy and resistance. So I invite you to hear these stories and reflections that speak to Bianca's personhood, our relationship, and how this is all a cornerstone of how this book has come about and how it may connect to you.

Dr. Laureano is an AfraLatina sexologist, rabble-rousing educator, and passionate human who brings a glowing fullness to every space that's blessed to have her. I have seen how she reaches out to people when they're struggling, how openly and vibrantly she discusses her wins as well as her challenges, how fearlessly she approaches uncomfortable things, and how tenderly she exists behind an exterior that some superficially reduce to "fierce-haired, larger than life, big personality." I have seen her grieve for her mother, grieve for our shared homeland(s), grieve for our communities in ways that are multifaceted, artistic, personal, narrative, and more. I have seen her navigate disabling conditions, complicated embodiment, professional betrayals, public success, and loss. I have witnessed her decked out in spectacular Halloween costumes, winning awards and commendations, pouring her heart into projects, loving on and laughing with her sweeties, and figuring out how to reel in her rage when it shouldn't be driving a situation. She has soared, she has fumbled, and she has continued. So, dear reader, know that's what this foreword is grounded in: personal and professional respect, radical love and care, deep friendship, transformative relating, tons of curiosity and silliness, and steady reciprocity.

Generative Conflict and Building Powerful Bonds

At the time of writing this, I had months prior connected two of my friends to each other: both people from different walks of life, but both of whom were part of the LGBTQ community and had ended up with horrible Long COVID and had their lives majorly disrupted. In the email I wrote to introduce them (after both agreed to the connection), I realized a huge thread that connected me to both: the intersection of being uncomfortably seen and lovingly called out while developing our relationship.

As I wrote the mini-bios and "how I know this human" in the email, I said about one friend:

> She was one of the humans who showed me a lot about boundaries for self care and the importance of taking care of the body even though I absolutely didn't implement much of that insight til years later; I was too busy going Hard AF. [laugh-crying emoji] She also called me out for my late night work email frenzies and I will never forget that [laugh-crying emoji].

About the other friend, a similar comment emerged as well:

> "They're observant AF and have (lovingly and snarkily) called my ass out multiple times when I've been trying to downplay feeling upset or uncomfortable which made me feel VERY SEEN and made an impression 4ever."

With each of these people I had moments of tension that yielded connection and collaboration rather than separation, and these cemented our friendship. That's not all it took, obviously, but it's an ingredient I've seen be key for me and many of my loved ones. To more fully trust and co-create with someone, I need to know that: we're here together, our liberation is seen and understood as collective, we can share compliments as well as critique, we can attune to each other in deep ways rather than following superficial scripts that don't serve our relationship.

Similarly, the "origin story" for me and Bianca had moments of tension that ultimately led to connection, respect, and depth. While I honestly don't recall exactly when we first crossed paths, I remember one of the biggest initial milestones in our connection: navigating a very thorny professional issue, and especially its racialized dimensions.

I was working at a nonprofit that had a weekly blog feature highlighting sexuality professionals. As both the feature and the organization itself were started by a brilliant woman (raised as a self-described WASP— White Anglo Saxon Protestant, for further context) who at the time didn't have a strong anti-racist lens, a lot of the people she was featuring were close colleagues and, sadly, the list was overwhelmingly white. In efforts to expand and diversify that (some of which I spearheaded), we began to reach out to a wider group of professionals to highlight, Bianca among them. When Bianca was evaluating the proposal, she saw that a concerning person was featured the year prior and brought that to our collective attention. (Mind you, when I say concerning here, I don't mean someone who just made a little offhanded comment, but rather an academic and "famous male feminist" who had a long and very well-documented history of targeting and harming women and people of color, which included but wasn't limited to a violent murder-suicide attempt with his ex-girlfriend.)

Almost simultaneously albeit separately, another person we had contacted for the blog feature emailed with similar concerns. However, this person communicated her concern differently and also happened to more precisely mirror the identities and experiences of the nonprofit director and a large chunk of its staff at the time—white, femme, queer in similar ways, more inquisitive than declarative when in conflict, etc. Unsurprisingly, the messages were received and held very differently even though they were pointing in the same direction and naming the same issues. Many, many conversations followed to explore and debrief what was going on, especially when it came to tone-policing and how we as a staff weren't all receiving these messages in the same way. While ultimately this man's feature was taken down, a press release was written to acknowledge what and why that was done, and I worked to institute a new vetting process for these features—the treatment and care that the two women who brought it up received were wildly different.

At the time, I was the only deviation from New England whiteness on staff, and while I was making space for and asking the staff to more carefully and less reactively consider Bianca's perspective, in retrospect,

I still had a lot of learning to do when it came to combating assimilationist tactics. At the time that I was advocating against tone policing and internalized white supremacy, there was still a part of me that was uncomfortable with it, and simultaneously was drawn to and really challenged by the ways Bianca so clearly, unapologetically, and directly named issues. Even as I defended her tone, I still saw it as "unstrategic" rather than fully understanding how it was powerful and valuable in itself not just in contrast to how the other woman did it. I was used to operating with people so differently, and steeped in prioritizing whiteness in ways I wasn't aware of at the time! (Also, my stronger connection at the time was with my director, who was also a dear friend and trailblazer, and ultimately she was the person I spent hours talking to about this, not Bianca.)

But this entire debacle and process left a huge impression on me. As someone who was not often intimidated and who was used to dealing with others' passive aggression rather than direct communication, seeing someone so firmly stand in their values and do so in a way that challenged me made its mark. From there, our connection found fertile soil to deepen.

Style and Substance as Embodiment of Book Values

Many forewords for books meant to exist (even partially) in academic spaces don't discuss how the author or editor is as a friend, as a person, as a co-conspirator; they focus on the author as a subject matter expert as if the two were not deeply intertwined. So much of this book is about the entwining and hybridity, about the ways in which our personhood and sociopolitical positions both create and reflect our realities, about the ways some of us are treated as marginal or expendable when we are not and have never truly been either of those things... that it would be a disservice to not already embody and employ these frameworks in my writing this.

I've already spoken extensively on this—including a piece in the 14th edition of "Taking Sides: Clashing Views in Human Sexuality" making a case for intersectionality as a framework in teaching sex ed in schools— but this is a hill I will continue to fight on. And even though I studied a lot of this theory and philosophy in formal, academic contexts, the place where it felt most real and grounded was, coincidentally, in conversation with Bianca, during one of her freedom-school multi-week sessions on intersectionality. Reading and dialoguing about Patricia Hill Collins' work on the topic—and specifically how she challenged Eurocentric, Positivistic philosophical frameworks on epistemology—was resonant and clear in ways that have stuck with me for years and I seemingly can't shut up about!

Many of us in the West have been exposed to a very particular conceptualization of "how we know what we know" and how knowledge gets created. This is one that prioritizes a very narrow and specific version of the "scientific method," where subject and researcher are and should be separate, where the goal is to be unbiased and unemotional, and where knowledge builds through adversarial debate. This gets presented as natural and obvious truth, the way things just are, when not only is that false but also when we have other robustly theorized frameworks that directly challenge and contradict some of those assertions to their core. These are also some of the same philosophical foundations deeply entwined with racist ideologies, coming out of countries where the development of scientific progress has been long-tied to colonialism and domination, and that de-facto gatekeep and dismiss epistemologies that don't fit certain Eurocentric standards. This is a core reason why this book is so necessary: it challenges all these paradigms in both content and process.

The reason so many people, especially people occupying various dominant social positions, can be so allegedly unbiased and "clinical" and "removed" is that their stake is made invisible, their bias goes unquestioned, and/or they're empowered to craft both the game and its rules. It's easy to opine from an armchair or from a position of holding someone else's chains! It's easy to be "levelheaded" and "present a cool face" when feeling deeply removed from an issue, or when the status quo is so beneficial that challenging it seems "unwise." And that "distance" itself is twisted as a strength when it's not.

I would go so far as to say not having a personal connection to a topic and not having feelings about it are more often weaknesses rather than strengths. Connection and emotions themselves aren't a problem, it's connection and emotions without reflection and structures to protect from undue, negative influence. In this book, connections and emotions are celebrated and nuanced, and authors' positions are honored and acknowledged rather than hidden or dismissed.

In these pages, you will see more of a focus on dialogue and collaboration rather than competitive debate, an ethics of care where emotions have a place, an understanding that lived experience is critical to knowledge rather than aiming for some "objective separation," and the idea that personal accountability and belief are integral to all these processes. The structure of the book itself as well as the process of writing it exemplifies each of these points beautifully.

For example, the notion that we can be values-neutral and unbiased is a fiction. Everything we do is influenced by our explicit and implicit values. Key ways to mitigate negative impacts of bias include deep reflexivity, listening to and accounting for varied perspectives, staying curious about how others experience the world, understanding knowledge and facts as evolving processes and realities rather than unchanging truths, ensuring that any laws or policies account or how bias is showing up, and more. Rather than presenting this as some magically unbiased book, here we claim biases and work to mitigate negative manifestations. Rather than promoting the book as a standalone, static text, it was envisioned as part of a series and one that would deserve and necessitate regular revision and expansion.

Similarly, rather than pitching a singular-author book, Bianca chose to craft an anthology with a variety of voices, specifically paying attention to what experiences were represented and how that could be as expansive as possible while staying on theme. Lesson plans are included side by side with written pieces and transcribed interviews, and multiple ways of studying the information are provided and encouraged. On the backend, Bianca hosted ongoing collective writing sessions, offered 1-1 support, and brainstormed ways we could all participate given all the challenges we all separately and collectively faced while authoring through life and a whole damn pandemic.

These approaches are not new to Bianca even as they've evolved over time. Dr. Laureano has ample experience with uplifting voices that have been purposefully silenced and excluded from sites of systemic power and being able to use her own experiences and feelings as both fuel and foundation. From her work on The LatiNegrxs Project (and The LatiNegrx Sex Survey) to the Women of Color Sexual Health Network (WOCSHN) for which she was a foundress, from her nuanced curricula with Scenarios USA (*What's the REAL DEAL about Love and Solidarity?*) to the Academy

Award-nominated and Sundance Audience Award-winning documentary "Crip Camp," from her curriculum labs and lesson plan mixtapes (designed for supporting and mentoring emerging professionals) to her topic- and population-specific Sexual Attitude Reassessments centering people of color…and the list goes on. Bianca has decades of experience designing creative interventions and facilitating spaces of deep growth and nourishment. She's done this while facing conflict head-on instead of avoiding it, challenging herself to show up for her people and her values, and navigating a world that repeatedly and systematically oppresses her along many axes. This is yet another offering for the world we deserve.

Dr. Laureano once again shows these commitments here in crafting this volume and demonstrating the power and role of creating archives of our experiences in our own voices rather than being subjected to others' misperceptions and violences. This is poignant in any field, but perhaps so particularly in the realm of human sexuality—interdisciplinary at its core, fraught with "taboos" and the controversies around pleasure, so often silenced or used violently to control populations, and where contributions and experiences from people of color have been so co-opted, dismissed, disguised, misattributed, destroyed, and presented as "optional."

In closing…

As part of a legacy of Black womanist and feminist thought, this book is a perfect example of challenging eurocentric epistemologies. This is a hybrid text in honor of how our human lives truly are. We exist in multiple dimensions, along varied paths, and our fullness of experience deserves an equally full attempt at representation and understanding, especially for people of the global majority.

Furthermore, this is an anthology as it should be when it articulates justice at its core: collaborative and inspiring, not a means to gather praise for a single author, not as a means of ghostwriting-adjacent ownership of content others write, but as a way of sharing varied narratives and approaches all coalescing around ideas of equity, visioning for a future we deserve, and strategizing with creativity. May you be challenged in your reading and gain inspiration that other worlds are possible!

Aida Manduley, LICSW

INTRODUCTION

I read a tweet that asked if we had ever met with someone at the same stage of their career as ourselves and after talking with them we realized they were so far ahead of us. I immediately thought I probably had, but then I paused to really consider the question and my answer changed. I had not. I was different, too different. So different that I thought people were more advanced in thinking and doing than me because they had been published in journals and had books! And yes, that even included questionable and horrible publications. Books were celebrated as I grew up and are a huge part of my family and culture. My blogs, open letters, and guest articles were not considered at the same level of truth and validity because they were based on how my lived experience and how my training at elite institutions did not meet the needs my communities and projects had of me. This sharing and wisdom were less than what was expected. When I remember the books that were assigned for all my courses and training, it was all people who did not work with my communities but they were

DOI: 10.4324/9781003181927-1

the "key researcher" or "lead thinker". Their credibility solely due to their publication status considered them a celebrated scholar.

I am a gifted and skilled writer. My writing defies the expectations and rejects the assimilationists desires. Thus, my publications, my writing were not immediately valued in this field, in academia; it was valued in communities outside of those spaces which are so powerful it forced those spaces to notice. Today, things have shifted towards acknowledging how we stay connected through virtual spaces and places. My online article "An Open Letter to White People in the US Sexuality Field" published in 2012 is still relevant today and widely used in sexuality training programs. My peer-reviewed journal publications doubled even when many participants on peer review boards do not consider me their peer. The work I do is always collaborative and thus the production is stunning and undeniably an exciting visionary offering. These archives of our work are so very thick, juicy, prickly, and luscious.

Today, I've chosen to acknowledge and recognize the power that exists in curating as we create our own archive. It is unacceptable that the US sexuality field and its training programs rarely cite sexologists of Color. This is a dehumanizing practice, one that is violent through its erasure. This practice is corrected when relationships are prioritized with care. Yet, what has manifested are relationships of a select few scholars of Color; the idea that we are a checklist that once you have a Black queer scholar teaching or lecturing or on a panel you've built a relationship with Black queer community. This is part of the scam of white supremacy and settler colonialism. Inviting us to speak on panels for 50 minutes sharing some of our most intimate experiences to a group of strangers for the sake of "education" isn't always the flex people think it is, especially if the honorarium is under $500 per person. Our intimate narratives are valuable and worth more than a gift card for $25 and we know this! Those who collaborate with us and value our relationship usually receive a "yes" from us in such instances. End extraction and build relationships that honor consent so if we say "yes", "no" or "maybe" we know we are heard and respected.

This book is the present and the shape-shifting future! This book is the complicated messiness of being a human during a time of constant chaos and oppression. These lessons, narratives, and insights are evolved and evolving. This book defies and destroys labels and binaries. It is a textbook for the future. A map towards the practice of liberation, freedom, interdependence, and vulnerability. This book is only a part of an expansive beginning. This is a textbook for the world we are building towards.

These are origin stories and lessons often ignored and devalued in public, yet in private and in ceremony, our stories are consumed, stolen, and used to create a workshop or worksheet by outsiders. This happens to us more than we allow ourselves to admit. Our time together is precious. No matter how you have come to this book, you belong here now and for as long as you choose to be here with us. We offer sharing and guidance in how to engage with our brilliance. We offer you an example of what is possible in hopes you can build something fantastic. As you sit in ceremony and ritual with us as you read and engage, you are welcomed into a space that was intentionally built for us. We offer a new vision, rememory, and plan for the world we all deserve.

Introduction 2021

This book is an incredible gift. A gift we created collectively for ourselves, our communities, and our field. We created this gift during a pandemic. Many of us are still grieving, healing, and finding our ways in new changing bodyminds. The completion of this book is and was a relief, an exhale, a reminder we are still here. Some authors died before we could archive their work here. Others wanted to participate yet were overwhelmed, confused, unprepared for an unpredictable future and could not fully commit to such a project at the time.

There are many voices missing in these pages; and there is such rich and valuable wisdom here by the authors. Readers are invited to join us in conjuring that this is the first book in a series that will continue to highlight the brilliance, wisdom, and experiences of people of color in the sexuality field.

Here, we focus on North America: Canada, the United States, and Mexico. Our authors are living in and from these countries. There is a heavy focus on the United States because this is where many of us live and the country that impacts us the most. The United States has an impact on our lives in very specific ways, and we also recognize what is lost and what remains when we ignore the impact of colonialism, imperialism, and capitalism on our lived realities. For this reason, we move between using terms such as people of color (POC), Black Indigenous People of Color (BIPOC), people of the global majority, and specifically naming the race and ethnicity discussed as we have complicated experiences of the construction of racialization and relationships based on the dehumanization practices of colonialism.

This book came to be when Healther Evans at Routledge emailed me. She said she had been reading several of the sexuality texts Routledge had published, noticed my work in many of these books, and wondered why I didn't have my own book. I said "That's a great question Heather!" We met on a virtual platform in March 2020 with my accountability partner Cory Silverberg and she asked me what kind of book I wanted to create. I told her a book that was an anthology, one that would be updated every several years with new voices and perspectives, new brilliance based on vulnerability, lessons learned, challenges experienced, and solutions and resolutions that emerged. I wanted a book that would change the way we use textbooks, the way we engage with writing, and change the way we value the work of racialized people. A book where we are humanized, have full self-determination, and guide how to discuss, embrace, and learn from our work.

Heather invited me to submit a book proposal in 2020. It took me over six months to submit the proposal to her. Not because I wasn't sure about what we were building, but because of how the pandemic was impacting us, and how our writing and work has been critiqued, for me this way since I started working in the sexuality field in 1996. As many sexuality professionals may have experienced, when I was called on to do this work in this field, others did not understand. They questioned me and shrugged their shoulders believing I would never find success or financial stability. Then, I started to do the work and realized how color-free these sexuality spaces, training, and schools were/remain. They did not ever really fully represent the communities I was a part of or the communities I knew existed.

Why Did I Say "Yes!"

There were several questions I considered before and during the writing of the book proposal. First, I asked myself if I wanted to do this process. What would be missed? What did we have time for? How do I decide who to invite into this project?! How do we do it together during a pandemic? Is this even possible right now when the world is chaotic in a new way?

Do I really want to work with a traditional academic publisher? Would we survive this pandemic? What if I died before it was completed?

I spoke with Cory several times about these questions and it was Cory who helped me complete the book proposal over several months. I realized this was a gift, an opportunity, a way to strategically understand the power I have in this moment and to use it in a way that brings others along, that invites them to build and create the table and chairs they need for us to be fully together. This was a new attempt at interdependence, collaboration, and care for sexuality professionals of color. I knew I could not pay authors what I wanted to pay them for their time and work. I was reminded by Jadelynn St Dre that I was transparent with everyone who I invited, that I honored the "no" that I received, and the "yes" or "maybe let me think about it" that I received as well. Honoring the silence from those invited yet could not respond also occurred. Of the 20+ people who initially said 'yes' they did so because it was their choice. They had the information I had, they were given the contract and the book proposal to review for their own curiosity and clarity. They each had the opportunity to consider what I was inviting them into. And many said "yes"! This conversation with Jadelynn helped me clarify the work for myself. I was stuck with feeling I had asked for too much for so little. Then, I realized again why people said "yes" in the first place and it was aligned with why I said "yes" to Heather and Routledge.

Working with a larger academic publisher familiar with our field is attractive. There is power for many of us in being published. Our agreement includes speaking with editors and copyeditors to explain that the language in this book may not be the academic language in other academic texts. There is code switching and languages other than English that we choose not to italicize for the comfort of anglophone readers. We chose to have the language as we use it featured in the text. There is power in our writing and choosing where it can be published. Starting here offers more opportunities for the authors in this book to be invited to do their own work. This is the kind of access I want for myself and to offer to others if interested. Choices and access are essential.

I was never welcomed into this field. It was lonely. I knew I belonged even when others wanted me to leave, to be quiet, to stop challenging them to be and do better. Equity and justice are rare in this field. Some may think this is incorrect, yet they have never asked us why we believe and know this to be true. Those people never asked us what happened or tried to find ways to solve the problem of elitism, isolation, "professionalism", and racist misogynoir. Instead, they erased, ignored, and fought me, and us, through back-channeled emails or by creating threads about my work on "professional" listservers. They did not understand why it was important to evolve and grow with this field, that people who looked nothing like them could teach them something about their bland flavor and attempts of "inclusion" that only welcomed those who liked those bland flavors already. This too included people of the global majority.

Writing can be traumatic. In 2003, I was heavily recruited into a PhD program, a department led by Black women and a Latina. In my third year, with a 4.0 GPA, I was told my writing was not good enough to be moved through the program and graduate. I was given one more opportunity to demonstrate my writing abilities through a paper. I hired a white woman editor to help me, and she did. Those faculty members and leadership of color at the university pushed me out due to my writing. I was told my writing was too accessible. Too many people could understand what I was writing about and that's not what they thought a "scholar" should be. Trying to explain to my father how a 4.0 GPA led to me being pushed out of a PhD program remains difficult. I left with a terminal master's degree and a ten-page letter to the Provost about the violation of the process outlined for removing students as stated in the Student Handbook and Guidelines. I've been trained by historians, specifically Dr. Jessica M. Johnson, on building an archive and sharing it, which I presented in this departure letter.

Writing can be traumatic. It can also be a coping mechanism, a healing experience, a practice towards transforming trauma. And we may not find the healing experience we need. Writing may not be what we need it to be. We made this book into something we know we need in this field and across all other disciplines. This book is not only a dream, a conjuring in its own right; it is also a vision of possibility, a model of moving forward, a new path. A movement!

Our Process

There are endless ways to edit and support writers. I know this from my experiences editing and being edited. I chose the path of innovation and limitlessness. We used open access and free services such as Google Docs to write and draft our chapters. Once an author said "yes", I created a folder for each author that had two items in it: (1) A blank page titled DRAFT with their name and (2) A "feel good" document with their name. We held 90-minute virtual writing/accountability sessions through the summer, so we could complete our drafts and chapters. I updated the "feel good" folders throughout the process.

I describe these "feel good" folders as love letters. I've been sending love letters to the femmes of color in my life for over a decade. These are handwritten notes with an intentional stamp on the stationery that is so heartwarming to me in a world where we mostly get bills or advertisements. The way Erika Lopez wrote about letters and mail in her book *Flaming Iguanas* (1998) speaks to my love and experience of writing love letters:

> I don't think they truly understand the joy of writing a letter on cool paper, putting it in an envelope, and addressing it in a funky way that challenges postal workers. The stamp validates the whole thing somehow, and whew! -- Putting it in the mailbox and healing that blue metal flap swing shut is just about the prettiest sound in the natural world. The universal sound of closure. And a cancelled stamp is just about the prettiest sight. It's almost love, and sometimes it really is love. ... It means someone thought of you for more than the fifteen seconds it took to dial your number and leave the message for you to call them back.
>
> (p. 118)

These "feel good" docs were snapshots of how we met: at conferences, during panels, online sessions, in the middle of community events, or some other way! I wrote lists to people about why I love what they contribute, who they have become as we have grown together, and how I have learned from them. I wrote about the ways I imagine our work expanding this field and how we expand alongside one another as we do this work from our values and principles. When writing became a challenge, there was something for each author to go to and read, review, recall, and engage with so they could find and remember why they said "yes", and what this means for us as we do this together. This is an archive of rememory as Toni Morrison coined in *Beloved*. A rememory of the past alive in the present. We are always already here.

Transparency in the editing and writing process is important. We used the "suggesting" feature so that no writing was deleted without the consent of the author. This is one of the many ways this book is "trauma-informed" every part of the way. Because I knew my own trauma with writing, I knew what was possible with regards to harm and I knew there was harm I could not imagine too. It was only 6 short months ago that an all-white team of editors told me my contribution to their sexuality anthology was not well written and that one bad chapter ruins the whole book. My chapter was the "bad" chapter according to this white older man. I withdrew my chapter from that book. Often sexuality professionals discuss consent. Consent is always around us, just like power is all around us. Creating a culture of consent together was one goal towards honoring and healing from traumas that may be experienced or returned. Through this culture of consent, some authors changed their "yes" to a "not now" for completing their chapter or to a "no". These were welcomed and celebrated as a boundary, an act of caring for ourselves. Their folders were never deleted either. They remain in the archive.

As the editor, I chose love. I chose love to be the guiding principle when offering edits. I also expressed to each author that my goal with editing was to remain curious about their writing and stories and to support the flow and evolution of what they wished to share. Our vision was not to make readers more comfortable. Instead, it was to help readers to be uncomfortable as a radical form of consent to unlearn what they had been taught and trained to do in this field. As a reader there is power in choosing who to learn from. Power in who to build with. There is power in citation. #CiteBlackWomen. We honor the consent that may emerge for readers: to read or to choose to skip chapters.

Then, there are the lesson plans after each chapter! Whew! Get ready to be challenged in new ways. We worked to create lesson plans to guide the conversations that may emerge from each chapter. We know what we want people to engage with and we know we want people to be encouraged and given permission to go in other directions we may not know of at this moment. These lesson plans guide what is possible but does not stunt that possibility of what may happen in the future. We know that in sexuality programs in North America, there are not many of us: people of color, people who are visibly Black, Asian, Indigenous, non-binary, transgender, intersex, immigrants, working poor, or sex workers as faculty or students. We knew if this book were to be used in sexuality classrooms the majority of people engaging with our work would not be us. For this reason, we created lesson plans to guide this process without using the usual dehumanizing lens often employed to discuss us, our contributions, and our labor.

Practice, Theory, and Guiding Frameworks

This book has an abundance of theoretical frameworks and principles put into action. Each author chose the approach they desired to include in their chapters. Some theories are used yet not named. For example: Standpoint theory. The entire book centers this feminist theoretical approach which values our lived experience and positions in society to offer us a space to theorize from. Readers will notice authors positioning themselves in various ways throughout their chapters. Black Feminist Thought is also witnessed in action when the Black authors in this book speak to the issues and needs of Black communities they are a part of and offer some of the solutions to meeting those needs. When non-Black authors write about why they collaborate and listen to Black people and community members, consider where your intentional relationships need attending.

A theoretical framework and practice of understanding power and oppression, Intersectionality invites us to consider our relationships to ourselves, our identities, to each other, and to the institutions, systems, and ways we experience oppression and harm. Many understand Intersectionality by the work of legal scholar and activist Kimberlé Williams Crenshaw. Offered here is an opportunity to witness how this theoretical framework and practice has been implemented for centuries by Black people in the United States without the name "intersectionality" being used and outside of legal scholarship. This becomes an offering to witness what emerges in multi-and interdisciplinary ways, which is exactly what the Sexuality field is: interdisciplinary. It also invites inquiry to consider: what happens when we do not communicate across disciplines? What gets lost? What remains? What is redone or revisioned?

Our queer, trans, non-binary, intersex, gender, and sex-expansive authors are engaging in and practicing Queer Theory as the most authentic primary sources: our experiences and work. You will find a qualitative approach embraced and celebrated. We invite readers to consider how we can create our own understandings of what emerges from the testimonies and lessons offered in each chapter.

Testifying and testimony are central to this book. As the Latina Feminist Group (2001) offered us an approach to Testimonios, we follow many of their practices but not all. The ones we follow include storytelling as a collective and offering collective feedback to tell a fuller narrative of not only our story as individuals, our stories of our collective community experiences. Readers will find the embracing of Testimonio throughout the lesson plans, in how we have chosen to be in conversation with one another through chapters that invite readers to engage this text in a non-linear way is intentional. Oral narratives, storytelling, and sharing are not often linear and neither is the expectation for readers engaging with this text.

In their writing, many authors are practicing autoethnography. They may not use that term or any of the language in this theory and framework section, but that does not mean theory and practice is not being done, created, or reimagined! We challenge ideas of who our "scholars" are and what "scholarship" is considered valuable. The vulnerability, nuance, and reflexivity found in this book and encouraged through the lesson plans, is essential and what we all said "YES" to offering. As you read, consider what behaviors were discussed, presented, engaged as reading continues, as we wrote, as we un/learn together? What is the exchange each of us as authors and as you, beloved reader, receive? This is power and it is all around us all the time. We invite readers to consider the power held and experienced in these moments with this text. Consider what your response or reaction is and, if you choose to share, what you receive in return. In the same spirit that Chela Sandoval created Methodology of the Oppressed (2000), we are guided by and encourage readers to consider revolutionary love!

Sections

The book includes three sections: Origin Stories of Safety and Care, Movement for BodyMinds, and Oral Narratives.

Origin Stories of Safety and Care

Historically, safety in sexuality and sexology has been narrowly understood to cover a few issues (STIs, reproductive choice, sexual violence). And historically, safety has been built by and for white people in this field.

We begin with safety because it's something that we as people of color, Black people, Indigenous people, mixed race people, racially ambiguous people, people in non-normative bodies, disabled people, queer, trans, gender expansive, and intersex people have only found in rare instances and exclusively when we are together. Safety for many of us has only been offered in the field unless it was created by us for us. White spaces have never been safe for us. Again: White spaces have never been safe for us. We start with safety to build a new foundation that demonstrates what we have done historically and how we continue to elevate work around safety in ways that benefit all of us. As the prison abolitionist and author Mariame Kaba reminds us "safety is a community responsibility", we invite readers to consider what is possible when we envision and create safety in this way.

Across their essays and chapters, writers share where and how racialized sexuality professionals find safety. When examining state-sanctioned violence that disproportionately targets people of color and BIPOC, disabled people, youth, queer people, sex workers, and working poor people, what are the strategies they have employed, and what are the ways they have modernized their inheritance and birthright of safety in a place their ancestors were enslaved, kidnapped, tortured, owned, and murdered; how do they make themselves visible and recognizable to themselves, their communities, and their ancestors? Exploring what representation and power means when hiring, training, and retaining people of color, queer, trans, and disabled people are welcomed.

These essays share strategies and healing maps that guide us towards a more expansive understanding of healing than what is often offered in Western therapeutic approaches. What are the solutions we have created ourselves and what must still be done? Creating a culture of consent for ourselves and our children on our terms, there is much work to be done and leading movement creators will share their solutions and paths forward.

Movement for BodyMind

When we discuss sexuality the conversations are very much around the body and society. Yet, what is often excluded is a focus on the body and mind as a unit of reality, safety, need, disability, and humanity. This section is a mixture of historical memory and archiving, the ways many sexuality professionals have affirmed their work in the face of global white supremacy. Readers are reminded that this book is created and offered at a time when movement is ripe in all areas, where a reckoning of racial justice and equity is explored collectively and publicly, and at the height of a pandemic and climate crisis. What are the ways forward? What do we learn from the past movements and labor? How do we keep from burning out?

This is the growing up love James Baldwin wrote about. This is the archive from the wars and battles we have fought, survived, and thrived in. These are our paths forward and we welcome each reader to join us where possible along the way. Discovering the voices and narratives of moving our bodies as a way to come back to ourselves, abortion, immigration, queerness, religion, and craft a plan for healing from this body trauma is provided. This section complicates the bodymind by engaging with the ways we may be perceived as we do our work, how we must collaborate to move forward, and find healing paths with our families of origin.

Oral Narratives

Media Justice lives in this book and in this section. Media is an enormous part of how many of us learn about sex and sexuality topics. It is also a space where complex stories are woven that tell a tale of white saviorism and the exclusion of those most like us. The section focuses on how the media is impactful for sexuality professionals and the populations we work within.

This section expands on the ideas of media and includes narratives from perspectives of queer ephemera and archival practices, how storytelling and oral narratives are shifting the way Latinx queer and trans communities find virtual spaces of freedom and wholeness, an interview with an activist who share their reflections of connecting on intersex justice, and a new model for using fashion as a tool in the community education and therapeutic/healing environment. We create the messages and opportunities we know are valuable and these narratives share how we do it in expansive and innovative ways.

Each section includes Media Literacy. Often ignored, excluded, and removed until the past decade in the US sexuality education curricula and teaching programs, Media Literacy offers a foundation upon which to make the learning environment significantly more accessible, engaging, and lively! It has also become essential in supporting teachers, parents, and trusted adults in discussing sexually explicit media and pornography. Media is powerful and to know the US sexuality field has often ignored this important educational framework is a reminder of how limited many view the field of sexuality within the public school system or after-school space, locations where a majority of youth find themselves five days a week. That other anthology where I withdrew my chapter, the editors suggested I completely remove a discussion about Media Literacy as it didn't "fit in" to me discussing why justice frameworks are needed and helpful in expanding our work, specifically my practice with my communities and how I create curricula and training experiences.

Succession Planning

Death is the guarantee in this life. Since my mother died in 2016, I've been getting very comfortable and close with death and dying. For over two years, death and dying consumed all parts of my life as I grieved and mourned publicly and without shame. I was honest when people asked me "how are you" my response was and is often "my mother is dead".

Death is not a fear for me as an individual, and I know I've spent a lot of time with death, finding a death doula, preparing for the death I want to experience if I am given the opportunity to die with dignity I identify for myself. Living in a country where mass shootings are a routine experience, and many sexuality educators may go into schools unprepared with knowing the safety plan of that school upon a shooting, puts us at unique additional risk of death due to isolation and gun violence.

As a disabled person with a compromised immune system when the pandemic began we saw it coming in early February 2020. Disability community in the Bay Area of California organized to get masks, hand sanitizer, groceries, and other needs to one another. I was on the receiving and organizing end of this work due to my relationship with activist and disability justice organizer Stacey Park Milbern who co-founded the Disability Justice Culture Club (DJCC). Stacey welcomed me into the DJCC as a facilitator to help establish goals and build relationships and connections. When the pandemic hit the United States, especially California where we live, DJCC organized and I received masks, hand sanitizer, and disinfectant wipes. I was welcomed to present on a topic for a DJCC Brunch where presenters were paid when we lost income due to the pandemic.

Then, Stacey died on her 33rd birthday in 2020.

Stacey and I had connected online long before we met in person. We were young girls of color online writing about ourselves, our bodies, our sexualities, our needs, and desires. We met through writing. We met in person at the Allied Media Conference. We reunited in California when I moved and relocated after my mother's death. We then collaborated with DJCC and as one of the Netflix Crip Camp Impact team leads where I co-wrote the official curriculum for the film with Dr. Aiesha Turman.

A large group of Stacey's friends led by her estate and legacy holders created a memorial service for her that was fully accessible in under a week of her death! This may have been one of the first large public car movements and rallies during the pandemic which was socially distanced, masked, sanitized, archived via posters, video, and photographs. I stayed home and held space online for those across the globe who could not attend the rally in person and offered audio and image descriptions of what we were witnessing through the filming of the rally. Over 300 people attended. I learned death is also a celebration of love, collective grief, and movement. The young women of color at the Radical Monarchs, a group that Stacey had been a mentor and instructor discussing accessibility and disability justice, gave us the #StaceyTaughtUs as a form of hashtag activism (Jackson, Bailey & Foucault Welles, 2020) and digital archiving that extends across multiple platforms.

As I began to continue the work on this book, I knew I could die if I contracted SARS-COVID-19. The news and hospitals were already reporting turning away fat and disabled people and choosing to focus on helping those who medical teams deemed worthy of being saved. I knew I was not considered worthy of being supported, saved, or helped. This was when my succession planning began.

I've often discussed succession planning, especially as I knew I was expected to go into an "executive" decision-making position sometime in my life. Yet, of all the projects and organizations I've founded or co-founded, I always knew I didn't want to be there forever. I still feel this way. Organizations, projects, ideas, they must grow. That cannot happen if the same people remain in leadership for extended periods of time. My personal number is eight years before I know I have become "stale" and need to move on.

When thinking about who I trust to continue this work and who would honor the vision that I've shared with the writers, I immediately thought of my friend, chosen family member, radical person of color, writer, and organizer Rosana Cielo Cruz (RC). Similar to how Stacey and I met, so did RC and I meet: online via writing and blogging. I remember first texting RC if they would be open to me asking for help with a writing project. RC immediately said "yes" and I wrote a longer email that started with an "I may die or become very ill and need help completing this if I do" and outlined the vision for the book. I was relieved when RC affirmed the "yes" via text with a "yes" in writing. I was ready and prepared for what was possible.

RC and I connected in June 2021 to discuss updates and details. I had already gotten my Pfizer two-shot vaccination in May and was incredibly ill for both injections. My body took over 7 weeks to recover and to this day, I believe there are some parts of my body that have been activated that my immune system is still figuring out. I shared with RC where our writing was at and we agreed that I will ask for help by the end of July/early August 2021! That the help I may need is in editing, clarity, and general "get it done" support!

And then Dani died.

I had reached out to Dani to write about their experience as a dark-skinned Black Ghanian non-binary sex worker living in Chicago. They were one of the co-directors of SWOP (Sex Workers Outreach Project). Their death was sudden, unexpected, and raw like Stacey's and all the other deaths that occurred in a short time. Before Dani confirmed their participation, they were no longer on the planet. I found myself attending their virtual altar, homegoing, and Instagram Live community events that were created for them. Death is the guarantee. This is how I prepared.

If I Die Before This Is Published ...

The intention that was central to this creation is one that I hope is archived, widely read and consumed, and objectified. Yes, objectified! I hope you beloved reader hold this book in your hands, feel it, smell it, listen to the pages as you turn them, and have a fully sensual experience with this book! If you get this in the audio version or in an online version, listen with your whole body, read with your whole body. Use those media literacy skills and notice what techniques attract you and keep you reading. We did as we created this book. I call on us to organize to create another edition of this book, another example of what it can mean for us to write ourselves into the history we have created and been a part of establishing. Another way forward to learn and unlearn and correct the missing parts that exclude so many of us already.

The ways the trauma of writing and being pushed out due to my writing from a variety of spaces, has changed me. I decided that the trauma of writing was from a Western colonial and white supremacist value that I do not ascribe to any longer. I choose to pass down joy and pleasure not trauma. This is a new version of epigenetics. Feel what you feel as you read this book and allow your body to rejuvenate and reconnect with the wisdom and pleasure your ancestors have provided to you through your DNA. Think of the wisdom and pleasure your ancestors found as you bring in the wisdom and pleasure as you read these words.

There is no expectation this is a linear read. We have actually made it so that you must move between the pages to get to other parts and lesson plans to find the gems that are intertwined and challenge a Western way of reading, storytelling, and sharing. We ask that you begin here at the introduction. Consider this invitation. This is afrofuturism, this is epigenetics, this is movement, this is possible. You are here now. You have already begun. We welcome you.

Bibliography

Hill Collins, P. (1990). *Black Feminist Thought: Knowledge, Consciousness, and the Politics of Empowerment*. London: Routledge.

Jackson, S. J., Bailey, M. & Foucault Welles, B. (2020). *Hashtag Activism: Networks on Race and Gender Justice*. Cambridge: MIT Press.

Latina Feminist Group (2001). *Telling to Live: Latina Feminist Testimonios*. Durham, NC: Duke University Press.

Lopez, E. (1998). *Flaming Iguanas: An Illustrated All-Girl Road Novel Thing*. New York, NY: Simon & Schuster.

Morrison, T. (1987). *Beloved*. New York, NY: Alfred A, Knopf.

Sandoval, C. (2000). *Methodology of the Oppressed*. Minneapolis: University of Minnesota Press.

SECTION 1

ORIGIN STORIES OF
SAFETY & CARE

White spaces have never been safe for us. Here, we demonstrate that reality and how we moved away from those narrow oppressive unsafe spaces to create our own. These are narratives of freedom, self-determination, and liberation; a breaking from colonial settler practices.

DOI: 10.4324/9781003181927-2

1

TRANSFORMING SEX EDUCATION CURRICULA THROUGH MEDIA LITERACY, MEDIA JUSTICE, AND POWER

Bianca I. Laureano

The evidence-based sexuality education curricula I was required to use in the early 2000s as a sexuality educator rarely recognized me as a fat queer disabled LatiNegra femme sex educator supporting a group of youth who shared many of those same identities and experiences. The curricula did not have the results and outcomes expected for our populations due to the embedded elitism, misogyny, racism, and ableism that still remains in many curricula. In many ways, this form of sexuality education failed the students and failed me as the sexuality educator implementing the curricula. This is what led me to creating my own curricula based on my knowledge and relationships with what students desired and were interested in learning. The curricula I create are always about collaboration, positive youth development, and power.

My training was very standard to how many sexuality educators are still taught. We were taught within a white supremacist settler colonial framework of what should and should not be taught. It was a very binary way of being trained and expected to implement curricula. Never

DOI: 10.4324/9781003181927-3

talk about yourself as a human being, sexual person, or educator. Never self-disclose. Never make it (the education/lesson plan) about you. These are still core elements of how we train educators, especially peer educators. This approach dehumanizes us!

The reality for me as an instructor pre-pandemic 2000s being in front of a group of participants meant they were consuming me! They were looking at me, my body, my gender expression, creating questions and stories about me, and I was not prepared or encouraged to engage with that reality. I was expected to say "I'm not going to answer personal questions" and smile while getting our discussion back "on track."

The track was never considered to be those moments of inquiry, curiosity, and reality for many students who did not often have a teacher speak to them about these sexuality topics and who also had a job, had a life outside of work. Yet, as someone who has almost always lived in the area where I taught, meeting my students outside of the classroom and being introduced to their parents and extended family at the grocery store or subway/bus stop meant this imaginary wall was shattered. The reality is we are trained to dehumanize ourselves and erase the markers and information of who we are in this world as a way of upholding racist ideas of "professionalism."

These ideas of "professionalism" are everywhere and they continue to dehumanize all of us! It's a misuse of power. I have experienced this so many times in my 20 plus year career as a sexuality educator and trainer.

I'll share one recent example. In a training for professionals I led during the pandemic, I shared my experiences of ableism, and how I had lost work because of the ableist approaches upheld at an organization. A young white woman who was present complained to the white director of the space where my class was offered. This young white woman reported that the discussion of my reality was "unprofessional." She believed that I was wrong in sharing what my lived reality was while publicly proclaiming that "Black Lives Matter." Without communicating with me, the white director allowed this person to be removed from my class, denying me the opportunity to do my job, which would be to educate this young white woman about boundaries and accountability. The director's actions upheld a white feminist lens that harms and violates me everyday. The student who complained and left my class chose to continue to follow me on social media. I chose to block her, and a year later she created a new account and attempted to follow me again. Neither she nor the director understood their actions as being a form of consumption without consent or accountability.

This cannibalistic violence happens often. Historian Vincent Woodard writes it best in *The Delectable Negro: Human Consumption and Homoeroticism within U.S. Slave Culture* about cannibalism

> [t]his desire was less about literal consumption and more about the cultivated taste the white person developed for the African. Whites often satiated this taste and appetite through acts of violence, sexual exploitation, imagined ingestion of the black, or through staged rituals designed to incrementally harvest black spirit and soul.
>
> (2014, p. 18)

In a country built on the exploited sexualized violence and labor of tortured kidnapped enslaved people, it is not hard to understand when white people create something it will be to consume our spirit and soul as they misunderstand what "diversity, equity, inclusion, justice, and belonging" mean in action. And most especially when they do not learn to offer an intentional apology followed by changed behavior.

My personal approach to education, collaboration, facilitation, and creation is to recognize when dehumanization occurs and challenge it directly. I do this through building intentional relationships. This means I had to intentionally remove myself from spaces and places that did not value me or my contributions. It was very lonely. It still is sometimes. Yet, this is how I survived living in and doing work in a cannibalistic field that wanted me alive to feed off my brilliance and not attribute me or my colleagues. I began to create my own spaces, places, and curricula!

One of my major critiques of many sexuality education curricula is how it rarely ever considered and presented Media Literacy and Media Justice elements. This is what happens where there are only white people at the table using a white supremacists settler colonial framework, expectations, outcomes, and parameters. Things always go missing and omitted. What is important to understand is that many curricula at the time came with VHS tapes, then DVDs, then online links and content, and often had activities where participants created media! Yet no discussion of Media Literacy or Justice. It seemed like an odd omission. Here is where I begin to recognize how sexuality education has become such a niche subject that we don't even collaborate with teachers and educators leading "traditional core" classes. If we did we would realize Media Literacy was a component of many of those classes!

I was introduced to Media Literacy in the early 2000s by author, creator, and Ivy league homegirl Sofia Quintero. My introduction to Sofia was a few years earlier when I was introduced to her novels by RW when we were doctoral students at the University of Maryland. Sofia's book *Picture Me Rollin'* was written under her Black Artemis pseudonym and rocked my world! I then found ways to welcome her into my radical woman of color "feminist" class and offer an honorarium as she shared with us her craft and creating of media. We have remained homegirls since. I remember we were sitting at the Riverdale Diner in the Bronx sharing a meal and I had asked how I could support the work she was doing in collaboration at Chica Luna Productions where they were supporting emergent storytellers and creating short films. I had just been "laid off" from my work at a Harlem school-based health center as the sexuality educator, a story too common as sexuality services are often the first to be cut from a budget. With the new time I had, I was encouraged by my homegirl Irish Lookout Ryan Shanahan to inquire about volunteer positions.

The article Sofia gave me was Skills and Strategies for Media Education by Elizabeth Thoman of the Center for Media Literacy (CML). Here, I read Thoman stated the goal of the CML "must be to help people become competent, critical and literate in all media forms so that they control the interpretation of what they see or hear rather than letting the interpretation control them" (2003). Reading that quote was connected so much to power and self-determination which was at the center of so many of the ideas I had and kept to myself about teaching, engagement, pedagogy, care, and liberation. My personal teaching philosophy includes all of these components and each time I update it so it remains relevant and alive, media literacy and justice have taken root.

At the core of Media Literacy is reflexivity and body autonomy. Thoman shares

> media literacy is not so much a finite body of knowledge but rather a skill, a process, a way of thinking that, like reading comprehension, is always evolving. To become media literate is not to memorize facts or statistics about the media, but rather to raise the right questions about

what you are watching, reading or listening to. At the heart of media literacy is the principle of inquiry.

Asking harder questions is one of my core ways of remaining accountable to myself, my community, and our future. Some of the hard questions I ask myself included: who has power in the situation? What power do I hold? What am I going to do with my power? Am I ready for the impact?

Sofia gave me a PDF article by Elizabeth Thoman "Skills & Strategies for Media Education" that I have used and shared ever since! During our lunch, Sofia shared with me in plain language how Media Literacy impacted her work and was so essential to creating the stories we share. It was at that moment I realized there was a term and framing for what I knew was needed. It was a relief! It was an opening up of what was possible. There are five core areas of focus in Media Literacy: (1) Media messages are constructed, (2) Media uses language and symbols intentionally to capture our attention, (3) Values are embedded in all media, (4) Different people will have different perspectives, (5) Something is missing or has been omitted. Each of these points has a question that helps us understand what we have been exposed to at various times. When I apply these same areas of focus onto the sexuality education curricula I was required to use, I did not like the answers that I noticed were deeply connected to an assimilationist approach to the western way of "knowing" and "understanding," the roots of a white supremacist settler colonial framing. I knew creating my own curricula meant collaborating with youth and listening to what they were saying they needed and doing the work to find resources, which includes creating them myself!

While I was at the Harlem school the stop and frisk practices of the NYPD (New York Police Department) had impacted and targeted the youth in my classroom and many of them were read as "problematic" due to racism, elitism, ageism, and surveillance. Many had questions of how to avoid police, if at all possible, and what to do to remain alive and "safe" after school when police were surrounding the school area. I chose to find a video to help them learn about their rights and what to say to police officers that were in alignment with those rights. Then, we discussed the video and what we learned, saw, what was useful, and not realistic. The teachers in the room were engaged more than they usually were when offering more specific sexuality lessons. None of the curricula

I was trained to use in sexuality education included how to engage with police and law enforcement. Yet, this is the lived reality for all of us in that space no matter our age. Plus, police and law enforcement are often identified as "trusted adults" in many curricula, another example of what is not realistic or meeting the needs of our communities and upholding a white supremacist settler colonial ideology.

Media was and remains a vital part of my sexuality education approach. Media Literacy is one of the guiding frameworks for my curriculum development and creation. Media Justice is as well especially when creating engaging activities for participants. When we invite participants to create their own media and representations, we are inviting them into storytelling, sharing their experiences, and becoming creators of media, this is Media Justice! When we control the narrative, representation, and ways our media is received and consumed is a form of justice. Media Literacy and Media Justice are not often a guiding framework in sexuality education curricula. Yet, we now have curricula using the language of "Porn Literacy" without ever identifying where that phrasing emerged from! It's wild to me how easily people will create something without the historical grounding or knowledge. Nothing is created in a silo and at a time when we live in a world with the internet, it's a choice to skip over Media Literacy for the more appealing and controversial Porn Literacy. When I collaborated with The Porn Conversation to build their Porn Literacy curriculum this was an important piece to identify as including in the teacher and parent guides. It offers an introduction for parents and caregivers to get comfortable discussing media with their children and youth before hopping to a larger topic of free online pornography. There is no Porn Literacy without Media Literacy.

And there's no Media Literacy without discussions and recognitions of power. Power is everywhere and it's all around us all the time! How are we avoiding discussing power in the sexuality classroom? That is a choice too. I believe this is one of the major reasons I am sought out for updating, editing, and writing curricula; I focus on power. There are many ways to do this and it doesn't have to be difficult unless we are committed to upholding a white supremacist settler colonial practice of education and knowledge production.

What comes with this knowledge and understanding of power is considering how to strategically use the power we do have to make our curricula expansive, useful, relevant, and updated. I'm often asked what I would change about sex education or what does sex education need. I share that sexuality education must be in all subjects embedded through and through from math class examining the statistics of HIV infections pre- and post-PREP access, or how the HPV vaccine has supported which demographics in avoiding gynecological cancers; to English and History classes that may offer an examination into the US Disability Rights Movement and how many disabled people's experiences of consent and pleasure have been impacted by medical abuse, isolation, and institution-alization. These are all topics for a sexuality education curriculum and a holistic approach to understanding the country we live in currently.

Media Literacy and Justice are at the core not only of my curricula but also my trainings. All the courses for the ANTE UP! Certificate that I offer uses these frameworks, my Sexual Attitudes Reassessment (SAR) is grounded in this framework which helps me identify what types and forms of media will be most useful for un/learning and discussion. Media Literacy and Justice also aligns with my teaching goals of using accessible forms of media that we may often be exposed to and finding time to reflect together. Media Literacy allows for all participants to consider their own gaze, position, and knowing. It is a powerful tool.

A strategic use of my power as a curriculum writer was to get my "radical" curriculum into classrooms as a useful teaching tool by incorporating Social Emotional Learning competencies as I learned from the CASEL approach. I also started to work with educators who understood the Common Core State Standard for different subjects and being guided by their knowledge of the standards to build a curriculum that embodied and embraced all of these. And it works! Building intentional relationships works.

And if we begin with valuing and building intentional relationships, understanding how a relational theory such as Intersectionality invites us to examine power becomes useful. As a trained scholar of Intersectionality, taught by some of the leaders in the social sciences today, I am witnessing a misuse of this theoretical framework and praxis in our field. One where the belief is if someone cites one legal journal and no other examples of intersectional work are considered enough to demonstrate mastery of the topic. We are at a time where people think Intersectionality is only about multiple identities and never about systems of power and oppression. Where people use the terms intersectional and intersectionality incorrectly and assume the use of the term "intersection" will invoke an understanding of an Intersectional analysis or lens. I'm tired of Black women's labor and gifts through a Black feminist and womanist lens being appropriated and deemed "easy" to do by watching one TED talk or (attempting to) read one legal journal. The archive of Black feminist and womanist brilliance is very thick and full, why are people only choosing one citation? Perhaps spending time in the Intersectional Research Database the Consortium on Race, Gender, and Ethnicity built with their fellows (myself being one of them) at the University of Maryland, College Park could help demonstrate how expansive the archive of this approach and lens is to and for our field.

The curricula I create are intentional in honoring the power the participants hold, expanding on their knowledge, and creating new forms of knowledge collectively. It is a grounding in interdependence, one of my favorite principles of Disability Justice, and an upholding of body autonomy a key principle of Reproductive Justice. It is not about the educator or instructor being the "expert" or holding "expertise" all participants must learn and absorb. Instead, it is a creative space to facilitate and offer care, correction, and ask for more of each other for the world building we need.

Bibliography

Thoman, E. (2003). *Skills & Strategies for Media Education*. Malibu, CA: Center for Media Literacy.
Woodward, V. (2014). *The Delectable Negro: Human Consumption and Homoeroticism within U.S. Slave Culture*. New York, NY: New York University.

Title: Books, Media, and Archives

Writers Names: Bianca I. Laureano

Note to Educators

This may act as the core lesson for introducing the text or any form of media. It aligns with every chapter of the book and invites participants to view the book as an object.

Learning Objectives/Instructional Goal

In this lesson plan, participants will examine the anthology as an object using a Media Literacy and Justice framework.

Learning Outcomes: By the end of the lesson participants will be able to:

- Define Media Literacy and Justice
- Interpret their own perspectives on various forms of media
- Examine the anthology as a living archive

Essential Questions

- What is Media Literacy and Media Justice?
- How do I consume, interpret, and receive various forms of media?
- What are living archives? How is the anthology an archive?

CASEL Social Emotional Learning Competencies

Self-awareness: The ability to accurately recognize one's own emotions, thoughts, and values and how they influence behavior. The ability to accurately assess one's strengths and limitations, with a well-grounded sense of confidence, optimism, and a "growth mindset."

Social awareness: The ability to take the perspective of and empathize with others, including those from diverse backgrounds and cultures. The ability to understand social and ethical norms for behavior and to recognize family, school, and community resources and supports.

Relationship skills: The ability to establish and maintain healthy and rewarding relationships with diverse individuals and groups. The ability to communicate clearly, listen well, cooperate with others, resist inappropriate social pressure, negotiate conflict constructively, and seek and offer help when needed.

Responsible decision-making: The ability to make constructive choices about personal behavior and social interactions based on ethical standards, safety concerns, and social norms. The realistic evaluation of consequences of various actions, and a consideration of the well-being of oneself and others.

Materials
Various forms of media to include social media posts, print media, visual media, that are accessible for participants.

Preparation
- Read the chapter and, if possible, find and read the Thoman article
- Remember everyone may have a different reception of any media shared
- Identify and examine various forms of media to offer and use for different activities, some invite more than one

Activity 1: Objectify the Book (15 minutes estimated)
The goal of this activity is to encourage participants to view the text as an object and how it is also a living archive.

Invite participants to bring their text to the learning space in any format they have it in (i.e. hard copy, audio, ebook). Ask participants to share what their definitions and understanding is of the term "objectify." If participants stay on a discussion of objectifying a human being encourage them to expand to what it means to objectify an object, such as a book. Create a collective definition of objectification. Notice how sexuality and the erotic emerge in the discussion.

Next, ask the following questions to participants:

- How were you socialized to engage with books?
- What does it mean to treat a book as an object?

- What sacred texts exist in our communities?
- How are those sacred texts engaged with/read/held?

Begin with the book cover and instruct participants to examine the front and back cover and spine of the book. What do they notice? Welcome in a sensual approach that includes vision, auditory senses, touch, or scent. What questions emerge for them as they engage in this activity?

Activity 2: What's in an Archive (20 minutes estimated)
The goal of this activity is to engage with and examine various forms of archives available, their contents, and presentation.

Invite participants to share what they understand an archive to include. Ask participants why archives are important. You may document key points or invite participants to create a document for note taking that will be shared with the group (encourage collective note taking!).

Share that participants will be examining some archives. From the selected archives you have in various formats, go through each format and offer participants 5–10 minutes to spend time and search in those archives on their devices. Partnering participants together may be one approach which may require more time for small group/pair discussion and then report back. Consider more accessible forms of media that participants may consider:

- Hashtags i.e. #DisabledAndCute #OscarsSoWhite #AmINext #FemmeInMourning
- Print Advertisements i.e. billboards and magazine ads
- Moving Images i.e. virtual videos, movies, TV ads

Bring the group together and facilitate a short discussion about what they found and learned.

Share that for the next activity, participants are expected to visit an intentionally created and curated archive and report back on their findings. Below is a suggested list to begin considering where to look.

The Lesbian Herstory Archives, The Leather Archives, The Library of Congress has numerous archives to examine, any museum, find what is available for scholars in our interdisciplinary field such as bell hooks, Audre Lorde, José Esteban Muñoz, Octavia Butler, Julia de

Burgos, Sor Juana Inés de la Cruz, Nawal El Saadawi, James Baldwin, The Schomburg Institute, and the People of Color Zine Project are a few to consider!

Invite participants to select an archive from a list you offer or assign the group one to spend time with. Remind participants of the time to help them conclude their review. Bring the group back together and offer these questions:

What did you expect to find? What did you find? What was it like to navigate the archive?

To conclude this activity invites participants to spend time in one more archive of their choosing from the list you offer or from the suggestions below with the question to consider: How do I build my archive?

Visit/spend time with social media accounts about or that archive. Some examples of websites and social media accounts are below:

- The Diaspora Solidarity Lab https://www.instagram.com/dslprojects/
- Gran Varones http://granvarones.com and https://www.instagram.com/granvarones/
- BuildYour Archive https://www.instagram.com/buildyourarchive
  Facilitate a conversation using these questions:
- Has your idea of an archive changed or expanded?
- Where would you archive this book?
- What other activities and discussions have we experienced about a sexology archive?

Activity 3: Media Literacy 101 (20 minutes estimated)
The goal of this activity is to engage with a Media Literacy framework and discuss the core questions in practice.

Begin by sharing that the author discusses Media Literacy as a foundational framework for their curricula. What do you believe are frameworks sexuality education curricula use? Do you agree a Media Literacy approach is useful for sexuality education and sexuality trainings?

Outline the five Media Literacy Questions:

1. Who created this?
2. What techniques are used to attract me?

3. What values and points of view are offered in this media?
4. How could other people understand the message differently from me?
5. What is missing?

After offering the questions, using media that you have selected (such as an advertisement or short video) engage with the media and facilitate a conversation guided by each question above. Be prepared to offer some information as needed about the media selected. You may need to review the media again for some questions if participants need a reminder/refresher.

If Media Literacy invites inquiry, facilitate a conversation with these questions:

• What is expected of us when creating and/or implementing curricula?
• How have we been trained to understand and perform "professionalism" as sexuality professionals?
• What power do we have in challenging narrow and harmful ideas of "professionalism"?

Activity 4: Media Justice
The goal of this activity is to discuss and consider how and if the anthology is a form of Media Justice.

Begin by asking participants that based on the discussion thus far about Media Literacy, what could be Media Justice. Participants may offer a range of responses. Offer the core principles of Media Justice followed by a definition offered below:

The Media Justice League was a collective located in San Antonio, TX working with south Texas communities which adjourned in 2012. During their organizing they outlined their Media Justice core principles to include:

1. Communication is a fundamental human right.
2. Communications and cultural infrastructure should be public and used to empower communities.
3. Media strategy and policy are core movement-building strategies.

4. Movement building demands participatory communications and organizing.
5. Strategic stories can change the game.
6. Media Justice is a powerful program for change. Not just to transform media rules and rights, but to claim our stories and frame our future.

The organization MediaJustice defines this approach for the 21st century as one that

> demands a fair economy, connected communities, a political landscape of visibility, voice and power. To achieve this we need a media and technology environment that fuels real justice. We call that 'Media Justice' and recognize this as a crucial moment in our struggle for freedom—freedom from oppression, freedom to communicate.

Pause for a moment and acknowledge the silence that exists. Invite responses from participants. Make connections to what was shared by the group prior to sharing these core principles and definitions.

Connect these ideas of Media Justice and archival work. Ask participants the following questions and facilitate a discussion:

- Consider the archives you examined today, which would you consider an example of Media Justice and why?
- What have you realized you have created or participated in that is an example of Media Justice?
- How is the anthology a form of Media Justice?

Bibliography

MediaJustice. (n.d.). Who We Are. https://mediajustice.org/who-we-are/.
Media Justice League (n.d.). What Is Media Justice? https://mediajusticeleague.tumblr.com/whatismediajustice.

2

WE VISION OUR DREAMS OF SAFETY INTO REALITY

A Conversation with Kalash Magenta Fire

Jadelynn St Dre, with Kalash Magenta Fire

Throughout most of my life, 'safety' has been a word that had no context. Unclear, intangible, and ephemeral, it existed as a concept I was aware of, but had no solid framework for in practice. A history of repeated violence, intergenerational trauma, and identities that left me vulnerable to harm – these truths taught me to distrust the promise of safety, righteously, whether it was being offered from others or felt in fleeting moments within myself.

When I began to organize in the movement to end sexual assault as a survivor, safety became something I learned to demand, for myself and others. Through the wisdom of my comrades; through the teachings of great thinkers and strategists such as Audre Lorde, Mia Mingus, and Leah Lakshmi Piepzna-Samarasinha; and through collective brilliance from Incite! or within *The Revolution Starts at Home*, I learned the ways safety is politicized, and how it is a strategic aim of colonization and systemic oppression to deny safety to marginalized folk, keeping us in a constant state of hypervigilance and dissociation. It was here I learned to feel

DOI: 10.4324/9781003181927-4

gratitude for the trauma responses I carry, not as pathology, but as gifts of survival. 'Safety' then became a self-generated, complex, and exquisite manifestation of my mind and autonomic nervous system, whose potency only increased when reflected by others who had experienced similar struggles.

It was within my training to become a licensed clinician I learned that safety is an industry. Indoctrinated into an institutional definition of safety, we were taught to provide it as a necessary 'container' that was predetermined and one-sized. We were taught to promise and sell safety, despite our obligatory ties with law enforcement, child and adult protective services, state boards, and federal government. We were taught to do this while providing no vulnerability of our own, offering only a hollow 'blank slate' in return. Further, we were taught to enact our clinical expertise as arbiters of others' healing, using our power to demand our client's trust and overshadow their right as the true experts of their own transformation and liberation.

Now, continuing my work in community as an organizer, an artist, and as a sex and trauma therapist, my definition of safety is far clearer, more complex and realized. The people I support, primarily LGBTQIA2S+ and/or BIPOC folk who have experienced sexual trauma, come into our work carrying scars from what are often multiple attempts at finding responsive support and experiencing harm in return. Part of creating a context of safety for the individuals and communities with which I work means actively deconstructing and working to abolish the violence that exists within institutional support work. It also means visioning, nurturing, and building paths to healing that are reflexive, site-specific, accessible, and truly safe enough to invite revolutionary transformation.

One oft-neglected path in work with survivors of sexual trauma is that of sex, pleasure, and desire. The incorporation of this path within anti-violence work, in particular within the nonprofit sector and the clinical worlds, is practically non-existent. While collaborations with sexuality educators can result in the necessary incorporation of sexual health models, it is exceedingly rare to encounter programming that centers liberatory, ecstasy-rich sexual support that utilizes pleasure and the expression of desire as bridges toward healing. Therefore, within the field, we miss vital opportunities to utilize interventions which incite expansive, exploratory, and intimate pathways toward healing, on survivors' own terms and at their direction. This begs the question – *What might the impact on survivors of sexual violence be if healing spaces were safe enough to explicitly invite explorations of pleasure and desire as strategies toward transcendence and transformation?*

The question above is not a new one. Communities of color, queer and trans communities, sex workers, and disabled folk have been emphasizing the need for more abundant, reflective, and safer spaces within which to explore pleasure and desire, in particular for people who have experienced ongoing objectification and oppression. Further, these communities manifest such places, understanding that the articulation of 'safe space' is a highly curated and temporal act of survival. A dance party, a friend's home, an organizing meeting, or an art event becomes a site for liberation, even if its potency may begin to dissipate as we begin the long walk home. This wisdom, unsanctioned by the institutions, is not peer reviewed and therefore its brilliance does not often enter our citation pages. Practitioners – in particular practitioners of power and privilege – who seek to create transformational, liberatory space for the people they support must look to those that have long been doing this work for inspiration and design.

What follows is a co-edited transcript of a conversation between myself and one such person – Kalash (pronounced Kaa-lish) Magenta Fire, CMT, MSW, ELC (they/them). Kalash is a Black queer unicorn, Bay Area scientist of the healing arts, community organizing savant, certified massaged therapist, and puberty and sex educator, who has long been an anchor in advocating for sex worker rights and decriminalization in the Bay Area, CA. Together, we explore the question posed above, expanding upon language, and envisioning the potential impacts of a world in which support for survivors unapologetically embraces pleasure, sensation, intimacy, and desire as essential companions to healing.

Currently, my definition of safety continues to expand. I am able to articulate that safety is both power and vulnerability. Safety is accessibility, shared language, and the space to consider the true meaning of our consent. Safety is multisensory connection, somatics, and breath. Safety is representation, resonance, and reflection. I can only imagine the impact my young survivor self would have experienced, getting to have someone like Kalash in my life; of being able to read their words, hear their voice in a classroom or to have them as a trusted confidant. The interview that follows calls on us, as sexuality professionals, to consider whose voices are uplifted in our fields and why. It calls on us to consider the necessity of subversion, decolonization, radical advocacy, and political action in our practices. Further, it asks us to consider the myriad ways that safety may better manifest in our client relationships, including humbly acknowledging the limitations of our practice.

––––

J = Jadelynn and K = Kalash

J: To start with this conversation, it's important that we get clear about the language that we're using. People often make assumptions about common definitions – words like 'survivor' and 'healing,' 'pleasure,' 'desire.' I want to just start by asking you, is the word survivor one that you identify with? If not, is there a better way to describe your experience?

K: I really appreciate this question. I think 'survivor' is an important word to have. My whole world is working in healing spaces and body work. I have also done sex work, which is always a healing space. You always carry 100% of yourself in any situation. So that means, if you're a survivor, you're carrying that sexual trauma with you into healing work as well, as a practitioner or as a client. When we're saying we're survivors, that's a part of the healing that we're giving. 'Survivor' helps to define what pleasure is. How do we bring in self-care and boundaries and all these yummy things that were torn away from us and then put good ingredients into that word survivor? You do carry it with you, but what are the tools to make that violence not stay with you?

J: I really identify with that. As a trauma therapist, the field teaches that I'm supposed to show up in the room as a 'healed' version of myself, however my identities, the histories that I carry, including my traumas, brought me to do this work and can often really serve as a point of connection with my clients. My full self is in the room whether I deny that I am in the room or not.

And that's another word, right? 'Healed,' or 'healing.' I prefer the word transformation or integration, because it emphasizes a process and movement. How have you come to understand healing in the work that you do?

K: I feel like healing is a self-responsibility. If you fall down and scrape your knee, you wipe off the wound, you clean it, you bandage it. There are steps on how you prepare to heal yourself, and then you wait for it to heal. I think that's the same way for sexual trauma. Mental health is so super important, and it's especially important for people that are marginalized and for people that don't feel like anybody wants to hear what they have to say. The last time I had a solid statistic about sexual violence it's one in six women in the US. This is a very limited demographic, not taking into consideration how much more common it is for BIPOC, LGBTQIA2S+ folk, or disabled folk, but it points to the fact that it's very, very common. So I feel like if you're a person of means that does this work, it's your responsibility to take it to the streets, to meet a person where they're at or invite them to an accessible location, because a lot of people don't know how to seek these opportunities out. With BIPOC folks, you've got to think about culture. Creating the steps for a balance is what's helped me. Now, this is assuming every person has access to safe people they can trust to talk to, or a therapist. There's a lot of privilege that comes with that, because so many people feel like they don't have anybody in their lives that they can talk to. Everyone should be able to have access to support and care.

J: Absolutely. It's the having access to those folk, but also for BIPOC folk, for LGBTQIA2S+ folk, finding therapists who reflect you is very difficult in a field that is, by vast majority, white, cisgender straight folk. When we think about people that live in rural communities, it gets even more difficult. We absolutely have to acknowledge how powerful access is. I think this is where resources other than traditional therapy become really important, too. Organizers, educators, sex workers, artists can be essential gateways. Therapy can be a barrier, because many marginalized people have had traumatizing experiences with therapists.

K: Organizing is a part of my therapy. Doing something for others is a part of therapy.

J: Yes! Healing looks like both the continual work that you do on your own, but also interdependence – which can look like being there to support other folks in their process.

What about the word pleasure? How would you define pleasure?

K: Pleasure, it makes me giggle because it seems like such a white word. Black people don't really get to receive pleasure. It's one of those luxury words. White people have been allowed to relax and go on vacation, while people of color, marginalized and Indigenous folk are the ones doing the cleaning, pampering, and serving.
      That's something that BIPOC folk have to train ourselves on – that we're allowed to do what causes us pleasure. I work in an industry where I try to be a catalyst for pleasure for other people. Mainly, the people I work with in my private practice are diverse bodies, and I'm proud of that.

J: I totally hear you. So does pleasure become a word that gets reclaimed somehow? Or deconstructed and blown apart to be something that marginalized folk can see themselves reflected in?

K: Pleasure can look differently for people. Pleasure could be sitting with a group of friends while you're laughing and drinking, it could be holding your baby after a long day's work, or just sitting next to a lover or a good friend. Pleasure could be sitting down on the bus after you just got off work, and nobody bothering you. So, I need to respect the ways that folks feel comfortable experiencing pleasure, and also maybe educate and nudge a little bit about other ways of receiving pleasure.

J: I totally hear that. When I support people who have experienced sexual violence and bring in this question of pleasure, I can't tell you how many conversations I've had about cheese. As sexuality support people, we often have to figure out a way to bridge the gap, to make pleasure accessible again, emphasizing conduits to pleasure that aren't immediately addressing orgasm or even just getting a great massage. Asking folk to take something that they know fills their body with a sensation that they can name as pleasure, like a delicious food, can be one of the places that we can start to build the muscle of allowing pleasure back in. Then, we can ask – can your body also feel open to receiving pleasure in other ways, including sex, if sex is something you have in your life?

K: You start with what your body is able to manage, to be really honest with yourself by saying "no" to things that just are not your bag, and taking your time. I want to start from where they're at. If I am talking to a person who is recovering from re-traumatization, I want to start from outside of the scope of the main problem. I might start with, "What kind of touch is a good kind of touch for you? Do you like the feeling of when you get into bed? Do you like a warm shower? Do you like feathers?" Giving all kinds of descriptors, focusing in on the pleasure factor that is currently present. The goal is to try to take some of the trauma away and also elevate the good stuff that's yours. It's kind of like a delta sandwich – start with the pleasure points, then get into a bit of the darker moments, then reminding them of some of those pleasure points – that sometimes you just like to hold someone's hand and that's pleasure for you, or maybe you have sex with your partner and that feels safe for you.

   If you refuse to talk to people about sex, or if you feel uncomfortable talking to people about sex, you're taking away their sexual autonomy which has already been taken away. Where then is the opportunity to get the healing around your sexuality?

J: I want to highlight your work as a support person and as an advocate with survivors of sexual assault, and also with sex workers. How did you make your supportive spaces safe enough for survivors? What do the clinical fields get wrong about making spaces safe enough? How can we do better?

K: If it's one on one – I can't reiterate enough – you need to do the back-end work, and not make your client have to teach you. I have a therapist right now and I like her because she's a Black therapist and sometimes she gets what I'm talking about. But she doesn't know anything about being a former sex worker, she doesn't know anything about being a queer person or a person who is non-binary, a person who is intersex or a person who is asexual. I've been a body worker and massage therapist for 20 years. I maintain my freshness because I keep learning. Be clear and honest, humble and inquisitive, excitedly curious and non-judgemental. And do your homework.

With sexual violence, you can't lead a person to come in thinking that the healing process is quick and easy, that you can see this person for just six sessions and they'd be fine. Have a client-based, client-centered approach. I have been a sex worker and have experienced sexual violence on several different levels. If you are a person who has also experienced trauma, you've got to think within yourself if you have the spoons to offer support. Always have a good reference or resource on hand that you feel very confident about. Remember that in marginalized communities, especially sex work communities, people know each other. Use community agreements, and keep some sort of frame to keep things confidential, focused, and centered.

Also, support workers need to make a livable wage. But in your practice, try to incorporate maybe ten percent pro bono clientele, where you can allow space for someone who can't afford your services and give them top notch support. I have one client who pays me in oranges because that's all they can give.

J: Yes! A sliding scale is not enough. And yes! We have to expand our education and our referral database. It's not just clinicians that should be your referrals. As licensed practitioners, we can't truly offer a 'safe space' to our clients, because the systems we work within undermine even the best intentions.

As a former sex worker, can you talk about the power of sex workers working with people that have experienced sexual harm? Why is this something that there should be more space for?

K: I call sex work, intimacy work, intimacy care. Not all sex work necessarily means sex. It could be sensual work, or it could be having a conversation – there's so many different levels. Everything about sex work is therapeutic, is healing. Sex workers may be more therapeutic than what a therapist can provide, through that level of intimacy.

J: Which is why every licensed practitioner needs to be advocating for the decriminalization of sex work. If clinicians and sex workers were able to collaborate together out in the open, the impact on everyone, not just survivors of violence, would be tremendous.

        That brings us back to the initial question, which I'm going to change a little bit based on this conversation. What do you think the impact on survivors of sexual violence could be if our healing spaces were safe enough to invite sexual autonomy and pleasure as strategies towards transformation and liberation?

K: That would be a dream – to be able to speak freely about what brings you pleasure. Even bringing up that word, as I said, as a Black person I think, "That's not for me." As a sexual violence survivor, as a Black person, my body has been on display and has been a point of pleasure for others. When you're the catalyst for pleasure all the time, you don't feel like pleasure is for you. How do you take that ownership? Like we were saying earlier, it starts with the small things, like eating cheese, and then goes into, "I love fisting" (both laugh).

        Goodness, it would be a dream – just being able to express your boundaries. When you don't have the protection of education, safety, or being able to speak up and out about your sexual trauma, you're more susceptible to folk breaching those boundaries. All body education at an earlier age helps us to connect and have more confidence in protecting our bodies. I'm an intersex person and my puberty class did not mention anything about intersex, trans, non-binary, or BIPOC bodies. When I was teaching puberty and sex education, I'm really glad that we were always teaching so everybody was included. Having autonomy and representation is a privilege that should be available to any person who has experienced assault.

J: I love what you said. It's like a dream. The vision becomes a dream, which then becomes reality. I want to end by coming back to this question of safety. What does safety mean to you?

K: This whole thing is about safety. The last time I felt safe was when I was with my parents. But, for 25 years now, I've defined safety within myself. You can't always find safety in other humans, unfortunately. I have people that I absolutely love and cherish – partners and best friends and pets galore. But if I don't feel safe in myself, if I don't feel rooted in myself, then I'm going to be running around wild. Self-autonomy is where it's at. Within that, safety is making sure you're taking your meds, that you're around the right people if you can, making sure your container is safe. Sleeping is safety. The core of it starts in yourself and how you may take care of yourself, whatever that may look like. The more you know and the more you feel safe in your body, the more things are not in the shadows or in the closet.

I've been on both sides. I've had the courage to speak up, then there have been times where I feel like I couldn't speak. Those were the times I was having the worst struggle in life, because I was too afraid to speak up. It's hard, it's really, really hard to do things by yourself. Keep on talking until somebody listens. It becomes frustrating, but eventually somebody will listen.

Title: Creating Safety in Our Realities

Writers Names: Bianca I. Laureano, Jadelynn St Dre, Kalash Magenta Fire

Note to Facilitators

It is important for facilitators to begin by considering their personal relationship(s) to 'safety,' in addition to the ways that they understand their responsibility for creating a "safer" space for the participants in this group and/or discussion. Challenge yourself to clearly assess what a "safer space" can feel like for the purposes of this lesson, considering the bounds of confidentiality, location, co-occurring relationships, power differentials, the presence of consent, and accessibility concerns. As facilitators, we invite you to only offer 'safety' as it is concretely attainable, not aspirational. We highly recommend co-facilitating this group, and allowing yourselves process time both before and after. Engage somatic exercises, body mapping, ritual and community support as it is available to you. Employ the survival skills that serve you well and release, with gratitude, the ones you have outgrown. Remember your living, breathing body-mind is also in the room and deserving of holding and care.

Learning Objectives/Instructional Goal

In this lesson plan, participants will engage with the topic of safety as it connects to their work.

Learning Outcomes: By the end of the lesson, participants will be able to:

- Define what safety means for them and their work
- Create a safety plan for offering sexuality support
- Establish a gratitude practice

Essential Questions

- How do I define safety for the work I do?
- What and who needs to be included in my safety plan?
- What am I grateful for as I do this work?

CASEL Social Emotional Learning Competencies

Self-awareness: The ability to accurately recognize one's own emotions, thoughts, and values and how they influence behavior. The ability to accurately assess one's strengths and limitations, with a well-grounded sense of confidence, optimism, and a "growth mindset."

Self-management: The ability to successfully regulate one's emotions, thoughts, and behaviors in different situations – effectively managing stress, controlling impulses, and motivating oneself. The ability to set and work toward personal and academic goals.

Social awareness: The ability to take the perspective of and empathize with others, including those from diverse backgrounds and cultures. The ability to understand social and ethical norms for behavior and to recognize family, school, and community resources and supports.

Relationship skills: The ability to establish and maintain healthy and rewarding relationships with diverse individuals and groups. The ability to communicate clearly, listen well, cooperate with others, resist inappropriate social pressure, negotiate conflict constructively, and seek and offer help when needed.

Responsible decision-making: The ability to make constructive choices about personal behavior and social interactions based on ethical standards, safety concerns, and social norms. The realistic evaluation of consequences of various actions, and a consideration of the well-being of oneself and others.

Materials

What is Not Happening worksheet

Preparation

• Review the reading to familiarize yourself with the content and what is expected to facilitate this conversation.

- Consider offering preparation for the participants before doing this lesson plan. Inviting participants to create a collage or other symbolic artwork, a mix tape that they all upload to spotify for a playlist. This can be powerful to share as connected to the access check-in.

Activity 1: Introduce Topic (five minutes estimated)
The goal of this activity is to introduce the topics discussed and presented from the essay.

Share with participants that you will be discussing a chapter that examines sexual violence and responses to care by sex professionals. Encourage participants to remember they are the expert on their bodyminds and to care for themselves first as a way to care for the group.

Invite participants to share three words that describe their reading of the essay. Write these terms on a board or shared document for all participants to view and access. Use these terms to guide the next activities. Consider asking the group and yourself for moving forward:

- What can we do with these words after we have them?
- What if critical words come up?
- What do we do with any confusion or need for education?

Activity 2: Safety for Sex Professionals (20 minutes)
The goal of this activity is to support sexuality professionals in defining safety for themselves and their communities.

Share with participants that often we use the word "safety" to mean a variety of things in various contexts. Generate a list of ideas from the question: What are some meanings of "safety" as we use them in our work?

Notice that safety may mean access to condoms, consent, body autonomy, clean drinking water, and more. Notice the ways participants may have mentioned physical safety from violence that targets them. If there are none, remind participants that in the United States, it is a common occurrence to experience gun violence in schools, that accidents happen i.e. car accidents, and that there has been a steady and consistent rise of hatred rooted in white supremacy culture and settler colonial practices such as anti-semitism, trans hatred, anti-Blackness, and anti-immigrant. With this movement of hate comes targeted attacks to comprehensive sexuality education, transgender, and gender-expansive communities through anti-trans legislation, and social emotional learning competencies being questioned. Invite a discussion to the following question:

- How do we find safety as targeted individuals?
- How do we engage with those who are not targeted individuals?
- Are those who are not targeted invited to speculate?

Read aloud, or have a participant read the following excerpts from the essay:

> Sleeping is safety ... Safety is both power and vulnerability. Safety is accessibility, shared language, and the space to consider the true meaning of our consent. Safety is multisensory connection, somatics, and breath. Safety is representation, resonance, and reflection.

If there is safety in shared language, what is the collective definition of safety the group agrees upon for using throughout the session. You may offer this activity in a variety of ways. Here, we suggest a few:

First, have participants write quietly their response to this question: What is their personal definition of "safety." Allow 5–7 minutes for participants to write and think about this question.

Next, reflect and remind participants of the group agreements for your space. This may be reading them aloud or offering time for participants to review them in the space. Invite participants to consider and discuss: How is the creation of a group definition of 'safety' different from creating group agreements?

Another option is to place the large group into smaller groups for ten minutes to discuss and present their findings to the larger group. You may do this as a large group and offer a standard definition to build upon. This discussion may require you to come back to it and reflect at another time or make a decision to continue the conversation until a draft definition is agreed upon.

Use the following questions to discuss this process:

- What did the participants notice about their discussion about defining safety as a collective?
- How did they notice their personal definition of 'safety' interacting with the collective?
- Were there things that needed to be compromised or shifted?
- How did participants gauge their consent in this activity?
- How do we make sure we're safe to make safety agreements?

Activity 3: Creating Collective Safety (25 minutes)
The goal of this activity is to consider how safety is a community responsibility and to consider if such practices are possible to establish for our work.

Remind participants of the collective definition created about safety. Ask participants if there are any comments or updates they wish to offer to the definition. Make those additions if offered.

Next, invite a conversation of their understanding of the phrase "safe space." Use these questions to guide the discussion:

- What is a "safe space"?
- How do we know if we are in one?
- Is it possible to create one with others?

Note the differences and similarities in the responses participants offer. Assess how participants are discussing the topic and consider if they would benefit from defining words such as comfortable v safe. Invite participants to discuss how they may manage conflict in their spaces (classrooms, therapy room, community gathering). Is it possible for conflict to exist and it still be a space that may be "safe"? Make a list of responses and ideas to the question:

- How does a space shift from a questionable space to a safer space?
- Could a space that was previously 'unsafe' become a safe space again? Could this happen in spite of interpersonal dynamics?

Some responses may be: embracing silence, all-gender restrooms, scent-free spaces, comfortable seating for all body sizes, modeling vulnerability, etc.

Share with participants that often we are taught to do our work with a focus on inclusivity. It is important to understand and note what is being excluded or avoided before we can discuss what is inclusive. This may also be received as an example of a content warning for some participants. Invite participants to complete the What is Not Happening worksheet to begin to think and write about what they may say verbally for the classes or sessions they create. Offer 5–7 minutes for this worksheet to be considered. Remind participants this activity is a living document and draft to help them practice before they find themselves in a specific situation again where safety must be addressed.

You may partner students together to share their experience or offer the following questions:

- What was your experience thinking about exclusion?
- How is clarity on exclusion a practice towards safety?

Activity 4: Gratitude Practice (20 minutes estimated)
The goal of this activity is to establish a practice for gratitude.

This ritual is best done with a guide. You can choose to either have a trusted beloved read the following to you as you engage with the prompts, or to record yourself reading it to follow along. Please consider pre- and aftercare as a component of any ritual. What do you need to hold yourself through what may emerge? Consider this from a multisensory place. What are the tactile objects, scents, sounds, tastes, or support beings that best provide you comfort? What would you like to have greet you after completing this ritual? What might you need to communicate to others so that any boundaries that may arise are respected? How might you need to be held?

This is a ritual that can be accessed at any time, many times, and in myriad ways. It is meant to be shaped and changed to best fit and respect the uniqueness of you.

Don't worry.

This ritual will ask nothing more than you consent to give.

Only you know the shape that best suits your body, the one that brings you in the most direct contact with the ground, your bed, your chair. A position that you can sustain, or one that will provide you ease of access to any rhythms, tempos, or changes that you need to engage through the course of the next ten minutes. The intention is to keep you in active comfort to the extent it is possible for you, and in the most proximal relationship to the ground.

If you can access deep breath without pain, take one now.

If shallower breaths are all that is accessible, take a sip of air and release it with your lips parted so that you can feel the air as it leaves your body.

This is how we begin.

Without touching your chest or your pulse – can you feel your heartbeat? The answer may be yes or may be no. Neither is wrong. Listen for it. See if you can sense it. If you can't, allow yourself to touch into it for a moment at your chest, wrist, or nape of your neck to remind yourself of its cadence. If touching isn't possible, you can also imagine. Your instincts feed your imagination and are trustworthy.

Once you find it, remember – this is the rhythm that has kept you alive, from the moment your clustered cells produced your beating heart. It drummed through and with the body of the parent who carried you, which had been carried in the body that carried them, and before them, and before. This is the rhythm of your ancestors.

And like your ancestors, every emotion you have felt, every celebration, every hardship, every ounce of joy and pain has occurred in symphony with your heartbeat. It is your soundtrack, adjusting to your state of being with a swiftness only possible as a result of its deep knowledge of you, and its full respect and care for everything you are and everything you will be. Its purpose is not only to keep you alive but also to remind you of what you have had to do to stay alive. Its purpose is to pump the blood through your veins so that you can take action with the whole of your bodymind in the pursuit of your own brilliant survival.

Can you feel its respect for you? Can you feel its reverence?

There is no judgment toward us from our heartbeat. It responds to us, lightning fast, because it trusts our intentions, wisdom, and knowledge. It knows that we do what we must to stay alive. Our hearts are like the tree base of our bodymind, its veins spinning off as roots creating an intricate, interwoven network that is the super-highway of our cells, our blood, and all that flows between. Our circulatory system is akin to mycelium, our spinal cord, our trunk, our brain branches, our musculature and skin, the leaves and fruits.

A tree is a deeply active, yet sentient being. Within their pulp lies the collected wisdom of sometimes hundreds of years. Imagine how intimately a tree comes to know the ground around them through centuries of witnessing. Imagine the detail they are able to take in from their environment day upon day, year upon year, season upon season, the things they must know and secrets they must hold.

Now, in its sentience, imagine the level of acceptance they must bring to the world around them. There is only so much a tree is able to affect change. While it is certain that we humans often fail to access the depth, knowledge, and capacity for magic required to truly understand a tree, nor what they are capable of, we know that there are a great many things a tree cannot control in its environment. We know that a tree aspires to flourish with abundance and to grow and age, in community and lush. We know that a tree endeavors to protect themself and their sibling trees against parasites, disease, mammals, birds, even humans. We also know that there is a great deal out of their control. We know they cannot always keep themselves safe. We do not blame the tree for this, no. We know that they act in the interest of their own survival.

Now return to your heartbeat. Can you visualize it, like a tree? Begin by imagining its shape and movement as it pumps in time with your breath. Close your eyes and track its aorta, spreading out into vines of pulsating life, each serving a function, providing nutrients. Imagine your spinal cord, stretching through your back like a trunk, razor straight or curled or bowed. Like a tree, imagine how much your heartbeat has witnessed throughout the course of its history with you. This heart knows you and has been witness to your experiences, and impacted by the histories that came before you. Take in how intricately your heartbeat has witnessed you, in all of your ferocious brilliance and potent vulnerability. It has seen you in your hardest places and softest, shaking bridge and steady ground. It has seen the aftershocks in you, and consigned to the ways you have kept going, despite the unspeakable harms you have weathered. It has been there when you have acted out of pain, when you have caused harm to others and also to yourself. It has celebrated you when you have chosen to keep breathing by beating even more strongly. It has comforted you in grief by reminding you to slow down.

Do you see how well your heartbeat knows you?

Now, track back into that heartbeat. Allow yourself to feel/hear it in the ways that are accessible to you. Imagine this feeling, this sound, this rhythm present to you throughout every second of your story. Acknowledge that it has kept beating even in moments that you thought it might stop. Even in moments you may have wanted it to.

Remember to breathe in the ways that nourish you, beloved. Remember to breathe.

And now, ask yourself at this moment – what would it be like to trust yourself the way that your heartbeat trusts you? To believe that the place that you find yourself now, in this moment, is one that deserves your beating heart? Imagine knowing yourself the way your heart knows you, and truly believing that all you have done to survive has been done with purpose, and that purpose was worthy. Take a moment to honor this survival, the skill it has taken, the sheer magnitude of your capabilities, your depth, your creativity, your genius. Know that your heartbeat has seen this in you. Know that, even when you forget, it knows.

Now, locate your heartbeat again. Has it changed? Were you able to find them more easily? Take a few moments, minutes, hours – whatever feels right for you – to listen to it drum. Ask your heartbeat if you can borrow some of its acceptance, some of its reverence, some of its gratitude for you. Know that it will say yes. Believe it. You and your heartbeat are linked in a dance for your survival and, together, you can determine what directions to go.

————

The continuation of the ritual ends in the artistic rendering of a tree with many branches. Feel free to represent this in any way that you wish – collage, sketch, paint, sculpture, poetry, any way that calls to you. Be aware of any critical parts of your cognitive mind that arise, and gently let them know they are not needed at this time. With each branch you draw, name a way that you have survived – a survival skill – and record it along the limb. Next, adorn each limb with a fruit of your choosing, one that exists or that is imaginary. These fruits symbolize the gifts that continue to be useful provided by each survival skill. Last, include fruits that have dropped to the ground from each branch, symbolizing ways each survival skill may not be needed/helpful anymore, and can now be composted. Gaze at your tree, tuck it away some place safe, share it or erase it. You will continue to hold it in your bodymind.

What's NOT Happening Worksheet

Instructions: Take a few moments to consider how you identify what is NOT included in your work/approach/etc.

What communities do you NOT center in your work? Who would not fully benefit from attending your sessions?

What types of language will you NOT use in your space?

If there is conflict, what will NOT be done by the facilitator?

What type of people/offerings will you NOT refer to when offering referrals?

3

"BUYING PEOPLE EVERYDAY"

Power, Intimacy, and Money at Work

Christina Tesoro

Last night, I watched *Indecent Proposal* with my Salome, a sex worker and writer friend of mine. The 1993 movie stars Woody Harrelson and Demi Moore as David and Diana Murphy, a young married couple who are financially down on their luck after a recession hits them hard. In desperation, they go to Vegas, and in a random string of luck, David wins $25,000 playing craps. Meanwhile, Diana meets a coiffed and classically handsome John Gage (played by 57-year-old Robert Redford) while perusing designer dresses. Instantly captivated by her beauty, Gage offers to buy her the dress. "I'm not for sale," Diana tells him flatly. Gage calls her naive; "I buy people every day," he tells her. Diana returns to the casino just in time to see her husband lose all the money he won the day before, leaving them in worse straits than ever. After soliciting Diana to play his Lady Luck, Gage makes a big show of betting 1 million dollars on the line and wins his bet. Afterwards, he invites the couple out to dinner, and he makes them an offer they can't afford to refuse: 1 million dollars, to spend the night with Diana.

DOI: 10.4324/9781003181927-5

I don't remember how old I was the first time I saw the movie. I think I must have been at least in high school. Even as a young teen, I felt confused by it. The million dollars Diana and David received – and that Diana earned by sleeping with Gage – changes hands many times throughout the movie. Driven by jealousy and his own insecurity, David can't stop himself from asking invasive questions about the night Diana spent with the millionaire. Eventually, the couple separates and divorces. Neither of them want the money; nor do they want to split it.

Watching the movie with a sex worker friend, after six years of working in the sex industry on and off myself, the movie makes even less sense to me now. I remember as a teen asking myself how much money it would cost for me to agree to fuck someone. Before I was a sex worker, there were lots of factors to consider: How hot or gross is the customer? How guilty would I feel afterwards? And what amount of money would make the guilt or disgust I assumed I would feel be worth my while?

The feelings that came up for me around sex for money as a teen are feelings that are likely familiar to most non-sex working people, maybe even some sex educators and clinicians. Part of what I've learned from being a sex worker, though, is how to tease out the sex from the work. Indecent Proposal flops, in my opinion, because of the way it emphasizes (and, to my mind, blow out of proportion) agreed upon and consented to extramarital sex. By contrast, my experiences in the club were way less about sex and eroticism, and a lot more about how I felt about work. When I felt negatively about work as a stripper, it was in a nutshell, because I was overwhelmed, exhausted, frustrated, and annoyed about how hard it was to try to survive within a capitalist system and society, and how jarring it was to context switch between the institution of academia, and the culture of a strip club dive.

It's important to me to state in academic spaces that my time as a sex worker generally isn't something I regret – much of the time, I look back on those years with fondness for the company of coworkers I kept, and in awe of my own grit and determination. I learned more at the club than I ever learned inside a classroom in my social work Master's program. Now, I'm a somatic trauma therapist and sex educator in private practice, a self-employed small business owner in charge of my own schedule and rates. Before becoming a stripper, I worked 9 to 5 mostly in the field of hospital administration; this type of work didn't suit my neurodivergence, and I was incredibly unhappy in that role. Stripping gave me a way to break away from that prescriptive work/life balance in order to create a more sustainable life for myself under capitalism. In gratitude, I specialize in working with sex workers in an industry that, at best, ignores the needs of sex workers. At worst, institutional mental health stigmatizes sex workers, discriminates against them, and actively works against their well-being. Yet sex work shaped my understanding of power, work, money, and intimacy – all themes that come up regularly in sessions with all of my patients, sex workers, and civilians alike.

Some of my sex-working patients fall into the category that clinicians might describe as "survival sex workers." The academics who coined the term "survival sex work" primarily had in mind street-based youth who traded in sex in order to house and feed themselves, though since then, the term seems to have generalized to include anyone who does sex work as their primary source of income, or who relies solely on the money they make from sex work to pay the bills, rent, food, health care needs, et cetera. Many of the sex workers I work with as therapy patients disapprove of this term, though. Who among us, they insist, whether in the sex industry or not, isn't working to survive the oppressive capitalist system we all unwillingly find ourselves under?

They are, of course, completely correct. I got my license to practice about six weeks before the start of the COVID-19 pandemic, and my focus on money, power, and work within trauma therapy has only sharpened since then. The sex industry was hit hard by the COVID-19 pandemic, with in-person work becoming exponentially more dangerous, cam sites being flooded with newbies, customers navigating their own financial shifts as a result of the pandemic, and the difficulty of sufficiently documenting one's employment in an underground, cash-based economy in order to receive Pandemic Unemployment Assistance. When the pandemic hit, my club shut down, and overnight I was without two-thirds of my income. The club remained closed for about a year and a half, and within that time, I had to scramble to build a sustainable therapy practice for myself. I personally experienced the anxiety of applying for unemployment and grappled with the question of whether or not it was worth it to out myself on a legal document in order to receive unemployment assistance – something I had a right to, since I had been paying my taxes diligently in the years before I entered the sex industry, and continued to do as a stripper.

At the start of the pandemic, I was working at a well-known psychotherapy clinic. In fact, it was one of the first therapy practices that specifically catered to the needs of LGBTQ+ patients, and prided itself on an intersectional, anti-oppressive approach to therapy that stressed just practice. In spite of these purported values, I was being paid $25 a session as a fee-for-service therapist (an independent contracting position) out of the $105 per session the clinic charged. I saw between 14 and 17 patients a week and brought home $1,400–$1,700 per month as a therapist - something quite common for new LMSWs (Licensed Master of Social Work, the first social work license one can qualify for out of grad school). I simply couldn't afford not to do sex work, despite having a Master's degree in social work and a license, and had COVID-19 not shut down the club, I figured I would be working there for at least the years it took me to get my LCSW (Licensed Clinical Social Worker), the licensure I would need to finally open a private therapy practice, and retire from dancing. Most fee-for-service agency settings are like this; the only reason I was able to pivot from dancing to full time therapy during COVID was by finding supervisors who shared my values and worked with me to create a more equitable and sustainable financial agreement between us while I practiced as an LMSW.

In grad school, I sat across from speakers from the National Organization of Women preaching at me about how every form of sex work was by definition exploitation, which seemed ironic to me then as an unpaid intern, and continued to grate as a severely underpaid LMSW. I spent a lot of time thinking about how my $25 fee-for-service rate was also the price of a five-minute lap dance at the strip club (not including tip), and was just $2 more than what I was making per hour as a hospital administrator prior to getting my Master's degree. In school, I overheard classmates snorting about how they would never want to work with sex workers because they could "never work with anyone who had so little respect for themselves," again projecting their own feelings about sex onto sex work. But I didn't experience sexualization at work for the first time in the strip club, though the club was the first place I *consented* to that sexualization as part of my job description: At 16, I worked off the books for less than minimum wage at my local grocery store, where I took home an envelope of cash each week, and experienced frequent sexual harassment from the male employees. Sexualization and harassment at work is a distressingly common experience for femme presenting folks across industries, yet sex workers are the only ones who are presumed to lack self-respect when we encounter it.

Feminine socialization has been an integral part of how I experience work throughout my life. I worked in doctors' offices, homeless shelters, hospitals, and in high schools. I fared slightly better in hospitals ($23/ hour and decent benefits) than private doctors' offices ($11–$13/hour, no benefits), though neither rate was what minimum wage should be, if it were adjusted for inflation today.[1] I've scheduled abortions and mediated conversations between bewildered and furious parents and their sexually active teens. I've put my body between two boys much larger than me and begged them not to fight, so they wouldn't lose their beds at the shelter for the night. I've fried chicken and burgers and hot dogs and plated them for hungry, angry queer teens who had been kicked out of their childhood homes for being gay. And I've, mostly naked, before a bar of one, or five, or fifty men, some leering, others gazing with stars in their eyes, most of them reaching out for a caress, some catching themselves before contact, sheepish, chagrined. Others felt no such shame.

Most of the work I've done has been considered rote, obvious, a given: care work or intimate, erotic labor; the type of work that is hardly considered to be work when performed by someone femme presenting, as I am. Necessary but natural, according to my perceived gender. The doctors I worked for didn't interact with their administrative staff as if we were people with full lives and feelings. An office manager once walked up to my desk and helped herself to my snacks without asking, while I sat there silent and gaping as a fish. It's not an exaggeration when I say I felt more objectified as an office administrator than I ever did as a stripper. In offices and hospitals, I was a robot, a piece of decor, a scapegoat for delays in radiology or the chemotherapy pharmacy, an emotional punching bag. In the club, I was interacting with objectification willingly, playing with it creatively in how I did my makeup and put together my outfits. If strip club clientele acted up or acted out, there was no rule (the way there is in reception work and in the service industry) of the customer being always right. Contrary to popular belief, I experienced a lot more freedom in the club than I did in any office job, and common refrain among the sex workers I see as a therapist now. It's important for clinicians and sex educators to recognize these dynamics and include them in how we understand work dynamics more generally, regardless of industry.

This isn't to put the sex industry on some kind of pedestal or to glamorize it in any way. It isn't easy to interact with sexual objectification as part of one's job, the energy is frequently heavy, draining, and depleting, and tied to patriarchal violence that of course exists outside the club as well. And while there are some sex workers who discuss their work as though they are priestesses, healers, and Sacred Whores, in general, that has not been my experience. The space of the dressing room felt sacred to me, though. I sipped iced black coffee with sweetener and ate chicharron and avocado salads at midnight in the soft and scented arms of the femmes who loved me, perhaps the first group of people to make me feel like one of them. Dancing, I felt powerful, wearing makeup as armor, leather, and lace as battle regalia, watching myself with wonder and lust as I strutted across the stage. But most strip club customers are not consciously looking for a religious experience or even necessarily a healing one; most customers want to get as much as they can get away with, for as little money as possible. And while there is a part of me that will always long for a world or time in which money can be exchanged for sex, and healing be an explicit and intentional part of the exchange, I don't know if that exists under capitalism for most sex workers.

Effective work with sex workers means challenging ourselves to hold both/and as deeply and gently as possible. I encountered violence at the club at times, and in many ways, stripping was the best job I'd ever had up until that point. I was, for the most part, in charge of my own schedule and was able to pick shifts that more or less fit around my grad school obligations. I had fun with my coworkers. I loved being on stage, my body long and powerful, surrounded by mirrors and smoke and neon lights, something more than human up there in incomprehensible plastic heels. I got drunk, sometimes. Sometimes, I got lucky and clocked an extremely generous customer early in the night; occasionally, that customer could be converted into a regular, for a time. And…it was also tiring work. The male staff were creepy and misogynistic, and some of the house moms (managers who had once been dancers themselves) liked to play games and create cliques, which meant hypervigilance and meticulous boundary work was necessary to get through most shifts. The men I danced for, by and large, did not value the work I did. They didn't even see it as work, and – young or old, rich or broke, attractive or ugly – often treated the club as a place they could go to find someone who would be happy to fold herself into their lives, a vending machine perpetually dispensing sex, care, affection, attention, love, intimacy, all with no need for reciprocity.

Still, stripping paid better than any and all of my respectable jobs ever had, and taught me more about relationships, and about what I am capable of, than social work school did. For that, it was better than any job I've ever had, except for being a therapist.

***

Intimacy – which I define as the space to be authentically one's self, and be seen, held, and accepted in one's vulnerability, and one's flaws – is the one thing people want most in the world, maybe even more than money. Yet, it's also something we are most reluctant to truly value. In the sex industry and in therapy, intimacy (or the suggestion of it) is a core part of the relationship for which you're paying.

The desire for intimacy looks very different in each setting, and my relationship to it varies widely. When I was first starting out as a stripper, I confused men talking to me about their feelings for intimacy (a misunderstanding I've made in my personal life as well). I find that straight men confuse this too: At the club, they are the adored center of attention, and the energy flows in one direction – toward them. In sex work, the other part of the transaction/equation is compensation (money). Often, customers are resentful of this. It shatters the illusion. It forces them to realize, though they may not be aware of it, that this one-sided intimacy is not, in fact, what they are seeking, though in their "real" lives, they often don't know how to find or co-create mutual, reciprocal intimate relationships.

This, I think, is where the well-known aphorism of sex workers-as-naked-therapists comes from, but working as a therapist quickly disavowed me of this conceptualization. If strippers approximate any kind of therapy, then it is the old, outdated Freudian model (one I don't find particularly therapeutic): stripper as tabula rasa, the blank slate upon which men project their fantasies, their desires, and the emotions they themselves cannot hold or regulate or process: their desire, their shame, and their rage.

Intimacy, however, is mutual, reciprocal. When I was dancing, I didn't experience it, not even with my regulars. I offered a lot of things: fun and entertainment; the sweetness of being the placeholder for a girl next door; the opportunity for time travel ("You look just like my ex-girlfriend").

The experience I offered was somatic and relational: soft skin and beating heart to be cradled against, perhaps the way Mom never did; a stern, fond presence to crush and combat trauma under the heel of a leopard print boot. These were all gifts of my body and energy, but the vulnerability to be myself, the person I am and the years of my experience, my childhood self, my adolescence, my interiority, the way I have healed and am healing my own trauma, was not included in the bargain. Strip club customers know this; I suspect it's why so many of them beg us, over and over, to tell them our real names.

As a therapist, by contrast, all of those things do enter the room with me: the self as a tool, as an instrument. Perhaps this is why, after a long day of sessions, I sometimes disassociate: my instrument is tapped out, drained, frayed like a violin bow in need of resin, needing to be tightened and called back into itself, a stringed instrument in need of tuning.

In general, I don't share much of my personal life with my therapy patients, though they can find me on social media, and sometimes we talk about what reading my writing or interacting with my social media presence is like for them. I don't, however, outright lie, the way I did with customers at the club (to create a more perfect fantasy for a better payout, but more importantly, to keep myself safe). My interiority is very present when I work as a therapist. It's the key to my empathy, my ability to attune. To hum or vibrate in concert with my clients. To collaborate, to co-create, to improvise effectively together in order for the conditions for healing to emerge.

Because of the intimate nature of our work, it's not uncommon for therapists to have a hard time talking about money. Similarly, in grad school, many professors actively discouraged the clinical social work students who had plans to go into private practice. At the same time, any acknowledgment of starting salaries for MSWs in agency settings was conspicuously absent, though I've seen listings with salaries as low as the "high 20k" including job descriptions that ask for on-call time, sky-high caseloads, and have the audacity to state "bilingual speaking ability a must." Supervisor after supervisor has assured me that it's normal to find it awkward and uncomfortable, having to charge late cancellation and no-show fees, especially when you work with people who have diagnoses like ADHD, CPTSD, or cycling mood disorders that impact executive functioning and impulsivity. The session fee is not just a fee for services rendered. The therapeutic relationship is an intimate one, and the feelings that arise around a session fee, or charging for a late cancellation are clinically relevant to the work. At the same time, therapy is my job. It's what allows me to keep a roof over my head and food on my table, and there are limits to how much trauma therapy one person can do in a week and not burn out. Yet, learning how to talk about money in therapy is something I learned after I graduated from my program, in supervision after the topic had already been raised in session with patients.

I've seen and been adjacent to a lot of conversations about money mindset, both among sex worker social media and lately – and somewhat alarmingly – among certain therapy "influencers" on Instagram, some of whom come from a social work background. Strippers and sex workers seem to like money mindset, especially the more successful ones, or the ones who have a course to sell. Entrepreneurs are into it, too. So are many sex educators, and coaches. There are even courses now for therapists to hone their competency in "financial therapy," to hold space for clients around money, finance, scarcity and abundance, and the complex emotional and attachment-based experiences we have around them.

But our choices around money have to do with much, much more than mindset. My club opened up again in July 2021. The time away made walking into it challenging, something my coworkers and I discussed at length before that first night back. It was a trip for our nervous systems to be inside with so many people after a year and a half avoiding crowds like the literal plague. In the time away, many of us also discovered that we're not actually nocturnal creatures and that our bodies feel better getting adequate amounts of sleep at night. And stepping into the environment where we would interact with the heavy energy of other people's needs and desires required a profound readjustment after so much time away.

A customer showed up for me, a man who claimed he had spent the whole pandemic thinking of me, though I didn't think of him once, didn't send a text, didn't even remember his name. We sat in the VIP room, cozied up on the squashy couch with peeling velvet upholstery. He kept requesting to see me outside of the club, asking again and again and each time I said no. I remember being outwardly calm and still as I demurred again, though in the red light of the "Fantasy Zone," his eyes looked uniformly black, like a shark's. He cried. He begged. He cajoled. The emotional manipulation was potent and obvious, a front and an act of poorly disguised rage. Afterwards, I went into the dressing room, changed my outfit to wear all black, and pulled back my hair into a severe ponytail – dominatrix hair, according to a coworker. I didn't speak to him for the rest of the night, taking instead a younger, submissive customer, and gagging him for a quarter of an hour with the heel of my shoe. The first customer left, in a fit and a huff. At home the next evening, I wrote his name on a piece of paper and put it in a jar with the diamond necklace he gave me, bound it in salt and black wax, and canceled the rest of my shifts for the month to recalibrate my safety.

The only reason I was able to do this was because in the time away, I had built up my therapy practice within relationships with supervisors that prioritized my emotional health and safety. Because of this, I was able to navigate the complicated algebra of safety at the club much, much differently. I was also able to walk away from someone who made the hair on the back of my neck stand up a little bit in warning. Had I been in grad school, I probably would have continued to entertain that client as a regular, at least while he was spending, regardless of how uncomfortable he made me.

None of the choices I've made in sex work had anything to do with my self-respect; all of them were informed by what I needed to pay my bills, which I think is partially why Indecent Proposal stood out as so outlandish to Salome and me. We griped for a while after the movie ended. How it's obviously written by a straight man, because all the conflict hinged around male insecurity and fragility, the toxic masculine inability to tolerate the thought of "their" woman enjoying herself with someone else, and allowing a different man to enjoy her body. The idea of "dirty" money, and how ludicrous it was to think that anyone in the world would turn their nose up at a million dollars cash for one night's labor – especially if you factor in inflation: 1 million dollars in 1993 is just over 2 million dollars today in 2022. I'd need at least as much if I ever wanted to buy a house in my hometown of Queens.

As a palate cleanse, we switched to marathon to the British-American television drama Harlots, which came out in 2017, and was written and produced by women. Though parts of the show are as over-the-top and salacious as Indecent Proposal, the topics of work, money, and power rang so much more true to me, and the scenes depicting sex work onscreen were clearly more about work than sex. The show was also clearly well-researched.

Most of the sex-working women in London in the late 1700s were doing so due to some blend of circumstance and coercion. They were "ruined" or "fallen" by having sex out of wedlock (sometimes consensually, sometimes they were assaulted). Often, these women were "ruined" before they even reached puberty, through the violence of male family members, duplicitous lovers, or simply by being born into abject poverty. More than once, the sex workers on the show struggle to hold both the fact that their experience within the industry generates much harm and trauma and that sex work is often the best way for them to survive the crisis of extreme wealth disparity that characterizes the time they're living through. In most cases, there weren't any other good options for single women and queer people, due to changing social dynamics that worsened with the privatization of land and the commons, the switch from a feudal to a capitalist economy, and the elevation of (white, male) doctors over the traditional knowledge of midwives and wise women with the advent of institutional medicine, according to Silvia Federici in *Caliban and the Witch*. As Europeans began their colonization efforts, they brought these economic and social dynamics with them, where they continue to shape people's lives to this day.

As we watched the show, Salome and I winced with recognition at some parts and cheered on the harlots' ingenuity, resourcefulness, courage, and resilience at others. We talked about how much sex work has made possible for us: Assuredness in our bodies, savviness and discernment in our interactions with so many different kinds of people, confidence in our ability to alchemize patriarchal violence and objectification into what we need to get by, and the most vibrant, loving, and wise community of friends and coworkers we've ever known. I thought about the students I went to grad school with, the ones who were so condescending in their assumptions about sex workers' self-respect. I snidely wondered how much they have left on their student loans, because mine are paid off. While I may have occasionally worried for my safety at the club, I have never once worried about my self-respect, and I've gained insight into human sexuality and desire that might've been difficult to come by otherwise. If I had to choose it again, in a heartbeat, I would.

Title: Power, Intimacy, and Money at Work

Writers Names: Bianca Laureano

Note to Educators
This lesson plan aligns with several other chapters in the text.

Learning Objectives/Instructional Goal
In this lesson plan, participants will engage with topics of money, value, professionalism, and expectations for sexuality professionals.

Learning Outcomes: By the end of the lesson, participants will be able to

- Identify how to collaborate with and learn from sex workers
- Discuss the work and compensation of sexuality professionals
- Create scripts for responding to questions about sex education in schools
- List how professionalism, assimilation, and power are defined by western and colonial models of knowledge and education
- Build an understanding of more expansive and liberatory pedagogy

Essential Questions
- What may I learn from sex workers and how do I collaborate with them?
- What work do sexuality professionals do? What do I want to do in the sexuality field?
- What are some ways I may respond when asked about sex education?
- How do I understand expectations of professionalism, assimilation, and power?
- How do I create an expansive and liberatory pedagogical approach?

CASEL Social Emotional Learning Competencies
Self-awareness: The ability to accurately recognize one's own emotions, thoughts, and values and how they influence behavior.

The ability to accurately assess one's strengths and limitations, with a well-grounded sense of confidence, optimism, and a "growth mindset."

Social awareness: The ability to take the perspective of and empathize with others, including those from diverse backgrounds and cultures. The ability to understand social and ethical norms for behavior and to recognize family, school, and community resources and supports.

Relationship skills: The ability to establish and maintain healthy and rewarding relationships with diverse individuals and groups. The ability to communicate clearly, listen well, cooperate with others, resist inappropriate social pressure, negotiate conflict constructively, and seek and offer help when needed.

Responsible decision-making: The ability to make constructive choices about personal behavior and social interactions based on ethical standards, safety concerns, and social norms. The realistic evaluation of consequences of various actions, and a consideration of the well-being of oneself and others.

Materials
- Stay Curious worksheet
- Paper and something to write with for each participant

Preparation
- Review the work of bell hooks and be familiar with the text *Teaching to Transgress: Education as the Practice of Freedom*
- Consider your own biases regarding sex work, capitalism, and western forms of knowledge before facilitating this conversation

Activity 1: Introduce Topic (ten minutes)
The goal of this activity is to introduce the topic and what is possible for us to learn when we collaborate and learn from sex workers.

Begin by inviting participants to share what their immediate responses and thoughts were to reading the article. Share that the major themes of work, value, money, intimacy, and power will be highlighted during the discussion today. Ask participants:

- What do we learn about work, money, intimacy, and power from sex workers?

Activity 2: WORK, Work, Work (30 minutes estimated)
The goal of this activity is to discuss the work of sexuality professionals and create scripts for responding to sexuality education in school.

Building from the list generated from the question above about what we learn about work as sexuality professionals from sex workers, ask participants

- What do you believe the work of a sexuality professional includes?

There may be a range of responses from participants. If it is not shared, remind participants that our work is also about safety, care, empathy, harm reduction, self-determination, and love. Remind participants that these are essential elements to our work and when we remove them from the work we do that is when we begin to align with a western colonial model of work, expectation, and is not sustainable.

Reminding or sharing about how some communities and families respond to sexuality education in the school system, ask

- What are reasons offered for why a young person is not allowed to join a sexuality education space.

Document the responses offered from participants where they may access. You will hear a range of responses from cultural and personal values to myths. All of the responses are valid when generating this list.

Reviewing the list, identify which suggestions offered are ones that may require a response by the educator. An example is given below. Do this for at least four responses listed as either a large group or as a quiet writing activity. Then, share it with the larger group.

Example:

Reason: Sexuality education and topics should be taught at home not at school.

Response 1: I agree sexuality education begins at home and also is affirmed at home for young people. May I ask you some questions? (if consent is offered ask) How may I support you in preparing to discuss sexuality topics at home? Do you need a resource or training? What books are you using? What topics are you not feeling fully prepared to discuss?

Response 2: Thank you for sharing. Your child will not be attending this class, and here is a sample assignment they may be invited to complete during this time. (give an example of assignment)

You may offer time for participants to practice sharing these scripts in front of the group or in pairs depending on your time.

To complete this activity ask participants:

- How do responses from some community members mirror negative ideas of sexuality i.e. shame, fear, morality, and confusion that extend to/are aligned with how sex workers are treated/supported?

Activity 3: VALUE & MONEY: Professionalism or Assimilation? (30 minutes estimated)

The goal of this activity is for participants to make connections to professionalism, assimilation, and power as understood by western and colonial models of knowledge and education.

Begin by inviting participants to take a piece of paper and fold it in half creating two sections on the paper by the crease. On one side of the crease, participants are to write "professional" and on the other side of the crease, participants are to write "unprofessional." Without defining these terms, instruct participants to take 60 seconds and create a list of the types of clothing sexuality professionals wear that may be in each category. After 60 seconds, invite another round for the same amount of time to generate a list of topics to be discussed in a sexuality education/professional space that may be in each category.

You may pair participants to share their list or invite some participants to offer what they wrote down to the larger group. Record the responses and note any similarities or trends that may emerge. For example, you may notice what is considered "unprofessional" for the clothing section may include specific examples based on stereotypes of gender, class, race, culture, immigration status, sexual orientation, and disability. Do the same for the category on topics to discuss.

Facilitate a discussion about the lists generated and offer some suggestions on how they understood "professional" and "unprofessional." Next, invite participants to take some time and respond to the sentence stem:

I feel powerful and know I'm powerful when I am dressed in ....
I am powerful when I adorn and decor my body in/with ....

Connect to how the author discussed their choice of attire when engaging in sex work and choosing their battle regalia. Connect further to how the author discusses the way they were trained to understand their work as an emergent sex therapist to be a "tabula rasa"/blank slate for clients to project their desires, needs, etc. upon. Share that if we use a Media Literacy approach to how we adorn, decor, and present ourselves to our clients and participants, they consume us and our bodyminds and how we present ourselves to them. Ask participants:

- If we are encouraged and expected to not present in ways that are powerful for us, what messages are being shared to participants?
- What stories may they make up of us if we are not encouraged to present in our full power?

Remind participants that often these expectations of professionalism are rooted in a very western and colonial approach to work and capitalism that upholds a hierarchy of power and control.

Connect to how the author discusses the shift in their mindset regarding compensation for their work. Ask participants what annual income they believe a sex professional they aspire to be may make and write that number down. Next, ask participants to write the annual income they believe represents a thriving wage/

salary. Discuss the difference that emerges in the two numbers. Ask participants:

- What is a thriving wage/salary?
- What training or education about salary, negotiation, compensation, and finances exist for sex professionals?
- Who are the sex professionals that make a thriving wage/salary? What are their practices to sustain that wage/salary? Which of those practices are tied to western and colonial approaches of work and compensation?

Activity 4: INTIMACY & POWER: Asking Better Questions as Pedagogy (20 minutes)
The goal of this activity is to build on the conversation of work and money to welcome in what a sexuality learning space could be when guided by engaged and liberatory pedagogy.

Keeping the previous conversation of thriving wages, power, and sexuality work present in the space by keeping notes for all to view, share that you will be discussing how sexuality professionals may practice a more liberatory form of pedagogy. You may need to define the term pedagogy for some participants. We suggest using bell hooks' definition of "engaged pedagogy":

> to be actively committed to a process of self-actualization that promotes their own well-being if they are to teach in a manner that empowers students.
> (Teaching to Transgress: Education as the Practice of Freedom, 1994, p. 15)

Ask participants the following questions and facilitate a conversation:

- What is your response to this passage?
- What must occur or is needed to make possible/create the learning and healing space the author describes?
- What are some ways to elevate the questions we offer when creating educational spaces or sharing knowledge?
- Why is a focus on questions and curiosity a violation of how we are taught to understand education, pedagogy, and knowledge?

Next, use the Stay Curious worksheet. Read the instructions to participants and offer five minutes to work on the worksheet. After the time has ended, you may partner participants up and come up with a new question they collaborated on to create. Have each pair share back to the group their new question/s.

To wrap this section up, invite participants to write one question that they have for the future of their work.

Activity 5: Wrap Up (ten minutes estimated)
The goal of this activity is to invite participants to think ahead to the future and imagine a world that is possible and respond to this sentence stem:

The future of sexuality work and healing is ....

Citation/Attribution

hooks, b. (1994). *Teaching to Transgress: Education as the Practice of Freedom*. England: Routledge.

Stay Curious

Instructions: on the right column is what is considered a "closed-ended question" which only invites a yes/no or fixed response. On the left, you are encouraged to reimagine this question with one that

Original Question for the Past/Present	Reimagined Question for the Future
EXAMPLE	EXAMPLE
Did you enjoy the sex education you received?	How would you describe the sex education you received?
1. Do you talk about this topic a lot?	1.
2. Was this lesson useful?	2.
3. How often do you think people should be tested for HIV?	3.
4. Do you know where to find an abortion provider?	4.
5. At what age do you think children should learn about masturbation?	5.

invites curiosity and care in response. Sometimes this is considered an "open-ended question." There is an example in the first row to offer support.

Note

1 According to the Center for Economic Policy and Research, the minimum wage should be $24 an hour if it had been adjusted to keep pace with productivity. Minimum wage workers would make $48,000 a year, working full time.

4

SEX ED *HAPPENS*

Francisco Ramírez

Sex Ed *Happens*

Whether or not it is formally implemented in a school or part of a curriculum, sex ed still happens. It is all around us, whether we like it or not.

When I talk about sex and sex ed, I like to start off by acknowledging that "sex ed happens" as a way of helping us recognize that the messages are out there, whether or not someone attends a school where comprehensive sexuality education is taught or not.

Sex ed happens through everything from: porn that people may deliberately watch (or catch glimpses of), conversations we have with loved ones and peers, and, of course, media. Media can mean anything from television and film to social media (including the content that's created, the messages in the comments sections, as well as the absence of content, when important and life-saving content is banned and removed by Facebook, Inc., for example).

DOI: 10.4324/9781003181927-6

When it comes to messages around sex and sexuality, the media is uniquely powerful because messages and information about sex are often restricted, off-limits, or entirely banned from our view (on social media or elsewhere). I recall very well when I was growing up as a young queer person, listening every night to the radio show, *Loveline*, like my life depended on it. Dan Savage was critical. Sue Johanson's *Sunday Night Sex Show* was my lifeblood. And yet, the one and only time I called in to *Loveline* and made it on the air of this nationally syndicated program, the host Adam Corolla made fun of my voice and said homophobic jokes about me for a full minute. As a struggling 16-year-old queer person, I was mortified. Moreover, it was clear to me that as much as I loved sexuality-focused media, it wasn't an inclusive space, and it wasn't okay for me to be me.

This notion that media spaces are not inclusive enough is something that I would continue to find for the years that I have been working in media (whether broadcast, print, or digital). While working on, or auditioning for, different projects, I have been told I sound "too gay," use too much Spanglish, and that I shouldn't be talking about sex work or immigration because I should instead be focusing on a single (and often reductive) message about sexual health.

Interestingly enough, the most meaningful and memorable conversations as part of my sex ed as a teenager were when I became a pen pal with an incarcerated Latinx queer activist. Through hand-written letters, I learned all about his life and the ways in which white supremacy, xenophobia, homophobia, and the policing of brown people led to this wildly kind and creative person being incarcerated. He taught me everything from the diversity of desire to how to re-envision sexual health and happiness. This interactive, print-form messaging to me *was* sexuality education. It was nuanced. It was relatable. It was safe.

The thing that people outside of our field often get wrong about sexuality education – including and especially sexuality education in the media – is that we are here to share cold, hard facts and stats, peppered with the occasional warning. In reality, our work as sexuality educators in the media is often about larger – and more complex – issues. For this reason, the content of these messages in the media, and the way we approach our media really does matter. The way in which we are intentional about our messaging, delivery, and inclusivity really makes a difference.

***

In the late 2000s, my desire to be intentional and innovative around the messaging and delivery of sex ed messaging led me to start what I called Free Sex Advice. I packed up a folding chair, and a hand-written sign that said "Free Sex Advice: Relationships, Sex & Dating" and went out to New York City parks, street corners, and subway stations, while people lined up to talk through their most secret beliefs, doubts and misadventures – all with the hope of being heard, helped or healed.

I aimed to create a space that was: (1) not mandatory, that is, something that people can opt in for, (2) not immediately linked with diagnostic testing or any other typical public health agenda of some sort – at least at the beginning, (3) non-threatening, (4) decidedly without cost or donation, and (5) accessible in a unique way that allows it be fully embedded in the community.

Unlike other sex ed projects I have designed or helped out with up until this point, this one is entirely unique: part street art/art project, part pop-up shop, part motivational talk/coaching session, or late-night slumber party tell-all. The personal and dynamic quality is unlike anything I've done on television, on a stage, or in a classroom. It is an entirely new medium.

And in this new medium, I am able to curate and consider elements of media justice within the work. This manifests in everything from choreographing the look of the chairs and sign to the autonomy and freedom of my messages and how I choose to use my voice, as well as the voices of people who join in on the conversations and ask questions along the way. Engaging in this medium allows me to call in people to these conversations who are not often invited: people of all ages who are experiencing homelessness, people who speak Spanish and languages other than English, teens who I might not be able to reach in schools, and people of marginalized or stigmatized experiences (including queer people, and people working in the sex industry, for example) who may not readily share about their personal experiences in settings that are not both intimate, as well as "anonymous" feeling as people often feel at Free Sex Advice.

Also, being able to choose when – and *where* – I put out my chair and sign has been critical. Being able to "take up space" with sex ed, to bring it to the public forefront, and to make it more accessible, are hugely critical elements of the work as well. Whereas information and support related to sex and sexuality is often relegated to a "back page" somewhere, shushed from the public view, or consent checklist, or banned altogether, Free Sex Advice is actually embedded into the fabric of society. Deliberately choosing, for example, to set up my chairs in the wide-open, dead center of Union Square Park, allows me to not only encounter and speak with people who might not have been actively seeking out spaces where they can talk about sex and sexuality, but it also allows the physical landscape to shift. The women, the trans people, the queer folx, and the people of all ages and experiences who sit down in the chair are in some way making their own semi-public statement about what it means to seek out information and support about sex and sexuality. The friendly, but also to-the-point, sign as well is in many ways a declaration that *the time is now* and, yes, *this conversation is happening right now.*

One of the usual comments I hear from people is their delight/ appreciation to be able to talk through their stories with a queer person of color. In many ways, this is not surprising. For people of marginalized communities, it is powerful to be able to say *we were here*, to have our voices echo and resonate. It is, in fact, urgent and necessary. That our voices have a moment, and continue on, is important when we are dying more quickly than others.

What I find most noticeable about practicing sexuality education in this new medium is the twists and turns of the conversations – their energy and their rawness – are vivid, dynamic, and *real*. This is in great part because it's a human-led and human-driven experience and exchange. In fact, I aim to update the title of the project soon to reflect that it is not actually "advice" or advisory conversations that we are engaging in. We are living. We are actively participating. We are exposing. We are taking risks, being vulnerable, and challenging ourselves to discover or confront what's here for us right now.

Said another way, in creating this medium that connects with people, there is *emotion*. There is true delight, surprise, and joy – and also, at times, sadness, pensiveness, and courage. In practicing a form of sexuality education that is in many ways "3-D." I created *Sex Probz* with Dirty Lola as a way to make inclusive, accessible, media and wonder: what would it look like if our media were more inclusive of, for example, people in the sex industry, different dating configurations, non-English speaking, and immigrants?

I also co-founded OkaySo, an app connecting young people who have sex and identity questions with teams of caring experts, and I continue to support/design/innovate other mobile apps for people with questions about sex. Throughout this work, I emphasize agency, empathy, curiosity, interaction, and inclusion.

The future of sex Ed it isn't me telling you what to do, it's us having a conversation. Media – and a new medium or space for these conversations – has the power to reflect that.

Title: Sex Ed Happens Lesson Plan

Writers Names: Bianca I. Laureano

Note to Educators
This lesson plan goes well with the Media Literacy lesson plan and chapter. Be prepared to model some of what is being asked of the participants around building trust and vulnerability with the group.

Learning Objectives/Instructional Goal
In this lesson plan, participants will discuss media, create media, and discuss unlearning dehumanization that the sexuality field still maintains.

Learning Outcomes: By the end of the lesson, participants will be able to:

* Identify what components of sexuality education are essential for their work and communities
* Define media and media justice
* Recognize how and when a dehumanization approach is being used
* Practice imagining the future of sex ed, creating origin stories, and vulnerability

Essential Questions
* What are the components of sexuality education that I value and enjoy?
* What is media and media justice?
* How may I challenge a dehumanization approach in my work?
* How do I imagine a future in the sexuality field?

CASEL Social Emotional Learning Competencies
Self-awareness: The ability to accurately recognize one's own emotions, thoughts, and values and how they influence behavior. The ability to accurately assess one's strengths and limitations, with

a well-grounded sense of confidence, optimism, and a "growth mindset."

Self-management: The ability to successfully regulate one's emotions, thoughts, and behaviors in different situations – effectively managing stress, controlling impulses, and motivating oneself. The ability to set and work toward personal and academic goals.

Social awareness: The ability to take the perspective of and empathize with others, including those from diverse backgrounds and cultures. The ability to understand social and ethical norms for behavior and to recognize family, school, and community resources and supports.

Relationship skills: The ability to establish and maintain healthy and rewarding relationships with diverse individuals and groups. The ability to communicate clearly, listen well, cooperate with others, resist inappropriate social pressure, negotiate conflict constructively, and seek and offer help when needed.

Responsible decision-making: The ability to make constructive choices about personal behavior and social interactions based on ethical standards, safety concerns, and social norms. The realistic evaluation of consequences of various actions, and a consideration of the well-being of oneself and others.

Materials
- Afterworld Worksheet (included)
- Blank paper to write on
- Stamped envelopes

Preparation
Review the activities and make sure you have the materials needed. You may wish to offer additional resources to discuss these topics such as the National Sex Ed Standards.

Activity 1: What Kinds of Sex Ed Exist? (15 minutes estimated)
The goal of this activity is to allow participants to discuss what aspects of sexuality education they enjoy, value, and find critical and to identify what aspects of sexuality education they find destructive, of no value, and dehumanizing.

Begin by sharing with participants what they believe sexuality education must include. What are the essential things to do, share, and create? As you generate this list, make a note of what is a common area i.e. anatomy and physiology or relationships. Note what may be excluded i.e. what is the experience of having a particular body part. Next, ask participants to generate a list of what should not be included in sexuality education. Encourage participants to consider why something is not to be included. Facilitate a conversation about what was offered.

You may introduce some of the recommendations that have been created by national organizations in the United States or other countries to review. Notice how these may depend on certain systems (i.e. education, healthcare) that have failed our communities. Complete this section by asking "is it possible to offer sexuality education within systems that harm us?"

Activity 2: What Is Media? What Is Media Justice? (15 minutes estimated)
The goal of this activity is for participants to discuss how they are defining Media and understand Media Justice.

Invite participants to discuss what they mean in very specific and clear terms when they say "media." What is included and excluded? Consider writing responses on the board or make this interactive and invite participants to write their ideas on large pieces of newsprint around the room or on a shared virtual document.

A volunteer may read what is shared on each piece of newsprint or on the board. Do you notice any similarities or differences? What are themes that may exist? Notice if there are new or more common forms of media. New media may include forms of social media and apps, and more common forms may include books or other printed materials such as magazines and billboards. Notice what is missing:

are there photographs, quotes on t-shirts, makeup application? If not, offer these and invite a conversation if their definition of media includes these practices.

If participants may struggle with where to place suggestions such as makeup applications and quotes on clothing, welcome a conversion about Media Justice. What do they know or understand about Media Justice? Share this definition of Media Justice by the organization MediaJustice.org:

Freedom from oppression, freedom to communicate

Invite participants to share responses to this definition. Use the following discussion questions to facilitate the conversation:

- How does media fit into our work as sexuality professionals?
- What forms of communication are valued in our sexuality spaces?

Activity 3: Humanizing Sex Ed (25 minutes estimated)
The goal of this activity is for participants to consider how they are trained to dehumanize themselves and others.

Remind participants that building trust takes time, especially as sexuality professionals where people seek out our care and support for some of the most vulnerable parts of their lives. Distribute the Afterworld Worksheet and invite participants to complete the Afterworld Worksheet by offering them 6–10 minutes. Pair participants together for five minutes and have them share what they wrote. Bring the group together and ask what it was like to complete this worksheet and share what they wrote.

Share that storytelling and origin stories are some common ways people begin to build trust and practice vulnerability with each other. This may be one way to begin to unlearn the ways we have been trained and socialized to dehumanize one another. Invite a conversation using these questions:

- How do we unlearn a dehumanizing framework and put the human back into human sexuality?
- What does vulnerability look like for the sex professional?

- How does this challenge how we have been trained to be robotic and clinical?
- How do we bring our own humanity into our knowledge-sharing spaces?

Activity 4: Love Letters (ten minutes)
The goal of this activity is for participants to work on their own practice of vulnerability and building trust with themselves.

Distribute blank paper and blank stamped envelopes to each participant. Instruct them to write their preferred mailing address on the stamped envelope. Next, give them ten minutes to write on their blank paper a love letter to themselves. Only they will read and receive this. You will put these in the mail at some time in the future. If participants need prompts, invite them to consider the following:

1. What are you proud of having completed/accomplished?
2. What are reminders of things that bring you joy?
3. What are the parts about yourself that you love and enjoy the most?
4. Share an affirmation.
5. Create a plan for something that has been a challenge to begin/complete.
6. Offer yourself an apology for something that you can release to move forward.

Activity 5: Future of Sexuality Education (ten minutes estimated)
The goal of this activity is for participants to consider and imagine their place in the future of sexuality education.

Offer two minutes for participants to complete this sentence stem to begin the conversation. Remind participants to continue to rewrite the sentence until the time has completed.

I imagine a future where sexuality education ....

Consider partnering participants into small groups to share some of what they wrote. As a large group, invite participants to share some of what they imagined was possible. Note any themes shared. Highlight common vision and future goals. Wrap up this session with the following discussion questions:

- How do we create environments where people feel heard, helped, or find healing as sex professionals?
- What did the author do to create this space?

Glossary
Media Justice

As defined by MediaJustice.org "Freedom from oppression, freedom to communicate"

Afterworld Worksheet

The year is 2153. Your ancestors are learning about you. They read from this letter you left them that offers all the information you believe they need to know about what you accomplished and experienced.

This letter is all about _____ who was a very _____ and _____ person.

Known for _____, they found a way to enjoy their life and were often found celebrating at _____. When they were _____ years old they discovered a new way to _____ that lead to a new way of

_____.

Often told, they were like _____, especially _____ because their

_____ and _____ were so similar! Yet, they had their own unique

_____ and that made them stand out in a crowd!

One of their favorite things to say was "_____ _____" because it reminded them so much of _____.

They were often

successful and had many accomplishments. Here are five of the most important ones they were most proud to experience:

1. _____
2. _____
3. _____
4. _____
5. _____

Printed with permission from Bianca I. Laureano 2016©

5

SOLIDARITY AS LIBERATION

A Queer Mad Legacy

Elliott Fukui

We never tried putting it into words before, but if we had to this is the way it goes: We live by sharing what little we have with those who are needier still. We know that others will do likewise. Call it living by faith if that suits you. Call it whatever you please, but don't knock it; we've lived by it for years and we aren't dead yet... It's like being part of a river we pass on to those below us just as we received from above, the flow continues without end.

Gay Post Collective, How We Survive, Gay Post, May/June 1975

Solidarity Is Liberation — We Are Our Most Valuable Resource

I learned how to give and receive care on children, adolescents, and adult Psychiatric units across Minnesota and Ohio, from other mad, poor, disabled, racialized, and abused people, starting from the age of 12 until my last hospitalization at the age of 19. I learned how to care for and survive from foster kids, queers, trans folks, addicts, survivors, Houseless people,

DOI: 10.4324/9781003181927-7

Disabled kids, immigrants, and "delinquents." We were all set down the same path from such an early age in life – Institutionalization or Incarceration. Chemical Lobotomy or a Cage. Submission or Punishment.

We had no control over anything that happened to us; our bodies, education, and lives were entirely decided by doctors, nurses, teachers, cops, judges, social workers, clergy, and guardians. We could not refuse, and no one cared what we wanted anyway. Surviving required solidarity, alliances, strategic resistance, compliance, or completely shutting down and shutting off. I learned to survive in a world where my brain chemistry, body, and agency could be taken, changed, adjusted without my consent at an adult's whim, and where I was gaslight to believe my understandable protest to these inhumane and unjust treatments were signs of my need for them.

It sometimes takes every ounce of my energy not to break down from the grief of it all – my people's collective suffering, which I carry with me every day.

Discovering social justice movements and people's history helped me to understand that what I was experiencing was not isolated or my fault, but rather that I was a part of a more extensive system that was set up to keep some of us segregated, pathologized, criminalized, and vulnerable to maintain power for a few rich white guys on top. I am eternally grateful to have found inspiration, reflections, and consciousness building in books and zines when there was little else to keep hope alive. It made me remember I wasn't alone, even in my loneliest and most shame-filled moments.

You do not need political analysis, organizing training, or a Ph.D. to understand that this culture of control and suppression is destructive to our shared humanity, health, and safety. I am sure the millions of our children and youth in detention centers, prisons and jails, refugee camps, orphanages, residential schools, military academies, conversion therapy programs, psych wards, and foster care homes could break it down for you if you took the time to listen to them.

The fact that we have normalized the idea of caging anyone should be terrifying and enraging enough for anyone who believes in human dignity and respects human life for us to change this. Unfortunately, abled people are more concerned about their perceived safety than neurodivergent and disabled people's actual safety. This has encouraged the continued state and interpersonal violence we face, particularly for those who lay at the intersections of Black, Indigenous, or Brown and disabled, or immigrant and disabled, or trans, intersex, or gender non-conforming disabled.

Those of us who survive light candles and incense, pour whiskey onto the ground, take to the streets and continue to love and care for each other. We feed each other and put gas in each other's tanks, and sit with each other on our sick, mad, and death beds. We make different playlists and chip in ten bucks for care packages, make meal trains and gofundmes, leave nugs in mailboxes, and hold each other through the waves of shame, anger, and grief.

We keep each other safe. We love each other, and when we go too soon (because my people almost always go too soon), we mourn together as we honor our mentors and friends and lovers and family who left too young, too fast, still full of ideas and sass and potential and dreams and love that could change the world, if only the world would let us love it and embrace us.

We take our rage to the streets, to the doctor's office, to the welfare office, and to the courts, and hit joints on back porches and in living rooms after the vigils and rallies and hate violence since we can't hit the medical industrial complex and prison industrial complex or these angry men that keep killing us off. This slow genocide has taken many of our people over the years, the army of white coats or the good old boys in blue and white ladies with their clipboards and good intentions and their illusions of grandeur – the demi-gods who find pleasure in controlling the lives of those less powerful than themselves.

We try to remember that we have to keep going, keep pushing, keep fighting, even though sometimes there doesn't feel like a lot to keep going for. If I am honest, I don't know why I keep fighting, only that I know it's what LL would have wanted. It's what Stacey, Musa, Deja, Elandria, and Brandon would have wanted, and all the comrades who gave their lives fighting and surviving in these systems would have wanted.

I fight because I am Mad. I am Mad because I care, and I refuse to give up now. Caring is resistance.

We are worth protecting, we are worth fighting for.

What I learned about the world as a kid and youth guided me towards organizing and social justice and the foundations of how I want to be and what I want to practice in the world – Radical Consent, Disability Justice, and Transformative Justice.

Radical Consent – We Are Worth Protecting

Treat every person in this space as though they are a survivor.
—Lucia Leandro Gimeno

I first learned about radical consent through zines and Riot Grrl music. I found zines like *Learning Good Consent*, *Strategies for Survivors*, and *Supporting a Survivor of Sexual Assault* on opensource platforms like ZineLibrary and fell in love with the idea of radical consent, something that I had never experienced in my life. Reading zines from across the globe from all different kinds of people exploring ways to have better communication and more autonomy and agency in our relationships with each other changed my life and how I thought about myself and others. I learned a lot from listening to and reading punks and anarchists, queers and trans people, Marxists and mad pride organizers, trans and queer smut and safer sex guides, sex worker tips for safety and care, feminists and womanists, and people working in anti-war movement and pro-choice movements about bodily autonomy.

Understanding that the abuse and harm I experienced, and the abuse and harm I have perpetuated, was a part of a pattern and culture that impacted so many different people in so many ways helped me to understand the importance of learning how to set and hold boundaries, ask questions, and apologize for the harm I cause, even though that was not something I experienced growing up. It has been a many-decade journey at this point, and I'm still growing, still messing up, and still trying to kill this cop in my head and this judge in my heart. I am also still trying to shake that small feeling I get when I know I need to speak up and protect myself, and remember that I am a person, too, sometimes.

Coming from a consent-based framework has been important in my ability to support other people in meaningful ways. I do not always get it right – in fact, I have made many terrible mistakes, just like everyone else. I am still learning my own biases, growing edges, and ego trips and how they show up. Radical consent takes a lot of work, consciousness raising and self-examination – learning our own boundaries, and learning how to set them with others is a task in and of itself. But this must be the foundation of how we love and protect ourselves and each other by honoring each human beings' right to dignity, self-determination, and agency over their bodies and their lives.

Disability Justice – All People Deserve Care – Period

It's not about self-care—it's about collective care. Collective care
means shifting our organizations to be ones where people feel fine if
they get sick, cry, have needs, start late because the bus broke down,
move slower, ones where there's food at meetings, people work from
home—and these aren't things we apologize for. It is the way we do
the work, which centers disabled-femme-of-color ways of being in the
world, where many of us have often worked from our sickbeds, our kid
beds, or our too-crazy-to-go-out-today beds. Where we actually care
for each other and don't leave each other behind. Which is what we
started with, right?
                    — Leah Lakshmi Piepzna-Samarasinha, Care Work:
                                        Dreaming Disability Justice

Sometimes the riskiest and most subversive thing we could do on the
wards was offer care to each other; to offer a forbidden hug or handhold
in a moment of crisis, homesickness, or breakdown; to hide food for
someone on punishment so they could eat later; and to distract the nurses
so someone could get a break from a terrible group or an abusive therapist
by throwing a fantastic fit and taking the hit.

We also fought and hurt ourselves and each other. We were kids who
had never had models of boundaries, consent, care, or conflict resolution.
Almost all of us were abuse survivors and poor. Many of us understood
that survival meant fighting, manipulation, or dissociating because that is
what surrounded us and what we were taught by the adults in our lives,
including the therapists, social workers, and psychiatrists who were "caring" for us.

Add a bunch of drugs to that mix, and it is not surprising how many
of us were driven mad by the madhouse itself.

I learned that you only received care through performance, through
denying the truth, through lying, and by complying. Unfortunately, the
way our societies are structured makes it very easy for us to fall into traps
of groupthink, and honestly, I can understand wanting black and white
answers to huge complicated 4D HD technicolor problems we're facing.

The desire to belong, the desire for care, and our ability to erase the
hard and ugly parts of what it means to be living (and for some profit-
ing off of and making our livings off of) the violence and crisis of white

supremacy, capitalism, imperialism, and misogyny so we can sleep better at night.

Disability Justice honors every person's humanity and dignity. Disability Justice doesn't ask us to be who we are not or value one way of being over another. We will not get liberated without a Disability Justice framework at the center of our collective movements.

Transformative Justice – Turning Poison into Medicine

I still have nightmares. Still hear the other kids screaming for help and knowing I cannot do anything. Still see the blood on the walls and feel the rashes on my wrists and I still feel the weight on the back of my neck, the pressure on the chest, and the bruises on my ass and legs. I still taste the chalky tangy pills and feel the cold of the hospital bed nylon pressed against my wet cheek.

There will always be survivor's guilt. Questions about who made it out alive. There will always be drug hazy memories that haunt me, and the dark patches where my memories were stolen from me by whichever pharmaceutical bought out the doctors that month.

There is no apology, no DEI training, no amount of money that can ever do justice for the millions of children who have been thrown away, locked away, tortured, and murdered in the service of capitalism, colonization, imperialism, medicine, white supremacy, patriarchy, and G-d, Jesus Christ, and Allah. We were all disposed of because our survivor truths were too painful for the adults in our lives to face. We carried your shame and violence on our backs until it broke us and then you threw us away.

There is no way our current justice system could ever hold for how many of us have had our childhoods, our lives, our dignity, and our agency stolen from us because it is this very same justice system that cages our people in the first place. That breaks apart our families. That justifies eugenics and colonization. That justifies our subjugation and oppression.

Transformative Justice aligned with my own desire as a survivor. And with my own realization that nothing would ever happen to these individual white men. That theirs was a power that I as an individual would not be able to touch. When I realized there was no path to accountability for the individual doctors, nurses, cops, security guards, bus drivers, teachers, clergy, and therapists I decided I'd have to find a way to bring the whole system down, and I am committed to the project of liberating all people from all cages.

This would be the justice I require. This would be the transformation I would find acceptable for the pain I, and so many, have endured for centuries at the hands of normies, typicals, and ableds. Please let my people go. Let us be.

It turns out healing cannot be monetized for personal gain. Healing cannot be prescribed. Healing cannot be put into a timetable or made to fit your golf schedule or your planned vacations. Healing cannot occur under the weight of power dynamics or capitalist fantasies. Healing cannot happen in a void, without acknowledgment of the social constructs that create the conditions of our struggle.

Bibliography

Gay Post Collective. (1975). How We Survive, Gay Post, May/June.
Leah Lakshmi Piepzna-Samarasinha, Care Work: Dreaming Disability Justice.

Title: Solidarity as Liberation: A Queer Mad Lesson Plan

Writers Names: Bianca I. Laureano, Elliott Fukui

Note to Educators
This lesson plan invites a variety of reflections, generation of lists, and resources. If you are unaware of some of the social movements and people's history presented in this chapter please take time to review what is available online from these communities as named in the chapter and this lesson plan. Consider offering what your experience was like seeking open source information when the lesson plan activities offer that opportunity.

Learning Objectives/Instructional Goal
In this lesson plan, participants will discuss the chapter and key components of community collaboration, care, and interdependence.

Learning Outcomes
- Identify key social movements to the sexuality field
- Define solidarity and collaboration
- Generate a list of resources for consent and accountability
- Create a plan for care offered and received

Essential Questions
- What are key social movements that impact the sexuality work I do?
- How do I define solidarity and collaboration?
- What resources exist to help me with consent and accountability?
- What forms of care and from whom would I receive care from and offer care to?

CASEL Social Emotional Learning Competencies
Self-awareness: The ability to accurately recognize one's own emotions, thoughts, and values and how they influence behavior. The ability to accurately assess one's strengths and limitations, with a well-grounded sense of confidence, optimism, and a "growth mindset."

Self-management: The ability to successfully regulate one's emotions, thoughts, and behaviors in different situations – effectively managing stress, controlling impulses, and motivating oneself. The ability to set and work toward personal and academic goals.

Social awareness: The ability to take the perspective of and empathize with others, including those from diverse backgrounds and cultures. The ability to understand social and ethical norms for behavior and to recognize family, school, and community resources and supports.

Relationship skills: The ability to establish and maintain healthy and rewarding relationships with diverse individuals and groups. The ability to communicate clearly, listen well, cooperate with others, resist inappropriate social pressure, negotiate conflict constructively, and seek and offer help when needed.

Responsible decision-making: The ability to make constructive choices about personal behavior and social interactions based on ethical standards, safety concerns, and social norms. The realistic evaluation of consequences of various actions, and a consideration of the well-being of oneself and others.

Materials
- Touch It, Feel It worksheet
- Writing materials or sticky notes for documenting if in person
- Virtual space to document generated lists all participants may access

Preparation
- Review and remind participants of group agreements for the session
- Recall the chapter by Vulgar.MX and the activities on community collaboration may be useful
- Review the Touch It, Feel It worksheet

Activity 1: Introduce Topic (ten minutes estimated)
The goal of this activity is to assess what social movements participants understood was presented in the chapter.

Begin by inviting participants to share what movements they recall being discussed in the chapter. Make a list where all participants may access the information. You may note a range of responses and be sure to include the following: disability rights and disability justice, transformative justice, Queer History, abolition of prisons and institutionalization, people's history, immigrant rights, health justice, and net neutrality.

When a list has been created review the list with participants and note where and how each movement is informed by and supported by other movements. This is considered "cross-movement organizing." For example, you could state:

How is the US abortion justice movement connected to abolition, people's history, health justice?

Activity 2: Collaboration and Solidarity (30 minutes estimated)

The goal of this activity is to discuss and identify what solidarity is and is not, identify what collaboration may be for their work, and generate a list of resources.

For this section, referring to or connecting to the chapter by Vulgar.MX and the activities on community collaboration may be useful to reflect on.

Invite a conversation of what participants understand the term and practice of "solidarity" to be. Take notes or write important themes somewhere all participants may access. It may be helpful to recall the cross-movement organizing discussed in the first activity.

Next, invite participants to share what are some examples that are NOT a form of "solidarity" to them. There may be a variety of responses here and some may contradict others and that is ok to note and invite further discussion, remember participants are sharing from their perspective.

Offer about five minutes for participants to generate a personal list of who they believe they must collaborate with as they do their work. This may include names of individuals or organizations as well as titles of jobs and roles. After the time has passed, instruct participants to review their list and mark with an "s" those they believe they must be in solidarity with.

Pair participants together to discuss with their partners how they came to identify their list and those they highlighted as wanting to or being in solidarity with. Offer about five minutes for discussion and sharing. Next, invite participants to add or edit their lists if needed for about three minutes. Remind participants it is ok if their conversation impacted their considerations and that editing and updating is a common experience when ideas are shared. Remind participants to cite and attribute if they are impacted by their partner to add to their list.

Mention to participants that the book this chapter is featured in is about archiving the brilliance that is often omitted, erased, and silenced in the sexuality field. Facilitate a conversation about building an archive of zines, books, films, media, and texts that hold the brilliance participants believe is important to their sexuality work. You may do this as a large group documenting responses or you may invite participants to write down suggestions on a shared document virtually or on sticky notes if in person. If needed, assign people to capture the shared resources.

Consider offering these questions:

- What are the important texts, resources, oral narratives that you believe are essential to doing our work?
- How many of the resources listed uphold a western approach to education or sexuality?
- Who and what is missing from the list?

Activity 3: Radical Consent and Accountability (20 minutes estimated)
The goal of this activity is to identify useful resources for consent and accountability as sexuality professionals.

Remind participants that the author writes about radical consent. Invite participants to consider what does "radical consent" mean in this context and how is it different from the consent work they imagine or are doing. Invite them to include where and how accountability for our impact emerges in these examples.

Ask participants where they would find the age of consent laws in their state or country. Offer them three minutes to search for this information online using a personal smartphone, computer, or tablet, or writing down who they would ask.

Invite participants to share (1) where they searched, (2) what they found, and (3) how they interpreted "age of consent" before searching. Be sure to ask what decisions or behaviors participants understood the age of consent to be for. You may want to note if there are differences between the age of consenting to sex, marriage, military service, abortion, accessing reproductive health care, and more.

Ask participants how consent plays a role in the work they wish to do in the sexuality field. Consider some of these examples if they are needed to help discussion:

- Parental consent for attending sexuality education classes
- Signing a contract for working together and creating content on sexuality topics
- Accepting a salaried or consulting job where you are a mandated reporter

Next, invite participants to respond to the following questions:

- Who has power in these circumstances? (may identify one example at time)
- Who has the least amount of power?
- How may power lead to harm if misused?

Facilitate a discussion on coping strategies especially online resources. You may need to explain what open source is and may compare it to a paywall requesting money or signing up to view information. Ask:

- How is a resource being open source important for sexuality professionals?
- What happens to you when you try to access a resource but there is a paywall? What feelings emerge? Where do you find information?
- How may these paywalls impact access to information and knowledge on sexuality topics?

Activity 4: All People Deserve Care (15 minutes)

The goal of this activity is to support participants in considering what topics challenge them when offering care or being reminded that we all deserve care.

Say that as sexuality professionals we are often given the impression that we must be prepared to discuss any type or kind of sexual activity, behavior, or experience. Remember this is a direct violation of consent, boundaries, and an unrealistic idea of what is sustainable for sexuality professionals offer. We all decide what our boundaries are and when to offer a referral if we are not the best fit for a client or need.

Invite participants to take about three minutes and write down what are "hard no" topics for them to discuss. They will not be sharing what they wrote unless they choose to with others. "Hard No" topics are ones that they are very clear right now on not being comfortable, interested in, or wanting to engage with in their work.

There may be some people who claim they do not know what to write or they do not have any "hard no" to list. Usually, people think they have been exposed to everything there is or they are not sure what they have not been exposed to that is a "hard no," or they have never been offered the space to consider. Remind participants if this is where they find themselves it is ok to always update and review this question and our personal and professional boundaries.

Next, instruct participants to review their list and think of and write down what their somatic, physical response and feelings are that emerge when they consider being required or forced to engage with these topics. Have a group discussion about what these feelings include. Remember participants do not have to share what the topics are or even what their somatic experiences may be.

To wrap up remind participants of the previous activity on collaboration, have them review that list and consider what other collaborations must be tended to and prioritized so they can maintain their own boundaries without shaming or harming a client. This is caring for ourselves as we care for others.

Activity 5: Solidarity and Collective Care as Liberation (20 minutes estimated)

The goal of this activity is to identify what forms of care participants are willing to offer and receive when experiencing challenges and difficulties.

Distribute the Touch It, Feel It worksheet to participants. Read the instructions which invites them to imagine being given $200 to spend on any form of affection or care they need and enjoy when experiencing a difficult time emotionally, physically, spiritually, or mentally. Mark what they would request with an X. There are several blank options with values in them for participants to add their own forms of care or affection if they are not listed. Offer about five minutes for this activity.

Next, invite participants to review the worksheet and mark with a check those forms of affection they would offer to others if they were asked for help. Offer five minutes for this review. Follow this activity with a discussion of what they notice are doubly identified forms of care they identified. Where are there similarities and differences in what they need and what they would offer.

There are numerous ways to continue or wrap up this discussion. Consider facilitating a discussion on how capitalism disconnects us from resources and care we may be able to find and offer one another to be more interdependent together. Invite a conversation about how we would request these forms of care and how we would honor the "no" we may receive as an essential part of radical consent.

Offer these questions to wrap up:

- What were you surprised to note or recognize through this worksheet?
- Why may we be hesitant to request what we need or want from those who care for us?
- How has cost and access to money and wealth separated us from one another?

Activity 6: Closing Activity

Invite participants to complete this sentence stem:

I have learned that interdependence is ....

Touch It/Feel It

Imagine being given $200 to spend on any form of affection or care you need and enjoy when experiencing a difficult time emotionally, physically, spiritually, or mentally. There are several blank options with values in them for you to add your own forms of care or affection if they are not listed.

Hold Hands $15	Snuggle/ Cuddle $25	Rub Scalp $20	Braid Hair $25	Hug Belly Button to Belly Button (No Arm in between) $25
Tuck into bed $15	Push hair behind ear $15	Lay head in lap $20	Wash hair $25	Being held while crying $15
Cooking a meal $30	Writing a love letter $25	Texting Thank You $15	Texting "I Love You" $15	Help with getting into shower/ bathtub $25
Body massage $30	Manicure $25	Lotioning body $25	Haircut/ style $20	Kiss on cheek or forehead $15
Squeezing body parts $25	Scratching body parts $20	Bathing $30	Foot massage $20	Help with getting onto toilet $20
Help changing clothing $20	Help with undressing $20	Help with brushing teeth $25	Head on shoulder $15	Doing activity where bodies touch $15
$15	$35	$30	$20	$25

Used and printed with permission from Bianca I. Laureano 2018©.

SECTION 2

MOVEMENT FOR BODYMINDS

To move through and in between borders and barriers is where we begin. Here are the pathways that led to new beginnings, new realities, and new movements. North America is the setting and our movements go beyond these borders. Beloved readers are encouraged to engage their bodymind and movement through the lesson plans for a sensual and full experience. Reading is not passive. What knowledge is your bodymind holding?

DOI: 10.4324/9781003181927-8

6

THE EROTIC POWER OF THE PROFESSIONAL NURSE, AND THE BODY THEY MOVE IN

Jessica Jolie Badonsky

I am a nurse. It is more than "what I do", it is part of my identity. Whether it is signified by the clothing I wear, the tools I use, or the language I speak, my observations, actions, and reactions are informed by my nursing identity. This identification informs my intercourse with patients and personal relationships. Yes, I said intercourse. The more intimate the interaction, the more erotic, because we have left nothing behind in the exchange. Unlike a sexualized exchange, there isn't any seduction, no flirting, no provocation. Instead, it's my presence, the creation of a container for healing that is the erotic element in nursing. By acknowledging our whole selves as nurses, we realize that nursing, as a profession, is exactly that intimate, sacred, and in that interaction, is where we move beyond skills and into the art of nursing.

When I meet another nurse, I quickly discover that their parent was a medical professional, perhaps a nurse, physician, or a medical assistant. I had a grandmother who was a nurse. I never met her. She died in the 1950s, I was told "her heart had exploded at work". No stories of nursing,

DOI: 10.4324/9781003181927-9

no homegrown resources, or tips of the trade. My parents were artists who made money by entertaining people. My mother is an actress, and my father was a producer of all sorts of things, including music and food experiences. Having grown up in that environment, I learned that to be valued, you create, cultivate beauty, make waves, find a deeper purpose, and disrupt. It made sense to me that I would eventually focus on healing beyond the pharmacology, beyond the pathology, and focus on the art of wellness through connecting with people's quality of life through the erotic.

If I tell you that nursing is an erotic profession, you may have images of the "Naughty Nurse", hear Gregory Isaacs singing "Night Nurse" or the countless Halloween costumes of latex like old timey nurses outfits with big red cross. These images are far from erotic and empower, and they are fetishized at the pleasure of the observer, the patient. In fact, the history of nursing is sexualized, before Florence Nightingale, older sex workers, and prisoners were the nurses. They were the untouchables of society, caring for the diseased, and they were Black women too. When understanding the creation of Western medicine and the impact on Black bodies, especially the Black woman's body, many imagine a speculum and the racist misogynist history of gynecology. Sex and medicine have never been separate. This essay is a conscious reclaiming of the erotic essence of the nursing profession, intuition, and connection that comes from understanding the self and the people we care for.

Years before I became a nurse, decades before, I was introduced to the work of Audre Lorde, poet and theorist who wrote about dismantling the master's house, redefining the self, and making the connection between the internal self and the outer political world. Specifically, Audre Lorde's essay *Uses of the Erotic: The Erotic as Power* where she defines the erotic as a deeply feminine knowing, what nurses call intuition, that guides the body and spirit. A piece that was published two years prior to Lorde's book *The Cancer Journals*, where she documented her journey through cancer, treatment, family, and transformation. Lorde share's about arriving home after her mastectomy:

> At home I wept and wept and wept, finally. And made love to myself, endlessly and repetitively, until it was no longer tentative.
>
> Where were the dykes who had had mastectomies? I wanted to talk to a lesbian, to sit down and start from a common language, no matter how diverse. I wanted to share dyke-insight so to speak.
>
> (Lorde, p. 49)

The erotic can be the catalyst to healing what is unseen. It is acknowledging the erotic essence of that person who is in the position of healer, the whole self that is brought to the bedside, not necessarily in an external form, much like the patient who is a full being beyond their diagnosis.

Healing and curing are different. Safety and protection are different. The surface versus the felt experience makes it possible to construct a fortress that ensures a sense of protection; similarly, it is possible to cure illnesses. The focus on the surface does not necessarily translate to safety or healing. Safety allows one to tear down the walls of the fortress, healing requires an inner power and self-awareness that Audre Lorde referred to as "the power of erotic",

> a measure between the beginnings of our sense of self and the chaos of our strongest feelings...[f]or having experienced the fullness of this depth of feeling and recognizing its power, in honor and self-respect we can require no less of ourselves.
>
> (Lorde, p. 54)

To work with the human body is to face the chaos of our strongest feelings, the beliefs that have been imposed on us. Some of these beliefs we defy while others we accept and they create separation and, sometimes, violence. The healing and safety are different from curing and protection.

The Chaos of Racialization

My formation and entry into the world would have been "illegal" past my birthday if I was born in South Carolina, the birthplace of my grandparents. Luckily, I was born in Illinois. Had I been born in any of the southern states my parents' union would have been illegal. It wasn't until 1967, for some states much later, that anti-miscegenation laws were ruled as unconstitutional; the Lovings were the interracial couple whose relationship became national interest in 1958 after they were sentenced to one year imprisonment. I was to be the embodiment of the new Loving Generation, the tangible form of the end of racism, the antidote to white supremacy. What an expectation to place on a body! A body that would inevitably stand out depending on the crowd. I'd be the golden raisins in the bowl of rice. A body to become a fetish of a future that cannot exist without radical change. Placed at the foot of the bassinet was my birth card, with footprints and my mother's name, my sex, and race "Negro". A body that would be assumed to be a bridge, some days a walking example of integration, and on most days a symbol of "other". It's impossible to ignore the existence of someone who challenges representation and all of the feelings that accompany its limitations.

> To share the power of each other's feelings in different from using anothers feelings as we would use kleenex...When we look the other way from our experience, erotic or otherwise, we use rather than share the feelings of those others who participate in the experience with us. And use without the consent of the used is abuse.
>
> (Lorde, p. 58 CR 2007)

I hypothesize there is a difference between those of us who are born of Black mothers yet biracial (Black & white), as opposed to those who are raised by white mothers. Hair is one example, the basic care for the physical crown. The Black mothers who have children, just a shade or two lighter than theirs, in the gaze of the white lens, hair a bit finer, looser, closer to the constructed scale of "good". Then, there are those whose birth babies barely passing the "paper bag test", pencils falling out of their hair because it is finer, the curl is looser, easier, maybe.

Growing up, Saturdays were spent in Arie's salon. I loved the smell of hair dye and perm, blow dryer, and hot combs. To this day, if I walk into a salon with the smell of smoke, sweet chemicals, and heated oils I feel a sense of calm. I wanted to be grown, I wanted a hot comb put through my hair too. Whether it was based on insistence or circumstance I distinctly remember standing at the stove, towel safely away from the burner and having my hair hot combed. The way my mother straightened her own hair, or as unruly as my hair was, my mom could see me, just as I was, just as I am, her child. You want to be seen by the one you love most.

My skin is "high yellow", light-bright and damn near white, and I'm a Black woman's child, a Black cisgender woman, also called a Negro woman. This unquestionable truth is my daily act of resistance to white supremacy, both internal and external. To survive in this world and the coming years, I gathered all of my strength and am still always on the offense, preparing for all the questions, comments, and explaining myself.

These comments ranged and included: "You don't look Black". "I knew there was something in you". "You got a bit of a spook nose". "Why don't you play with someone your own color?" "Oh, like white chocolate". "Are you together?" as if an eight year old would be at a wine shop alone. "Karenga says your partner should be your reflection, there's no way I'd stay with you".

A sense of belonging is always with us, and it develops into a longing to belong. There is no story here of another mixed or tragic mulatto. I am not a mule and the last five decades have been far from tragic for me. This is an affirmation of those who have been asked to stand for the oppressor and the oppressed, as embodiments of unity but scream out that our bodies are not yours. A fetishized body, high yellow, with patches of brown and pink in the hidden areas. I am the undercover negro. After being named, labeled, and given the choice of choosing "one", many choose "other", an act that goes against the human condition, to let others determine our bodies. I chose Black.

Our first erotic relationship starts at home. How we understand what it means to be loved and to love, is from those first relationships, where we begin as an extension of our primary care takers. I was an extension of my mother, our facial features, our expressions, our fear, and our discrimination was all the SAME, hers by how she was/is approached and mine because I am an extension of her.

> [W]e use each other as objects of satisfaction rather than share our joy in the satisfying, rather than make connection with our similarities and our differences. To refuse to be conscious of what we are feeling at any time, however comfortable that might seem, is to deny a large part of the experience, and to allow ourselves to be reduced to the pornographic, the abused, and the absurd.
>
> (Lorde, p. 59)

Before becoming a nurse, I was a doula. And before becoming a doula, I was a yoga teacher, somewhere in there I worked in the film industry as a dialect coach, and before that, before 9/11 I was a financial software trainer, self-taught from working in the restaurant industry, after being a tenant organizer in Central Harlem. I became a tenant organizer because I fell in love with grappling with the hegemony once I found my teacher who introduced me to the work of Audre Lorde, Adrianne Rich, and Mama Lola. It wasn't until I became a young adult that I was academically introduced to Voudo, specifically Ezuli, Ezulie, Ezili, Ezuli Freda, Freda, an Iwa from the Vodou tradition, who had many names, and many functions. Ezili had command of her power, a longing to belong, as Maya Darren writes, "capacity to conceive beyond reality, to desire beyond adequacy, to create beyond need" (Deren, p. 138). Ezili's erotic power is creativity, an ability to seduce while remaining centered in who she is. In the book *Mama Lola*, Karen McCarthy Brown describes Ezili as a shapeshifter, where on land Ezili appears white, a European ideal, perhaps due to the gaze of white supremacy; however, when Ezili is in the flow, underwater, you see her Blackness. While I am not a scholar or a practitioner of Vodou or Ezili, I carry her in my mind, my heart. On the most basic level of understanding, Ezili, in all of her formations, her love of love, luxury, fertility, health, passion, and strength,

> The white fathers told us: I think, therefore I am. The Black mother within reach of us - the poet - whispers in our dreams: I feel therefore I can be free.
>
> (Lorde, Poetry is Not a Luxury, p. 38)

Ezili was the erotic archetype for the body that I have been gifted. An almost secret representation of my kind, the "undercover Negro". She let me know that I was not alone, when I felt my loneliest, most invisible, and protected, with a powerful truth.

Black Nursing from the Erotic

What is our primary human need, belonging, and connection? What happens when the body is dismissed, through age, through race, through gender? Take sex, for example. For over a decade, my work as a nurse in all of its formations has been to approach the patient in their healing journey by directly addressing the erotic in terms that seem obvious, what people think of as sex. I did this by asking patients if they had any sexual health concerns following hip surgery, or if I noticed shame upon their face when they demanded that their partner leave while their colostomy dressing was being changed. There is an internal urge, a physical feeling, a tightening in my gut, voice, not auditory hallucinations, erotic power taking over, urging me to open the door to discussion. Creating space, at that time, for their healing, in that interaction I will care for all of them if they allow me to. My fierce devotion to my patients may have come from wanting to be "seen". To be healed is to have freedom and a sense of being made whole, and a large part of that wholeness is erotic energy. Art, delicious food, landscapes, revolutions, and people are from this energy, healing is no different. Quality of life is not only taking medication or a cure but to how we live our lives to the fullest. Our sexual expression is a tangible measurement. Medical establishments, nurses, perpetrate additional layers of violence when we ignore the erotic lives of the people we have sworn to care for.

However, this is not what I was taught when I was in the training to become a nurse. In fact, it was the exact opposite, if asked "how the nurse is to provide care and comfort" I was quickly trained that it had nothing to do with the erotic lives or patients, addressing their fear, allowing for space for their exploration, not grappling with the hegemony of the medical system, systemic racism, ageism, sexism and on, no the correct answer was "The nurse provides care and comfort by securing hydration, nutrition, pain management, and adjusting their body". Nurse was addressing the broken body that lies in the broken system. Which makes sense however, once you leave the classroom and step next to the bedside, you are faced with a person whose trajectory has landed them in your care. If you are reading this now, you understand the medical system in the 50 North American States is broken. You know the cost, you hear of the profits and you think why should anyone have to go homeless to have their insulin, lose their teeth because they don't have dental insurance or fail in school because they already lost or broken their second pair of glasses and the cost of a third means not enough for rent. You understand. Like much of the helping professional world, our focus is on the motivation of needs and the hierarchical structure of those needs, specifically Maslow. Where only once we have our physiological, and logistical needs met can we begin to address the needs of connection. You can have a check-up, but now the medicine to support you, well that may cost a pretty penny. Right there the path to healing is lined with inequity, those that are in need and those that have the means to fulfill the need.

> The principal horror of any system which defines the good in terms of profit rather than in terms of human need, or which defines the human need to the exclusion of the psychic and emotional components of that need – the principal horror of such a system is that it robs our work of its erotic value, its erotic power, and life appeal and fulfillment.
>
> (Lorde, p. 55)

To truly care for each other, we must acknowledge the psychic need and emotional needs of the patient, not only their bodies and this takes an interdependence of the patient and the practitioner. The consent of all bodies, allowing space for difficult conversations. For me, it was listening for hidden questions, the hesitation. I discovered that acknowledging the sexual being could be a catalyst for healing and moving through fear by observing what my patients needed, giving them the space to ask, which was about the erotic, desire, and to be fully seen.

There is a power dynamic in the provider-patient relationship: while the patient is the consumer, the provider wields the "cure". While nurses are usually in a race to be the most trusted professional, only matched with the fire department, there is still distrust in the medical establishment. COVID has shined yet another light on the distrust, studies showing that if your provider looks like you then you will be at ease, and ease creates healing. I am fully aware that when I walk into a room to meet a client I am classified into several categories, based on who I am taking care of. Some see my dark features and expect that I speak a particular language, read my last name and think I pray to a particular book, see my grey hairs and make assumptions of age and gender me in binary terms, but rarely are the assumptions correct. What we imagine a person's life to be is rarely what they experience.

I am the gatekeeper to my mother's health, attending appointments to make sure it is clear that this Black mother and grandmother is not to be dismissed, ignored, or toyed with. If I need to set people straight that she is loved, has people, and pull out my nurse card (I have one) I will.

I am the mother of second-generation biracial Black children, 50/50s, who are faced with questions about their personage. Questions about their hair, hips, and lips are asked, by a Black scholar, to create a Punnett Square to prove their identity.

It is not lost on me that, when we talk about statistics regarding the maternal mortality of Black women, it involves MY mother, who was told that she should not see her daughter after birth because she might die. It is not lost on me that as a daughter who presents very differently, getting her seen quicker, and attended more comprehensively merely from my presence. It is that erotic connection a deep feeling of connection that moves with me as a daughter, parent, and professional. I belong to "them", and "they" belong to me, empowered to live fully as a Black daughter, mother, partner, and professional, aware of how I appear and grounded in knowing that if I can face even the uncomfortable feelings, I will not be lost and therefore present and able to care for the whole person, including the private parts of their wellness.

I am a nurse. As I enter a room, an office, or a zoom call, my focus is to see the person beyond the diagnosis or medicine and allow them to tell me who they are. The intercourse between us, provider and patient, requires me to be fully present. So, to be fully present for "my" patients and see them, then I must be fully present, especially when we fight against a violent medical system. I am of course using my body, my senses, to care for theirs, my intuition to move beyond medicine, hoping to bring organization to the chaos of dis-ease through the erotic.

Bibliography

Deren, M. (1970). *Divine Horsemen: Voodoo Gods of Haiti*. New York: Chelsea House.

Lorde, A. (1980). The Cancer Journals. In A. Lorde (Ed.), *Part 2: Breast Cancer: A Black Lesbian Feminist Experience* (pp. 24–54). New York, NY: Penguin Random House.

Lorde, A. (1984). Sister Outsider. In A. Lorde (Ed.), *Uses of the Erotic, The Erotic as Power* (pp. 53–59). Trumansburg, NY: Crossing Press.

Mama Lola, M. C. (2001). *A Vodou Priestess in Brooklyn*. Berkeley: University of California Press.

Title: The Erotic Power of the Professional Nurse

Writers Names: Bianca I. Laureano, Jessica J. Badonsky

Note to Educators
This essay works well when partnered with the resources cited in the essay which include Audre Lorde's *Uses of the Erotic, The Erotic as Power* and excerpts from *The Cancer Journals* "Part 2: Breast Cancer: A Black Lesbian Feminist Experience".

Learning Objectives/Instructional Goal
In this lesson plan, participants will discuss nurses as an essential part of sexuality and erotic work.

Learning Outcomes
* Examine the role of nurses in the sexuality field and what expectations sex professionals have of them.
* Identify how nursing is part of an erotic approach to healing and care.
* Explain safety and healing differ based on needs, identities, and experiences.

Essential Questions
* What are the roles and expectations of nurses in the sexuality field?
* How is an erotic approach useful in healing and care work?
* How does safety and healing differ based on position in society?

CASEL Social Emotional Learning Competencies
Self-awareness: The ability to accurately recognize one's own emotions, thoughts, and values and how they influence behavior. The ability to accurately assess one's strengths and limitations, with a well-grounded sense of confidence, optimism, and a "growth mindset".

Self-management: The ability to successfully regulate one's emotions, thoughts, and behaviors in different situations – effectively managing stress, controlling impulses, and motivating oneself. The ability to set and work toward personal and academic goals.

Social awareness: The ability to take the perspective of and empathize with others, including those from diverse backgrounds and cultures. The ability to understand social and ethical norms for behavior and to recognize family, school, and community resources and supports.

Relationship skills: The ability to establish and maintain healthy and rewarding relationships with diverse individuals and groups. The ability to communicate clearly, listen well, cooperate with others, resist inappropriate social pressure, negotiate conflict constructively, and seek and offer help when needed.

Responsible decision-making: The ability to make constructive choices about personal behavior and social interactions based on ethical standards, safety concerns, and social norms. The realistic evaluation of consequences of various actions, and a consideration of the well-being of oneself and others.

Materials
- Audre Lorde's Uses of the Erotice, The Erotic as Power
- Audre Lorde's The Cancer Journals "Part 2: Breast Cancer: A Black Lesbian Feminist Experience"
- Gregory Isaacs "Night Nurse" song and lyrics (available with an online search)

Preparation
Review and become familiar with the suggested readings in materials

Activity 1: Introduction of the Topic (10 minutes)
The goal of this activity is to begin a conversation about the role of nurses in the sexuality field and what expectations sex professionals have of them.

Invite participants to consider what are the ways nurses are represented in the sexuality field. Depending on your group dynamics, welcome other shares about nurses here are some suggested questions to offer:

- How are nurses represented based on gender, race, ethnicity, class, etc.
- What expectations do people have of nurses regarding sexuality issues?
- What ways may sexuality professionals collaborate with nurses?

You are encouraged to consider the origins of the nursing field, how forced nursing/caretaking is a gendered and racialized experience for many in the United States, and any current events/responses to nurses during a pandemic.

Listen to the song referenced by reggae singer Gregory Isaacs "Night Nurse" who died of lung cancer at the age of 59. Invite sharing of what participants heard and noticed in the song. The Media Literacy lesson plan may work well to examine the song, lyrics, and impact.

Activity 2: What Is Erotic Nursing? (20 minutes)

The goal of this activity is to identify how nursing is part of an erotic approach to healing and care.

Bring in Audre Lorde's essay Uses of the Erotic, The Erotic as Power assigned for participants to read. Be sure to invite participants to share their understanding of how Lorde discusses and defines the erotic. You may write the definition for all participants to refer back to. You may also welcome participants to expand on the definition to include the work sexuality professionals do currently that may not have been included in the original essay.

There may be a conversation or question about Lorde's anti-pornography perspective in the essay to which you may offer: How do we expect our elders to expand and grow and un/learn? What expectations do we have of ourselves as elders if we are given the gift of aging?

To move the conversation forward, discuss the author's essay beginning with inviting participants to share what they understand is the positioning of the author:

- What identities does the author share with us?
- What do we notice about how these identities emerge? (i.e. language, age, race)

Bring both this essay, the Isaacs song, and Lorde's essay in conversation by offering:

- How is the erotic a part of the wholeness and quality of life?
- What does it mean to have an erotic essence of the nursing profession?
- How does the erotic essence in nursing align with how the nursing field was discussed in activity 1?
- What does it mean when someone does not want a cure or to engage with a Dr as Issacs sings?

Activity 3: Healing and Safety (20 minutes)
The goal of this activity is to consider how safety and healing may be experienced and different based on needs, identities, and experiences.

The following excerpt from *The Cancer Journals* "Part 2: Breast Cancer: A Black Lesbian Feminist Experience" was quoted in the essay:

> At home I wept and wept and wept, finally. And made love to myself, endlessly and repetitively, until it was no longer tentative.
> Where were the dykes who had had mastectomies? I wanted to talk to a lesbian, to sit down and start from a common language, no matter how diverse. I wanted to share dyke-insight so to speak.
> (Lorde, p. 49)

Here, Lorde offers what she was craving of community and "dyke-insight" and a desire to speak to those who have lived experience and would understand fully. If participants read the entire chapter, they will identify how nursing staff responded to her use of a prosthetic after her mastectomy. Facilitate a conversation using the following questions:

- What emerges for you as you are reminded of this quote and desire Lorde has?

- What are our primary human needs? How does belonging and connection fit?
- What happens when the body is dismissed, through age, race, gender, and sexual orientation?
- How was Lorde's body dismissed by her nurse and how is the nurse writing this essay divesting in such a response?
- How are healing and safety connected to the work and practice of nursing for Black women nurses?

Bringing in other essays from this section may be useful especially if defining terms such as safety and healing are needed.

Activity 4: Closing Activity (10 minutes)
The goal of this activity is to conclude the session with a focus on self-reflection of the erotic.

To close this conversation, invite participants to write down two ways the erotic guides their work in the sexuality field.

Partner participants and invite them to share one of the items they wrote.

Bibliography

Isaacs, G. (1982). Night Nurse [song]. On *Night Nurse* [album]. Island Records.

Lorde, A. (1980). The Cancer Journals. In A. Lorde (Ed.), *Part 2: Breast Cancer: A Black Lesbian Feminist Experience* (pp. 24–54). New York, NY: Penguin Random House.

Lorde, A. (1984). Sister Outsider. In A. Lorde (Ed.), *Uses of the Erotic, The Erotic as Power* (pp. 53–59). Trumansburg, NY: Crossing Press.

7

YOGA

A Liberatory Praxis

Serina Payan Hazelwood

I am Indigenous. I am a survivor of the products of colonialism and genocide. My matriarchal ancestors come from what is now known as Chihuahua, Mexico. Much of our Indigenous memories were erased and stolen. I do not know much about my father's settler-colonist ancestors; not because they were forced to forget or because their safety was threatened. My ancestors willingly left their Indigeneity on the soils of England and Scotland to embrace the romanticization of taming the Wild West. I am my grandmother. I am my mother. I am my daughter. The field of epigenetics suggests that the womb carries the traumas and memories of our ancestors. How I identify is relational to new understandings of my being and I am constantly in motion.

My chapter tells the story of how a decolonial approach to practicing yoga offered me many paths to liberation that connect me to the earth's womb, that which is inextricably connected to my womb. My life's purpose and responsibilities are to decolonize and unsettle spaces, bodies,

DOI: 10.4324/9781003181927-10

and souls through education, activism, and ritual as an act of resilience AND resistance from that which was stolen, erased, and forgotten.

In the ancient language of Sanskrit, yoga means "to yoke" or "to connect". Like culture, the rhizomes of yoga are always moving and reshaping. The reshaping of culture is intrinsically woven with power, similar to a rhizome. Deleuze and Guattari (1987) fashion the metaphor of rhizome in Assemblage Theory by supporting the idea that the transformation of yoga over the centuries can be imagined as Miller (2019) wrote:

> A rhizome, or the creeping rootstalk of a plant, spreads horizontally and can send out new shoots upward. The rhizome has no fixed bounds or conceptual limits and is based on the idea of multi-directionality and diversity.... When parts of the rhizome break off, they can survive on their own, meandering and re-forming or uniting with others, but always along lines that trace back". The metaphor of the rhizome also allows for a recognition of power, since we can consider the way such plants can be cultivated across time, their growth patterns encouraged or inhibited in unique ways, and how different positionalities might present actors with more or fewer opportunities to engage in this cultivation process.
>
> (p. 28)

The illustration below offers a visual of how the rhizome of yoga moved throughout time and nature:

These early systems of yoga were heterogeneous and included meditation, rituals, and philosophies rooted in "enlightenment, liberation, and isolation from the world of suffering" (Miller, 2019). Scholars traced the spiritual and philosophical system of yoga to the 6th and 5th centuries BCE through textual documentation formed by Buddhists, Jain, and Ajivika practitioners who rejected the Brahmanical orthodoxy (Bronkhorst, 2007; Miller, 2019).

Like a bowl, the womb carries the memories of our ancestors. Memories include trauma, pain, joy, and pleasure. These memories are important because they connect us to the roots that support our bodies and spirits in the ecosystem of life. Ancient yoga philosophy refers to the womb as Svadhisthana {sweetness}, the sacral chakra. The sacral chakra represents sexuality, movement, life force, creation, restoration, and pleasure. Pleasure is our birthright and pathway to liberation. When humans embody pleasure, we are free and in our power. When we are in our power, it is much more difficult for the systems of white supremacy to oppress our bodies, minds, and spirits.

For most of my life, I avoided yoga because my observations led me to believe that as an inflexible, large-bodied, queer, Indigenous-Chicana woman, I did not fit into the lifestyle of yoga. The lifestyle of yoga in the United States is rooted in capitalism that inevitably supports ableism, appropriation, and the commodification of yoga. The year of my 39th birthday, I experienced a compilation of life-changing, traumatic events that led me to attend a month-long yoga teacher training (YTT) program in Costa Rica. As an observer of the lifestyle of yoga, I ignorantly viewed the sacred practice as a product that I could use to survive financially. I invested the last of my financial resources in hopes of extracting what I needed to learn, so I could make living teaching students who were on the edges of the dominant culture.

During the month-long program, I quickly learned that yoga included much more than physical poses (asana). I experienced transformation and liberation in my body, mind, and spirit. Be that as it may, my experiences in the program reinforced my previous assumptions of yoga as a homogenous practice for slender, able-bodied, white, financially privileged women: a space I could participate in, but a community in which I did not belong. For a short time, I did not have the language and labels to attach how I was feeling and what I was experiencing in yoga spaces. The label I was seeking to validate and describe my observations and experiences was enveloped in white supremacy. Modern yoga in the United States is framed within a system of white supremacy that perpetuates a homogenous mainstream portrayal of straight, white, slender, affluent women, and actively excludes anyone who doesn't fit the mold (Payan Hazelwood, 2020).

Western modern yoga is built and perpetuated by the systems of white supremacy (Payan Hazelwood, 2020). Yoga culture is seeping with ableism, fatphobia, racism, and capitalism (to name a few). As people of color tend to do in spaces where white supremacy controls, hoards, and appropriates Indigenous Knowledges, I compartmentalized experiences and imagined how the practice could be accessible to "others". Others like me. I later understood this process as unsettling Indigenous Knowledges. Unsettling is an ongoing process in which I decenter myself from the power of ownership of yoga knowledge from a Western lens and recenter Indian Indigenous Knowledges of yoga. Some of the methods I used to unsettle myself from yoga were listening to the podcast series, *Yoga is Dead*, by Tejal Patel and Jesal Parikh, (2019–2020) and participating in a decolonizing yoga teacher training led by Susanna Barkataki (2020). I researched and wrote an essay on, *The History of Yoga and the Impact of Colonization in the United States* {2020} that centered on Indian scholar research and storytelling. Finally, with mentorship from India and BIPOC, I created a *Liberation in Yoga: A 200-Hour Yoga Teacher Training Program with a Social Justice Framework*.

My queer identity added another layer of complexity that was underrepresented in this predominantly cis, heterosexist space. Binary terminology like, "feminine" and "masculine" energy to describe poses; and penis (lingam) and vagina (yoni) were said to be the "perfect unions". This language was violent for me to hear because that meant I was not perfect in my body and spirit if I was not yoked with the "masculine penis". My queerness did not fit within the Western interpretation of yoga. It is through my scholarship of yoga from Indigenous Knowledges that I learned the oppressive language and interpretations of yoga philosophies were translated through the lens of colonialism and not in alignment with the root of yoga as a liberatory practice.

At the peak of ingesting the characteristics of white supremacy during the YTT, my body absorbed the violence of ableism and fatphobia. The harm caused to me from having to frequently ask for modifications became overwhelming to the point that I refused to participate in some poses. Opting out of a pose should have been acceptable too, but this was not an option. Why didn't the yoga leader have pose modifications readily available? It didn't occur to the leader that my stomach was "in the way" of the "ideal" twist. A simple modification or reframing of language could have felt liberating instead of oppressive to my body and mind.

I was exhausted mentally, physically, and spiritually from trying to fit into the ideal yoga body and yoga lifestyle. I felt the yoga lifestyle for an instructor came with more expectations of ability. The yoga blocks that I needed to support my body were viewed as a stepping stone on the way to the proper way of shaping the pose. The yoga lifestyle supported the notion that a yoga instructor *should* be able to model poses to perfection. I was told to "keep practicing" and "you will get there one day".

The characteristics of white supremacy include perfectionism, the binary, fear, one right way, individualism, paternalism, and worship of the written word. Like many yoga practices rooted in the yoga lifestyle, the erroneous message that folk is solely responsible for creating their own reality and peace is the epitome of spiritual whitewashing because this philosophy ignores how our multiple complex identities are impacted by power; the privilege of "creating one's own reality and peace". Yoga rooted in liberation invites the practitioner to self-reflect and examine their power. Yoga philosophy is a pathway to the liberation of all, not just one.

As the month-long training progressed, I committed to learning the modifications needed. I knew if I needed the modifications, there were many more who also needed them. I got up extra early and found hiding spots to practice yoga alone. Practicing solo allowed me access to my body in a way that was free from the non-consensual voyeurism of others who were consuming my body shapes as if I were an exotic creature performing for validation and unsolicited-well-meaning encouragement. I was not distracted by the need to take the shape of someone else's pose because their shape was more bendy and ideal to what was being asked of them. Rather than quickly moving from one pose to another in a hurried, competitive flow, I was able to hold a pose for as long as I needed. I supported myself with as many blocks and props as I needed to feel safe in my body. I received breath in a way that felt good to me and allowed me to connect more deeply to the earth's womb.

By focusing on connecting with the earth's womb, I was able to access the messages my body had been storing. Messages like, how unsafe I had felt in my body since I was eight years old when the adults at the Weight Watchers meeting stood me in front of the circus mirror and applauded as my reflection elongated my image of the ideal body. And, how I stuffed down my pain in the womb for the sake of being tough and picking myself up and moving forward. All lies, of course. The practice of processing the messages was something like this:

My belly (solar plexus) began to burn up the rotting emotions that were held down below in my womb. The sensations I felt in my body were a combination of heaviness, anxiety, and anger. The more I was able to access my body just the way it was, the more I felt the sensations that needed to rise. The sensations eventually rose to my lungs and heart space and I felt the fullness of toxic smoke that was from the rotting emotions and feelings stored in my body for too long. The smoke transformed into what I describe as a serpent in my throat. The serpent was constricted by my unspoken truths that needed to be shed. As I felt the serpent shedding, I could feel sensations, emotions, and feelings leaving my body. I wailed. My tears cleansed and transformed me into the person I am today. For a moment, I embodied liberation in my entire being.

Moments after this transformation, I took the shape of a reclined goddess pose (Supta Baddha Konasana). In this pose, I accessed the whispers of my ancestors. Literally. I asked myself, "why is this happening to me?" What I was asking had everything to do with the days, months, and years leading up to that moment. The answer that my body received was, "you asked for this". Not in the way in which spiritual whitewashing says I create my own reality; rather, it was the message that I had asked to be connected... yoked. I needed to burn some of the emotional trash that was no longer serving me so I could begin the journey of liberation.

With a sense of purpose and responsibility, I began to lead yoga classes in the same spaces I once felt marginalized. My classes were labeled "alternative" because they were accessible. Being an accessible yoga teacher led to harm as I experienced anger from "purist" yoga participants. My body was visually sized up with a scan from the body to toe. Two women were so upset I was substituting for the advanced yoga class that they whispered to each other, grumbled, and walked out in clear anger. Their protest was an example of how white feminism is dangerous to anyone else seeking liberation in body, mind, and spirit. White feminists' proximity to power (white supremacy and misogyny) has indoctrinated them to embrace competition, ableism, perfectionism, and other -isms that distance them from their own liberation. White feminism needs permission from their power-hoarding counterparts so as to not disrupt their proximity to power, rendering them in a position closer to that of the "others".

My classes were filled with "others". We practiced yoga in a way that gave all of us joy. The simple act of giving participants permission to focus on their body and not the reflection of their pose in the mirror and asking, "what does your heart desire" and "what sensations are you experiencing in your body right now" was revolutionary. I arrived early to classes so I could set up mats, chairs, and props for everyone. By doing this, nobody felt embarrassed or othered. The props were just part of the practice. Participants were given permission to take care of their bodies to dismantle the systems of paternalism. I avoided using language that was binary, cis-supremacist, and heterosexist by prompting the steps of making the shape of the goddess pose (Supta Baddha Konasana) but wouldn't give the name of the pose power; rather, I asked "how does this pose make you feel?". This style of teaching created a space where a person in a wheelchair could practice next to the athletic veteran who lives with PTSD. It was a space where participants could practice moments of liberation in their mind, body, and spirit.

Facilitating yoga for participants in a liberatory way is truly a gift. I learned so much about myself and my relationship with and to my body as well as to others. Yoga was the first access point to discerning the messages my body was holding. Through yoga, I reconnected with practices from my Mexica (Mēxihcah) ancestry such as curanderismo. I returned to higher education to learn about human sexuality and sustainability in education through decolonial praxis. Of all the liberatory practices yoga has led me to, my most beloved one is gardening. I always loved the smell of the earth and enjoyed planting flowers. Leveling up to gardening from seed to harvest helped me visualize a root extending from my body into the earth, connecting me. Gardening has been the medicine I needed to feel completely embodied and connected. As I harvest the calabacitas, I hear my grandmother's laughter, feel the strength of my mother's will, and see the beauty of my daughter's future. Gardening connects with the cycles of birth and death.

Yoga led me to discover many paths to liberation. Most importantly, yoga led me to the womb…home.

Bibliography

Patel, T. & Parikh, J. (2019–2020). *Yoga Is Dead Podcast.* https://www.yogaisdeadpodcast.com/home.

Payan Hazelwood, S. (2020). *The History of Yoga and the Impact of Colonization in the United States* [Thesis]. https://w.taskstream.com/ts/payanhazelwood/SerinaPayanHazelwood.html/k7eef6eu00kffafgfaf8ecfgfs.

Title: Yoga: A Liberatory Practice

Writers Names: Bianca I. Laureano and Serina Payan Hazelwood

Note to Educators
This lesson plan introduces and encourages a decolonial approach to facilitation, teaching, and learning. We encourage you to offer this when you are comfortable discussing (and engaging in) this process and open to sharing with participants some of your experiences. There are some somatic exercises woven through the activities that offer a script for you to read aloud or edit as the needs of your participants may be.

Learning Objective/Instructional Goal
In this lesson plan, participants will discuss and examine their impact in the sexuality field and consider a variety of healing modalities from a decolonial approach.

Learning Outcomes: By the end of the lesson, participants will be able to:

- Discuss how and why yoga is a healing approach to bodymindspirit
- Explain what a decolonial approach is in the sexuality field
- Identify the impact their work has on the land
- Create an action plan for limiting harm that embraces Indigenous Knowledge
- Outline approaches to creating a sense of belonging in their spaces

Essential Questions
- How and why is yoga considered a healing approach useful in the sexuality field?
- What is a decolonial approach?
- What impact does my work have on the land?
- What can I do to unlearn settler ways of being and knowing?
- How do I create a sense of belonging for my participants/students?

CASEL Social Emotional Learning Competencies

Self-awareness: The ability to accurately recognize one's own emotions, thoughts, and values and how they influence behavior. The ability to accurately assess one's strengths and limitations, with a well-grounded sense of confidence, optimism, and a "growth mindset".

Self-management: The ability to successfully regulate one's emotions, thoughts, and behaviors in different situations – effectively managing stress, controlling impulses, and motivating oneself. The ability to set and work toward personal and academic goals.

Social awareness: The ability to take the perspective of and empathize with others, including those from diverse backgrounds and cultures. The ability to understand social and ethical norms for behavior and to recognize family, school, and community resources and supports.

Relationship skills: The ability to establish and maintain healthy and rewarding relationships with diverse individuals and groups. The ability to communicate clearly, listen well, cooperate with others, resist inappropriate social pressure, negotiate conflict constructively, and seek and offer help when needed.

Responsible decision-making: The ability to make constructive choices about personal behavior and social interactions based on ethical standards, safety concerns, and social norms. The realistic evaluation of consequences of various actions, and a consideration of the well-being of oneself and others.

Materials
- From Local and Indigenous Knowledge Systems (LINKS) website https://en.unesco.org/links
- Environmental Violence and Reproductive Justice by Native Youth Sexual Health Network https://www.nativeyouthsexual-health.com/environmental-violence-reproductive-justice
- Impact On The Land Worksheet (included)

- Indigenous Rights in the Amazon (focus on Ecuador and Bolivia as they have laws with the earth) https://pachamama.org/indigenous-rights
- Berros, M. V. "The Constitution of the Republic of Ecuador: Pachamama Has Rights." Environment & Society Portal, *Arcadia* (2015), no. 11. Rachel Carson Center for Environment and Society. https://doi.org/10.5282/rcc/7131.

Preparation

Review definitions for terms in glossary and identify some examples of appropriation of Indigenous Knowledge in the sexuality field (they exist in abundance!). Next, review Environmental Violence and Reproductive Justice by Native Youth Sexual Health Network links and statements and additional readings and resources in the materials section. Make copies of the Impact On The Land worksheet.

Activity 1: Positioning Yoga (10 minutes)

The goal of this activity is to invite a conversation about yoga as a bodymindspirit practice and how it connects to sexuality work.

Begin by inviting participants to quietly share what some of the ideas, people, and places that come to mind when presented with the term "yoga". Honor the silence of this activity by inviting participants to write in a chat box if you are virtual, or write ideas on a sheet of paper or on a sticky note posted to the wall in the space. Offer about 3–5 minutes for this reflection.

Next, read aloud the shared offerings. Note any similarities that may emerge. It is ok to say you are unsure how to pronounce a term that is shared. Offer an overview of what you have noticed from the group. Here is a sample script to edit as needed:

> This is a great list of various places, feelings, people, and experiences! I noticed there are some similarities in how class, race, appropriation, and stereotypes emerge here.

Offer the following discussion questions:

- How does the author describe her experience entering the yoga practice?

- Are any of the experiences shared by the author represented on our group list?

Activity 2: What Is A Decolonial Approach? (20 minutes minimum)
The goal of this activity is to allow participants to discuss and consider what a decolonial approach includes and what forms of Indigenous Knowledge are a part of the sexuality field.

Begin by sharing that the author writes "My chapter tells the story of how a decolonial approach to practicing yoga offered me many paths to liberation that connect me to the earth's womb, that which is inextricably connected to my womb".

Ask participants to share their responses to this question:

- When you read/hear that sentence, what do you imagine as a decolonial approach?
- Does your idea of a decolonial approach match what you read by the author?

Allow participants to share voluntarily and be prepared for a range of questions and ideas shared. You may wish to engage with writing from additional Indigenous scholars and community members for this conversation.

Next, begin by generating a list of what they believe are examples of a "decolonial approach". What does this mean and how does it become a practice? You may also consider generating a list of resources that align or help sex professionals understand a decolonial framework. Some examples are included in the materials section of this lesson plan. Prepare for a range of shares and a long list!

Invite participants to share what they believe Indigenous Knowledge means and how it is described in the essay. Remind participants that indigeneity is a global experience and not limited to North American experiences. If participants need a definition of Indigenous Knowledge use the United Nations Educational, Scientific, and Cultural Organization (UNESCO) definition:

Local and Indigenous knowledge refers to the understandings, skills and philosophies developed by societies with long histories of interaction with their natural surroundings. For rural and

Indigenous peoples, local knowledge informs decision-making about fundamental aspects of day-to-day life.

Ask participants the following questions:

- What are some examples of Indigenous Knowledge in the sexuality field?
- How does erasure of Indigenous Knowledge become a form of violence and appropriation?
- Can we generate a list of examples that have appropriated Indigenous Knowledge? (some examples may be the misappropriation of the 4-D Wheel by Gina Ogden, performative land acknowledgments without action or connection to community, whitewashing of eco-sexuality, tantra, plant medicine (sage, palo santo, copal, etc.), rituals (cacao ceremonies, etc.), and terminology (Two-Spirit).

Activity 3: Considering the Land (30 minutes estimated)
The goal of this activity is to invite participants to consider how their work impacts the land they live on.

Begin by sharing that the guiding question for this section is to ask ourselves:

- How does our work impact the land/earth?

Share that this is often a topic that rarely gets addressed in sexuality training based in settler and Western values and this is a great example of what a decolonial approach may invite us to consider. Many are using the following website to help them identify who the stewards and original inhabitants of the land they are currently on are: https://native-land.ca. Invite participants to take a few moments to find the stewards of the land they are on by putting their zip code into the box. The Indigenous communities will show up below the box the zip code was put into.

Share now that participants are a bit more familiar with original inhabitants and stewards of the land, invite them to identify two actions they can do to continue to learn about these communities and how to support them. Offer 5 minutes for participants to write down and create two action items. Some examples may include doing additional research, attending public open to all local events held by the stewards, and contributing to Land Trusts. Remind participants that recognizing the land they are on is one of the most important first moves, and it is not the only approach to understanding our impact on the land.

Introduce the Environmental Violence and Reproductive Justice by Native Youth Sexual Health Network and offer participants a 7–10 minutes to review the website and click on links. When the time has ended, partner participants and have them share what they learned and understood during their review. Bring participants back as a larger group and welcome a few volunteers to share what they learned. Invite participants to consider why it is important to be guided by Native youth.

Next, invite participants to complete the Impact On The Land worksheet.

Activity 4: Earth's Womb and Our Bodies (20 minutes estimated)
The goal of this activity is to invite participants to consider the earth's womb or the earth as a womb and how this could provide another path to connecting one's body to the earth's.

Begin by sharing that the guiding question for this section is to ask ourselves:

- What characteristics of a womb are shared by the earth and our bodies?

Share that the mythos of the earth as a womb, or that the earth had a womb is an ancient and modern belief that is shared globally. Many cultures have evidence of their connection to the earth's body that includes ritual, art, music, and oral histories. In this activity, you will be facilitating the creation of a collaborative talking circle that invites participants to share their knowledge and lived experience of earth's womb and their body.

In the first round of the circle, invite participants to consider the characteristics of a womb. Ask these essential questions:

- How is the term "womb" received at this moment and how is it understood?

- What are the physical functions and characteristics of a womb?
- What is the sacred and/or spiritual significance of the womb?

Synchronize the essential questions above by asking the participants to consider at least one way the functions, characteristics, and significances of the womb can also be applied to the earth. What are the synchronicities in terms of the body, mind, and spirit?

In the next round of the talking circle, invite participants to consider the political, social, and spiritual aspects of the earth's body and how it mirrors that of our own? For example, individuals and systems of colonialism have a shared expectation that the earth's purpose is a source of endless resources (water, minerals, agriculture, and more); the earth's body is owned and controlled by individuals and systems; and regenerative practices are not required for the extraction of these resources. How are our bodies a resource?

In the final round of the circle, ask participants what curiosities and questions came up for them in this circle. How does their body feel at this moment? Invite a collective breath or release of some tension that feels good for participants.

A suggested script

> This is an invitation to close your eyes or soften your gaze. Notice your breath without changing your breathing. Notice your body as you receive breath, now, notice your body as you exhale breath. On your next inhalation receive a breath that feels good to you. Exhale. Receive breath two more times. What is your body feeling at this moment, has anything shifted? Gently open your eyes, notice the physical space outside of the circle. Bring your eyes into the circle. Who do you see?

Finally, offer the participants a two-part personal inquiry at home to

1. Find at least one story, ritual, or art piece of Indigenous peoples celebrating the earth's body.
2. Investigate how pipelines and the movement of Missing and Murdered Women, Girls, and 2-Spirit People (MMIWG2S) are connected
3. What action(s) can the participant take to connect their body to earth's body and how can they support social, spiritual,

and political movements that protect and honor bodies, minds, and spirits that are extracted?

Activity 5: Belonging As A Sexuality Professional (15–20 minutes estimated)

The goal of this activity is to consider how sexuality professionals find a sense of belonging in our field and how we create a sense of belonging in our teaching/learning spaces.

Begin by inviting the participants to participate in a daydream practice. A script template includes:

observe the physical space you are in. What do you notice? How do you feel when you notice the space? Receive an inhalation that feels good to you. Observe your breath. Observe sensations that are present and/ or arising.

Allow silence for 30–60 seconds.

Receive breath in any way that feels good to you. Allowing your body to answer, what does belonging in the sexuality field feel like in your body? Observe all sensations, even if there is an absence of sensation. Observe your body as you imagine, dream, or remember what belonging in the sexuality field feels like in your body. Receive breath in any way that feels good to you.

Invite the participants to share what emerged for them.

Facilitate a conversation guided by the following discussion questions:

- Why is it important to experience a sense of belonging?
- How can belonging in the sexuality field be liberatory?
- How can you be a beacon for belonging in the sexuality field?

Next, invite the participants to collaborate in small groups to create a list of ways a sexuality professional can create a sense of belonging for self and others? Discuss the highlights in a large group discussion. Invite the participants to share and expand on the list to use in their own practice.

Finally, ask the participants if they felt a sense of belonging in their body during the small group? Why or why not?

Activity 6: Emotional Trash? (15–30 minutes estimated)
The goal of this activity is to consider the author's description of emotional trash and how participants may or may not relate to this analogy.

Begin by reading aloud, or having a participant read aloud, the following excerpt from the chapter:

> "Moments after this transformation, I took the shape of a reclined goddess pose (Supta Baddha Konasana). In this pose, I accessed the whispers of my ancestors. Literally. I asked myself, "why is this happening to me?" What I was asking had everything to do with the days, months, and years leading up to that moment. The answer that my body received was, "you asked for this". Not in the way in which spiritual whitewashing says I create my own reality; rather, it was the message that I had asked to be connected... yoked. I needed to burn some of the emotional trash that was no longer serving me so I could begin the journey of liberation.

Offer the following questions for participants to discuss:

- How do you interpret and understand the phrase "emotional trash" in this context?
- What are other analogies that describe sensations, emotions, and feelings in their body?
- How do sensations, emotions, and feelings in their body inhibit their work in the field of sexuality?
- How do sensations, emotions, and feelings in the body contribute to their work in the field of sexuality?

Invite the participants to consider creating a form of art to convey their analogy of "emotional trash" as they interpret it based on this passage and the questions offered. Consider offering this as something to share and present at the next session together or separate some time in class to do this with a few art supplies. Some ideas include:

- Drawing, coloring, or doodling
- Sculpting with clay or dough

- Writing poetry
- Movement or dance
- Digital collage
- Creating music
- Making sounds (humming, growing, yelling out loud, etc.)

At the conclusion of the activity, invite the students to share their work in-person or virtually. Encourage playfulness and curiosity.

Glossary

Decolonial   A process with various global definitions that actively deconstructs and opposes the systems that colonialism that prioritizes landback, self-determination, interdependence, delinking, and resisting the systems constructed by and from colonization that are guided by empire, conquest, and exploitation (Ayame Hiraide, 2021; Mignolo, 2007).

Indigenous Knowledge   United Nations Educational, Scientific, and Cultural Organization (UNESCO) defines this term as "Local and Indigenous Knowledge refers to the understandings, skills, and philosophies developed by societies with long histories of interaction with their natural surroundings. For rural and Indigenous peoples, local knowledge informs decision-making about fundamental aspects of day-to-day life". From Local and Indigenous Knowledge Systems (LINKS) website https://en.unesco.org/links.

Womb   A place where something is generated (2022. In *Merriam-Webster.com*).

Yoga   The Sanskrit translation means to "yoke together" or "union". It can also mean technique or discipline (Gandhi, 2009).

Citation/Attribution

Ayame Hiraide, L. (2021, July 9). *Postcolonial, Decolonial, Anti-Colonial: Does It Matter?* New Voices in Postcolonial Studies. https://newvoicespocostudies.wordpress.com/hiraide/.

Berros, M. V. (2015). **"The Constitution of the Republic of Ecuador: Pachamama Has Rights."** Environment & Society Portal, *Arcadia*, no. 11. Rachel Carson Center for Environment and Society. https://doi.org/10.5282/rcc/7131.

Gandhi, S. (2009). *Translating, Practicing and Commodifying Yoga in the US* (pp. 1–240) [Dissertation].

Local and Indigenous Knowledge Systems (LINKS) United Nations Educational, Scientific, and Cultural Organization (UNESCO). (2022, June 16). https://en.unesco.org/links.

Mignolo, W. D. (2007). "Delinking: The Rhetoric of Modernity, the Logic of Coloniality and the Grammar of De-coloniality." *Cultural Studies,* 21(2–3), 449–514. https://doi.org/10.1080/09502380601162647.

Native Youth Sexual Health Network. (2002, June 17). Environmental Violence and Reproductive Justice. https://www.nativeyouthsexual-health.com/environmental-violence-reproductive-justice.

Impact on the Land Worksheet

Instructions: take some time to consider the questions and write your responses. The goal of this worksheet is to assist in identifying how your work may have an impact on the land you are working on and in.

Who are the stewards and original inhabitants of the land I live on?

What relationship do I have to these community members and stewards?

How do I be in service? Is my service digital? In person? A hybrid of both? Something else/more?

When I think of what "the land" means to me in my sexuality work it is …?

My current understanding of my impact on the land is …?

What are two commitments I can make to continuing to consider my impact on the land?

8

MY GRANDMOTHER, THE UNLIKELY ALLY

How Binary Thinking about Social Change Impedes Social Change

Karen B. K. Chan

I was 22 years old, still living at home, and hadn't come out to my mother yet. I'd thought about it – I'd been thinking about it since I was 9. Being the only child in a household of two (my Dad had gone back to Hong Kong after we emigrated), and the sole caretaker of my mother's happiness, I kept putting it off.

I was living a double life. I was active in the queer (East and Southeast) Asian communities in Toronto, doing HIV and queer youth work (in the late 90s, these things were closely entwined because of funding structures). In newspapers, on radio shows, and at conferences, I was endlessly talking about homophobia in Asian communities and racism in the queer community. I was telling the queer world many stories about my family, and yet I wasn't talking to my family about being queer.

That summer, I landed a great gig. A non-profit was going to pay for my hotel and train tickets to Montreal, and I got to speak on a panel about being queer, immigrant, and young. It was the first time I got to "travel for work" and it *really* floated my boat.

DOI: 10.4324/9781003181927-11

As we were preparing dinner, I told my mom half the story. "I'm going to speak on a panel about being a young immigrant". I knew she would be proud of me, and she was. But then, she did an unexpected thing – she invited herself along: "Wow, I'll get to visit Montreal finally!"

My mom never imposed and always just assumed she's excluded. This meant she was off her guard. Open and honest, yes, but also, vulnerable to being hurt in ways she normally wasn't.

I blurted out, "Who goes to a conference with their MOTHER?" The thought of her finding out that I was queer sent me into a panic. Plus, I had already invited my lover and planned a whole sexy hotel adventure.

Mom didn't look up. She mumbled, "Oh. Okay", while fussing with some mushrooms. I had broken an unspoken boundary in our family – you don't indignify your parents. We continued cooking and ate dinner without talking. I tried to engage her in one inane question after another and she wouldn't bite.

———

The day came and I left with my lover. We walked hand in hand through Montreal. We ate poutine by a fountain. We found sprinklers and ran through them. We jumped on the hotel beds.

I did my talk and it was well-received. But my heart was sunken. All my fantasies about my sexy Montreal work trip flattened against the wall that I had put between my mom and me. I couldn't enjoy any of it. I had hurt my mother, and not even with the truth! I let her think I was ashamed of her because I couldn't tell the actual truth.

Crying into a bowl of pho, I had finally had it (and my lover also had had it – it was as miserable for her as it was for me). I took deliberated on a napkin: "Queer" would be too hard to explain in Cantonese, maybe "gay" was a better choice? Should I start with saying how the panel went, or should I just jump into it?

Then, I called my mother. The most important bottom line for me was that I was sorry I had hurt her. I had no qualms in bringing her to Montreal. In fact, I would be proud to take her with me on a work trip.

In truth, I thought the coming out part would be simply confirming what she had always suspected. I had been an androgynous child and teen, and she was used to correcting everyone, "Not my son. She's my daughter".

So her reaction was a shock. She berated me on not being a decent person. "Why can't you just get a job and be a contributing member of society?". In retrospect, it makes so much sense that employment was how her deeper concerns were verbalized. Employment translates for her into goodness. But she also threw other jabs: That being gay meant hiding in dark basements doing drugs and parading down public streets dressed only in leather crotch pieces. (An interesting juxtaposition of two images, come to think of it.)

That call didn't end well. She hung up on me after a few rounds of pointless argument. I was too hurt to hear what she was actually saying, and she was too panicked to hear that my call was actually an act of love.

We didn't speak for the next half a year. We spoke, functionally, of course, being the only two people in the house: Did you take out the garbage; can you sign this form; please heat up the leftovers; by the way, one of the cats threw up. But we avoided talking so that we could avoid facing what happened.

———

One day deep into the winter, my mom blurted out over dinner, "My boss is gay". I didn't say anything. I just nodded, but in my heart, I knew this was big news. Not only that my mom had broken the silence, not only that she was acknowledging that I had come out to her, but most importantly, that the only other gay person she now knows is a highly educated lawyer who makes more than ten times what my parents make. It was a sign that stability, security, and safety would not elude me simply because I'm gay.

———

Throughout this period, I was being interviewed in English and Chinese language newspapers, saying much the same things that I was saying on that panel. Only now, I started to share the articles with my mom.

After a particularly busy week in the local newspaper, she asked me, "How would you feel if I called every one of our relatives and told them about you?"

I thought it was a rhetorical question, meant to scold me for causing my family indignity by being so public about my queerness. As per usual, I said nothing and waited.

My mom pressed,

> If your relatives read about you but hadn't heard it from your dad and me, they will assume it's a shameful secret and that we disapprove. It would give them permission to slight you or to treat you badly. I don't want that. So I'm going to call them and show them we are happy and accepting. We will set the standard for them to follow. I think it's smart.

I was gobsmacked. Bowled over by the incredible thoughtfulness, the self-less courage she would muster on my behalf, and by the terrifying idea of coming out to my 14 aunts and uncles and the nearly 100 cousins. I was also torn by the small yet significant lie that this entailed: Truth is, she wasn't all that happy or accepting. And this loving, courageous act was ultimately a crisis management move. It was how my mom was covering for me, making up for what I lacked in respectability to our extended family.

I defaulted to the safety of hiding – I shrugged and feigned flippancy, "I don't care. Do what you want".

And she did. Each auntie or uncle received a phone call and a loose recital of the same script. Yes, Karen is doing great at school. Almost finished her degree. Some kind of biology. Very hard work. Oh, she's dating now. Yes. A girl. No, no. Dating a girl. She's very polite, a good worker at a steady job. A Taiwanese. No, she doesn't speak Cantonese. Mandarin though. Well, young people nowadays are not old-fashioned like us. Ok, yes I will. You too. Eat more food, you sound thin. Ok, goodbye.

Over the course of a week, every night after the dishes were done, she would get on the phone. And then, it was done. Except for one.

My popo – my mom's mom – was nearly 80 and living in Hong Kong. Common sense seemed to say that we shouldn't trouble the elderly with this kind of trauma. My grandmother had an arranged (and highly unhappy) marriage to my grandfather, and she had never talked about things like love or romance or dating. My mom was reasoning that popo would simply not understand. What if she has a heart attack? Plus, my mother was probably scared to face her own mother, to report on the outcomes of her parenting efforts abroad.

But, now that she had told all her siblings, some of them may bring it up with popo. So really, she had no choice.

My mother told me about their conversation a few days after the fact.

———

Mom: I talked to *popo*, did I tell you?

Me: No.

Mom: She said to give you a message.

Me: Hm? [terrified of any message, wanting this conversation to stop]

Mom: She said that if anyone gives you problems for being "like that", remember it's not your problem, it's theirs.

Me: She knew what you were talking about?

Mom: Yes. Actually, she said that her sister, your *yi po*, was "like that" too. *Yi po* had girlfriends coming in and out of the front door so frequently they might as well have kept it open, she said.

Me: Oh wow.

Mom: *Popo* also said that if my neighbours give me any problems with your girlfriend, the trick was to adopt her as my god-daughter. An easy way to shut them up.

Me: Oh, that's not necessary.

Mom: Well, it's an option.

Just like that. Understated and avoidant as always, and leaving more unsaid than said, my mom and I ended what is now clearly one of the most important conversations of my life.

————

A few years later, my grandmother would come to Toronto to live with us. and the girlfriend in question was also living with us, due to a temporary housing issue.

By then my grandmother was in her late eighties and frequently forgetful. On more than a few occasions, like when I was dying her hair or driving her to an appointment, she'd say, "Well, that nice girl living with us, where is her husband?"

Each time I would "come out" to her again. Each time she would learn about my gayness anew, and ask, "Do the neighbours give us trouble?"

Title: How Binary Thinking about Social Change Impedes Social Change

Writers Names: Karen B. K. Chan & Bianca I. Laureano

Note to Educators
This lesson plan and chapter examine a range of topics. Be sure to review and become familiar with what is included. This chapter may go well with the chapter on Muslim experiences.

Learning Objectives/Instructional Goal
In this lesson plan, participants will examine how sexual orientation and attraction are impacted by western ideas and expectations.

Learning Outcomes: By the end of the lesson, participants will be able to:

- Define and explain the impact of Orientalism on the understanding of sexuality and sexual orientation, especially on diasporic Asian communities
- Define and explain the impact of colonial thought on the understanding of coming out, social change, and social justice
- Recognize a range of coming out experiences and when a Western perspective is elevated over others

Essential Questions
What are Orientalism and its impact on the sexual expression and lives of people in diasporic Asian communities

- What does it mean to out someone? Why do we expect people to "come out" in specific ways?
- What are the benefits of having a shared language regarding social change (like terms for sexual orientation and gender identity)? Who gets included that would otherwise be excluded?
- What are the limitations of having a narrow range of language or behavior deemed appropriate when it comes to social change (like using the correct terms or the latest concepts)? Who gets excluded?

CASEL Social Emotional Learning Competencies

Self-awareness: The ability to accurately recognize one's own emotions, thoughts, and values and how they influence behavior. The ability to accurately assess one's strengths and limitations, with a well-grounded sense of confidence, optimism, and a "growth mindset".

Self-management: The ability to successfully regulate one's emotions, thoughts, and behaviors in different situations – effectively managing stress, controlling impulses, and motivating oneself. The ability to set and work toward personal and academic goals.

Social awareness: The ability to take the perspective of and empathize with others, including those from diverse backgrounds and cultures. The ability to understand social and ethical norms for behavior and to recognize family, school, and community resources and supports.

Relationship skills: The ability to establish and maintain healthy and rewarding relationships with diverse individuals and groups. The ability to communicate clearly, listen well, cooperate with others, resist inappropriate social pressure, negotiate conflict constructively, and seek and offer help when needed.

Materials

Author Viet Thanh Nguyen On the Deep Well of Anti-Asian Racism in the US. Available at: https://www.pbs.org/newshour/nation/author-viet-thanh-nguyen-on-the-deep-well-of-anti-asian-racism-in-the-u-s.

Preparation

Review the lesson plan and identify any additional resources to include. Review the PBS resource listed above before introducing it to the class as a form of contemporary conversations of Orientalism.

Activity 1: The Role of Silence (15 minutes estimated)
The goal of this activity is to prepare participants for the activities and conversation presented by the author.

Begin this lesson by reading aloud the following passage by the author:

> As we were preparing dinner, I told my mom half the story. "I'm going to speak on a panel about being a young immigrant". I knew she would be proud of me, and she was. But then, she did an unexpected thing – she invited herself along: "Wow, I'll get to visit Montreal finally!"
>
> My mom never imposed and always just assumed she's excluded. This meant she was off her guard. Open and honest, yes, but also, vulnerable to being hurt in ways she normally wasn't.
>
> I blurted out, "Who goes to a conference with their MOTHER?" The thought of her finding out that I was queer sent me into a panic. Plus, I had already invited my lover and planned a whole sexy hotel adventure.
>
> Mom didn't look up. She mumbled, "Oh. Okay", while fussing with some mushrooms. I had broken an unspoken boundary in our family – you don't indignify your parents. We continued cooking and ate dinner without talking. I tried to engage her in one inane question after another and she wouldn't bite.

Offer the following discussion questions:

- What role does silence play in our lives and sexuality work?
- How was silence experienced by the author and their parent?
- When may silence be the most impactful action to take?

Activity 2: Power & Multiple Oppressions (20 minutes estimated)
The goal of this activity is to offer participants the opportunity to consider how multiple forms of oppression and harm exist at the same time and introduce them to the concept and lived reality of Orientalism.

Karen B. K. Chan writes "I was endlessly talking about homophobia in Asian communities and racism in the queer community. I was telling the queer world many stories about my family, and yet I wasn't talking to my family about being queer".

For this writing activity, invite participants to take three minutes to write their responses to this sentence stem. After completing one sentence, continue responding to the sentence until the three minutes have completed. It is ok if these responses are more of a list than complete sentences. Invite participants after the first sentence stem to do the same with the next sentence stem.

I have learned that racism is …

I have learned that homophobia is …

When the time is completed for both sentence stems, it is not required that participants share what they wrote, they deserve privacy. You may pair participants up and invite them to discuss the following questions:

- What was your experience responding to the sentence stem?
- What were you surprised to notice?

Introduce the term Orientalism and offer this description and definition:

> Orientalism is a term coined by Palestinian American postcolonial scholar Edward Said. His book *Orientalism* published in 1979 offered a critique of the way The West (i.e. empires, colonial settlers) often considers, depicts, and represents The East i.e. the Orient, which is often dehumanizing, harmful, and upholding Western supremacy. His work has led to scholars and communities reexamining how they discuss and interact with people from the Middle East and Asia.

Invite participants to expand the definition if they wish. This may be a good time to reflect on a reading or passage by Said, or a contemporary piece on anti-Asian racism if desired. We suggest an open resource PBS option with author Viet Thanh Nguyen.

Use the following discussion questions to facilitate a conversation:

- What are some examples of Orientalism that still remain?
- How does Orientalism impact the sexual expression and lives of diasporic Asian and Middle Eastern communities?
- How are "traditional" societies portrayed in North America? In the dominant culture, and also among diasporic communities?

- What is the function of those portrayals (i.e., notice not only what the portrayals do, but also what they allow dominant society to do, and what they allow diasporic communities to do.)

Activity 3: Coming Out (15 minutes estimated)
The goal of this activity is for participants to consider what "coming out" means, its impact on individuals and communities, the various ways we come out, and how a Western model of coming out is often encouraged.

Begin by asking participants what comes to mind when they hear the phrase "coming out". You may consider playing "I'm Coming Out" by Diana Ross to set the tone of the space. As you generate a list, notice themes that may emerge. Next, if you can identify the Western ideas and expectations for "coming out" are deeply rooted in proclaiming something about oneself. Ask participants what else we come out about in our lives beyond sexuality experiences.

Reflecting on the chapter, invite participants to discuss what some of the challenges Chan shared they had with coming out to their mother about their queerness? (i.e. language translation from English to Cantonese).

Conclude this section with the question: What other ways exist to come out that are not linear or vocal?

Activity 4: Binary Thinking (20 minutes estimated)
The goal of this activity is to recognize binaries when they emerge, especially in our thought process; to identify ways this leaves out many people, and how it may be in alignment with a dehumanization approach similar to Orientalism discussed in earlier activity.

Begin by inviting participants to share what they understand a binary to be, how it is defined. If you need a definition, here is one suggestion:

A binary is when describing something as having two and only two options.. Binary gender is having only two options for gender: Woman or man (or girl vs. boy). Black and white; right and wrong; on and off... are all binaries.

Invite participants to share other binaries they know. Invite participants to share synonyms for binary (which may include dichotomy or other more academic terms).

Binary Thinking is about simplifying complex concepts and situations into being one side or another. Nuance, complexity, and the parts about a situation or concept that don't fit neatly are ignored or forced into one of the two poles. Consider using these discussion questions to facilitate a conversation:

- What are the benefits of binary thinking? How does it make life easier or better?
- How does binary thinking manifest in the portrayals of marginalized cultures and peoples? How does binary thinking affect identity formation (racial, cultural, sexual)? What would complexity and nuance in their portrayals do? Where are the places where nuance and complexity can be introduced in sex education?
- Progressive sex education and sex-positive movements are committed to challenging binary thinking – moving away from binary gender, binary sex, normal vs. abnormal, away from heteronormativity, or even the assumption that all people are sexual. At the same time, progressive sex education can become dogmatic. What are some forms of binary thinking you can identify that are still prevalent in progressive sex education? What are ways to expand and complexify them?

Glossary

Body Autonomy   It is the human right to decide what happens to our bodymind and a principle of reproductive justice.

Binary Thinking   Simplifying complex concepts and situations into being one side or another. Nuance, complexity, and the parts about a situation or concept that don't fit neatly are ignored or forced into one of the two poles.

Coming Out   A process. A choice for an individual to share personal information with others. Often coming out is put in the context of sharing a queer identity, yet we come out about a lot of other experiences and lived realities (i.e. adoption, poverty, documentation status, relationships type, etc.)

Orientalism   A term coined by Palestinian American postcolonial scholar Edward Said. His book *Orientalism* published in 1979 offered a critique of the way The West (i.e. empires, colonial settlers) often considers, depicts, and represents the East i.e. the Orient, often dehumanizing, harmful, and upholding Western supremacy. His work has led to scholars and communities reexamining how they discuss and interact with people from the Middle East and Asia.

Bibliography

PBS News Hour. (March 18, 2021). Author Viet Thanh Nguyen on the Deep Well of Anti-Asian Racism in the US. https://www.pbs.org/newshour/nation/author-viet-thanh-nguyen-on-the-deep-well-of-anti-asian-racism-in-the-u-s.

Ross, L. (2017). *Reproductive Justice: An Introduction*. Berkeley: University of California Press.

Said, E. W. (2003). *Orientalism*. London: Penguin Classics. Vintage.

9

A VULGAR SEX EDUCATION

Melina Gaze and Sucia Urrea of Vulgar

Dear reader,

Greetings from January 15, 2022, well after the final draft of this text was due to the loving, revolutionary, and unabashedly human curator of this book, Bianca Laureano, who reminds us always of our own humanity and who gives us permission to feel our own vulnerability. Inspired by Bianca, we wanted to send a little note to you to let you know where we're at.

We're tired. We know you are too. We wrote the following text at the beginning of the pandemic, when it felt like what we were writing was still true. Now, two years in, we aren't so sure. We read, and re-read, edited and re-edited, and we still are feeling displaced in our own words. We are reminded how our social contexts, our connections, our collaborations, and our bodies hold and give life to our work. And this far into the pandemic, where we have largely gone online, where we haven't perreado wildly with our friends and collaborators, held them close, blurted out the wrong thing in public, been messy with an ex, run into our queer party friends in what always felt like the most miraculous serendipity (but of course they were going to be at that queer party—everyone was) a lot of what we write below feels...distant.

DOI: 10.4324/9781003181927-12

Through some notes from our tireless editor Bianca, we reflected that our writing didn't sound that confident, that we apologized a lot. The "we thinks" and "maybes" didn't fit the manifesto style of this piece. But the thing is, upon further review, we're not confident. We feel very much at the crux of a thing we can't even name yet, and we know it's changing our work. It's changing our priorities. Maybe we don't want to do sex education anymore, maybe we want to revisit what sexuality actually means and where it came from; how the thought of a compartmentalized "drive" actually limits our broader erotic, relational and sensual experiences of the world. Maybe we want to reframe our project not as "education", but as an offering of tools to engage critically with ideologies of sexuality. Maybe we want to not do anything ever ever again on social media because it doesn't permit the deep, in-person experiences that we crave. Maybe education isn't enough, maybe we need to take a more direct action approach. Maybe the world would be better served if we just shifted gears completely and dedicated the rest of our lives to the climate crisis. Maybe, maybe, maybe.

All this to say, take the following with a grain of salt. As an attempt towards coherence that admittedly is not coherent at all. As a text torn between what we thought we were, and what we don't know we're becoming.

Vulgar is a sexuality education collective based in Mexico City, Mexico. We work with educators and activists from Mexico and Spanish-speaking United States to facilitate spaces for collective learning about gender and sexuality. We also employ arts-based pedagogy that engages mind, body, and community because we believe learning is a full body experience with social and political implications. Mostly, we give workshops for people who are 18 years old and older.

While we are constantly in a process of reviewing our guiding principles, these are some that we're thinking about now:

1. Pleasure is political.
2. Learning and unlearning is an ongoing process.
3. We are more than individuals. We are deeply interconnected with people, contexts, and social structures.
4. Sex education can be a tool to challenge violences including racism, sexism and ableism.
5. We have a right to explore and know our bodies.
6. All of our decisions as sexuality educators have political implications.

Read on for more detail:

Pleasure Is Political

Yes, we mean this in the way it's used as a slogan within current sexual liberation movements. Many of us have been denied access to knowledge about our bodies or have suffered exclusion on the basis of our sexuality. So embracing our own pleasure can be an act of resistance. This has been one of the founding ideas of Vulgar: we want to help people develop tools that lead to more pleasurable experiences of sexuality, our bodies, and the world.

We also want to add some nuance to this understanding because the idea of pleasure in itself is not categorically good. It can also be used to justify acts that perpetuate harmful dynamics. For example, our friend Axel Bautista, who is an HIV activist and educator, talks about sexual liberation and pleasure on online dating apps, and how in the name of pleasure or "it's just what I like", people perpetuate sexist, classist, racist, ableist, and capitalist hierarchies. As Axel explains about his own experience, "if you are HIV positive, and you are a darker skin person, you are at the bottom of the list".

So, yes! In our work, we believe that exploring who we are, and what we like and don't is key towards living a pleasurable life. But that is not enough. It is important to interrogate pleasure, understand how it shapes our relationship to others, and undo harmful and violent social and cultural legacies.

We also recognize the way pleasure and a "you deserve it" attitude can be coopted and used against us to create harmful norms about sexuality: that we have to be having sex to be "liberated" (you don't), that we have to buy things to have a full sexual life (you don't), that our pleasure is top priority and people are dispensable tools towards that aim (they're not), and that our individual pleasure is important above all else (we hope to work toward collective liberation).

Learning Is an Ongoing Process

We recognize that everyone who decides to join our workshops is in their own processes of learning and unlearning. We all are. There is no final state of enlightenment, no final set of principles we can find for existing in this world. By acknowledging this, we hope we can foster spaces that welcome all sorts of people, including those we don't agree with. We don't tolerate harmful behavior, such as xenophobia, racism, or transphobia, and we try to welcome differences of opinion and come to a common ground. It's only by recognizing our vulnerabilities and the things we don't know that we can learn.

We Are More Than Individuals. We Are Deeply Interconnected with People, Contexts, and Social Structures

So often, sex ed operates from an individualistic stance that is just about one person – their pleasure, their well-being, their health outcomes. It's evident in the ways sex ed is taught with the premise that if you teach individuals about how to make "responsible decisions", then they will make better decisions that will in turn improve their health outcomes. Yet, we know that this doesn't always work, and many communities are more at risk because of structural inequalities, lack of access to medical care, and histories of social exclusion and oppression. That's why we try to incorporate a lens beyond the individual and incorporate a more social perspective. As Marbella Figueroa, cofounder of the Mexican anti-racist podcast *Afrochingonas* shared with us recently, "under capitalism we desire options that are present for us, and we are made to believe that we are free because we can choose out of those options without questioning why those [are our] options in the first place". We believe that a collective interrogation of the social contexts we inhabit and understanding how social conditions shape our intimate, sexual, and erotic experiences, can help us expand the horizon of what is possible and foster new ways of relating to ourselves and others. This acknowledgment of interconnectedness allows for a strategic vision of what collective change looks like. Just employing personal responsibility is not enough; we need to work at a social level.

Sex Ed Can Be a Tool to Challenge Different Forms of Violence

We know that gender violence, classism, racism, and ableism impact people's intimate, sexual, and erotic lives. We believe it's essential for sex ed curricula to unpack how access to safety, pleasure, and knowledge are unevenly distributed, and how that has violent consequences for many people. We believe acknowledgment is not enough, because that rings of complicity. We think sex ed can be a space to contest the violence, through some of the following activities:

a. Collaborate with workshop participants to develop media literacy tools so we can assess how messages and norms about sex, body image, pleasure, and relationships intersect with racism, sexism, and other forms of social exclusion.
b. Work with participants to cultivate scientific literacy, so we can better understand the sexuality information we consume.
c. Ally with anti-racist, disability rights, sex workers', and other movements to explore together the links between sexuality and social justice and expand possibilities for liberatory sex education.

We Have a Right to Explore and Know Our Bodies

We have a right to know and explore the full range of our bodies, including pleasure. These are some ways we try to bring in ideas that celebrate pleasure and move away from a risk-based approach. By no means is it a comprehensive list, but it's a li'l taste:

a. Help develop body and emotional awareness skills so that participants can better parse out their own boundaries or curiosities.
b. Discuss a wide range of sexual behaviors, identities, and experiences.
c. Include the wide range of variation in human bodies and genitals.
d. Discuss common sexual response models, how they were produced, and how they may apply to our experiences (or not!)
e. Explore pleasure beyond the genitals!
f. Talk openly about masturbation and offer resources for people to explore it if they wish.
g. Discuss porn and erotic materials and develop porn literacy tools so people can "read" porn critically.
h. Help people identify tools to create environments more conducive to their pleasure.
i. Practice consent conversations.
j. Discuss STIs without stigma.
k. Question the idea of a "normal" sexuality and where this came from historically.

All of Our Decisions as Sexuality Educators Have Political Implications

Everything has a political angle and historical genealogy. For example, as our collaborator Malicia, the founder of the transfeminist sex shop *Deseos Violeta* asks, "Why might some sex education teach about the erectile tissue and function of penises but not of vulvas?" Why does a lot of supposedly "comprehensive" sex education still not mention trans people or people with disabilities? And why is it that supposedly "scientific" anatomical drawings still only include young, thin, able-bodied white people? The omission of pleasure, the omission of trans people, the omission of BIPOC people, the omission of queers, the omission of people with disabilities: all have political motivations and implications. We do not pretend to be a "neutral" sex ed group. We understand sexuality education is intimately linked to our participation in and connection with diverse social movements invested in social justice.

Sex Ed Can Be a Fun and Pleasurable Experience That Involves the Body

We think learning is more fun and effective when it engages each person as a full being, including their body. We learn and enjoy more when we laugh, write silly poems about anatomy together, and dance with our *culos* so low they bounce "*hasta el subsuelo*", as our collaborator Natalia Lane from *Centro de Apoyo a las Identidades Trans*, would say. We also know that sexuality can be a painful experience, and that making room for our hurt is important for making room for pleasure and joy. Pleasure is not just a point of view, it is an ethical principle; a tool for enjoying life right now and for the sustainability of our project long term.

Thanks so much for reading our little manifesto. These principles are not set in stone. They are always tentative; changing as we meet beautiful and powerful people pushing the boundaries of education. These principles do not come out of our practice alone; they emerge from genealogies of activists and scholars and our work with our friends. If they resonate with you, it is because there are many people who have made it possible to do the work. If they are totally new, welcome!

Title: A Vulgar Sex Education Lesson Plan

Writers' Names: Bianca I. Laureano

Note to Educators
This lesson plan is partnered with a multilingual chapter. You are encouraged to decide if you wish to seek translation for the Spanish language parts as there are intentionally no translations offered in the text to suggest action for the reader: what will you do to fully understand?

Learning Objectives/Instructional Goal
In this lesson plan, participants will identify guiding frameworks in community collaboration and citation practices.

Learning Outcomes: By the end of the lesson, participants will be able to:

- List at least two coping strategies
- Identify guiding principles for their work/approach
- Create a community collaboration philosophy
- Recognize citations as accountability and love

Essential Questions
- How do I manage and cope with change as it emerges?
- What are the principles that guide my work?
- How do I imagine and put into practice collaborating with other communities?
- In what ways do citation and attribution help me understand who I have learned from and what communities I am accountable to?

CASEL Social Emotional Learning Competencies Met in This Lesson Plan
Self-awareness: The ability to accurately recognize one's own emotions, thoughts, and values and how they influence behavior. The ability to accurately assess one's strengths and limitations, with

a well-grounded sense of confidence, optimism, and a "growth mindset".

Self-management: The ability to successfully regulate one's emotions, thoughts, and behaviors in different situations – effectively managing stress, controlling impulses, and motivating oneself. The ability to set and work toward personal and academic goals.

Social awareness: The ability to take the perspective of and empathize with others, including those from diverse backgrounds and cultures. The ability to understand social and ethical norms for behavior and to recognize family, school, and community resources and supports.

Relationship skills: The ability to establish and maintain healthy and rewarding relationships with diverse individuals and groups. The ability to communicate clearly, listen well, cooperate with others, resist inappropriate social pressure, negotiate conflict constructively, and seek and offer help when needed.

Responsible decision-making: The ability to make constructive choices about personal behavior and social interactions based on ethical standards, safety concerns, and social norms. The realistic evaluation of consequences of various actions, and a consideration of the well-being of oneself and others.

Materials
- Guiding Principles worksheet
- Community Collaboration Philosophy worksheet
- Solutions to Online Violence FemTechNet Respect Wheel https://www.femtechnet.org/wp-content/uploads/2016/06/Respect-color.png

Preparation
- You may want to complete the worksheets before introducing them and share your own responses as examples.

- Review the following websites and become familiar with the content so you may facilitate a discussion with participants.
  - Cite Black Women https://www.citeblackwomencollective.org
  - Center for Solutions to Online Violence FemTechNet RespectWheel https://www.femtechnet.org/wp-content/uploads/2016/06/Respect-color.png

Activity 1: Coping with and Expecting Change (15 minutes estimated)
The goal of this activity is to discuss how we cope with change in our field, lives, and the work we do. Consider being in a circle if you are meeting and discussing in-person.

Begin by sharing that you'd like to begin the conversation about the essay by discussing the introduction from January 2022 that the authors offer. They bring in an understanding of the unpredictable impact of the pandemic and question what they wish to do for the future. If your group conversations are more fruitful when participants know the questions and can write quietly before sharing, trust your knowledge of your group. Invite a conversation guided by these questions.

1. How does change connect to sexuality topics and how do we discuss these changes?
2. What are coping strategies that work for you in preparing for and coping through change?
3. How do we understand sustainability for doing our work and caring for ourselves?

Activity 2: Citations as a Form of Revolutionary Love (20 minutes)
The goal of this activity is to encourage participants to elevate their citation and attribution practices.

Begin with a discussion on how participants noticed the citation and attribution practices of the authors of the chapter.

- Whose labor and brilliance was welcomed into the conversation?
- How did these citations become guides for their principles?

Ask participants what they believe the purpose of citation may be in their work. Why would they cite a source? You may hear a variety of responses. Document them on the board or in a communal document to reflect back on.

Next, visit the Cite Black Women website and invite participants to read aloud the "Our Praxis" section. Cite Black Women https://www.citeblackwomencollective.org

If participants are unclear what the term "praxis" means, please offer a synonym such as "practice". The "Our Praxis" section outlines the guiding principles for the collective. They write "think of them as practices to live by". Invite a conversation using these questions:

- Why is citation a practice to live by?
- Who are the Black women in the sexuality field that they may cite?
- How does accountability fold into this practice?

Visit the Center for Solutions to Online Violence FemTechNet Respect Wheel created by The Alchemists https://www.femtechnet.org/wp-content/uploads/2016/06/Respect-color.png and if possible distribute to each participant to review. Note and focus on the circle of Accountability which states the following questions:

- Who receives credit for their work and who doesn't?
- What are the intentions of the work being cited and what are the intentions of the work being created?
- What power do you hold over those you are citing?
- What power do you hold over those you are NOT citing?
- How do you plan to use the work? Did you inform the person you were using their work? Are you willing to have a conversation about how you may/not be able to use the work?
- Who are you citing from? Who aren't you citing from?

Read aloud the names of The Alchemists who created this resource which include Bianca Laureano, I'Nasah Crockett, Meagan Ortiz, Jessica Marie Johnson, Sydette Harry, Izetta Mobley, and Danielle Cole for the Center for Solutions to Online Violence. You may invite participants to do an internet search on one or two of these individuals to find their contributions to sexuality as an interdisciplinary field.

Note that the editor and forward are written by two of The Alchemists. Invite participants to share their understanding of what an "alchemist" is and what they do. Complete this activity with the following questions:

- How does the idea of alchemy, magic, creativity, and transformation connect to change as discussed previously?
- What ways does love for knowledge, community, and care emerge in this citation and attribution process?

There is a Power Wheel that accompanies this document and it may be found if a continued discussion is desired. https://www.fem-technet.org/wp-content/uploads/2016/06/Respect-color.png

Activity 3: Community Collaboration Philosophy (20 minutes at least)
The goal of this activity is to create a community collaboration philosophy.

Share the authors write that "Sex ed can be a tool to challenge different forms of violence". Invite a few volunteers to share their thoughts on this statement. Use the following questions for this conversation:

- What forms of violence may be challenged via sex ed?
- What communities must we collaborate with to meet these goals?

Distribute the Community Collaboration Philosophy worksheet. Read the instructions and offer participants ten minutes to begin. You may also revisit if participants need more time. You may want to do this worksheet yourself and offer what you created as an example. Partner participants and have them share what they created.

Wrap this activity up by inviting students to share their experience completing the worksheet. What emerged for them?

Activity 4: Guiding Principles (15 minutes estimated)
The goal of this activity is for participants to consider what guiding principles lead them to do their work.

Begin by reminding participants that group agreements are a common creation in the sexuality spaces we facilitate and build together. Reference the Cite Black Women website as the first time you discussed guiding principles during this conversation. Ask participants:

• When we discuss guiding principles what comes to mind?

Introduce and distribute the Guiding Principles worksheet and read the instructions aloud for participants. You may want to complete the worksheet before introducing it and share your own responses as an example. Offer participants 7–10 minutes to begin and complete this worksheet. Remind participants that this is the first of several times they will come back to this worksheet and offer revisions or updates. Revisit this worksheet with participants so they may think on the principles and become comfortable updating the document as their vision/needs/guidance shifts and changes.
Offer this discussion question for participants:

• What came up as you were writing?

Activity 5: Closing Activity (five minutes)
The goal of this activity is to encourage participants to think about the movements they know and that resonate with their ideas of community and collaboration.

Invite participants to take a few moments to think about what movements exist that guide their work and have them share at least one. (i.e. Reproductive Justice, Disability Rights, Abolition)

Be prepared for how to respond to those who may share more harmful and violent responses such as supporting anti-trans legislation or arming teachers with assault rifles or supporting genocide.

Citation/Attribution

Center for Solutions to Online Violence FemTechNet Respect Wheel. https://www.femtechnet.org/wp-content/uploads/2016/06/Respect-color.png.

Cite Black Women. https://www.citeblackwomencollective.org.

Guiding Principles Worksheet

Instructions: Answer the following questions to begin to identify the guiding principles that support your work in the sexuality field today.

What are ideas, theories, scholars, and work that inspire your creativity?

What have you learned?

What topics or issues do you care about and wish to focus upon?

What do you want? Why do you want it?

How do you plan to take what you learn and apply to your approach?

Community Collaboration Philosophy

Instructions: Use this worksheet to help develop your philosophy for collaborating with other communities besides your own. There are no right or wrong answers! This is your own living document that helps guide you in identifying the ways you wish to work with (and maybe for) others.

What communities do you want to connect and build with?

What can you offer in a community collaboration? Consider your origin story and position yourself (how you got here, who helped you, what identities do you have and what power do those hold). Think in a mutually beneficial way!

What is a quote/lyric that resonates with you in doing this work? Write about how that quote guides you to do your work in the sexuality field. What does the quote remind you of and how does the quote help you gain clarity on your work?

Come prepared to share part or all of your working community collaboration/building philosophy.

10

CHANGING THE NARRATIVE

Abortion as a Family Value

Sara C. Flowers

As a sex educator, I am constantly reconciling the evolution between my current, professional, and adult values, and the ones I learned from my family as a kid.

Growing up in the 1990s, my sex education was limited to puberty basics – which, at the time, was a bit left of center. My family also went to church every Sunday, and every conversation about sex happened in the context of heterosexual marriage. When I was around 12 years old, I remember announcing to my mom, a white woman, "I am not going to have sex until I am married because I don't want to get pregnant." Without skipping a beat, my mom replied, "You need to worry about HIV[1] – I can fix pregnancy."

That was the first time I was told, unequivocally, that abortion is an option available to me. I had NEVER heard someone suggest that abortion was an option without framing it in a debate. And because the words she used didn't explicitly say that abortion was an ok option, I wasn't sure if it was a punishment, consequence, or fine, no big deal. The message I

DOI: 10.4324/9781003181927-13

got from my mom was about 'fixing' an unintended pregnancy was not a clear positive one for me because at the moment, it felt like a threat or a punishment for pregnancy. And I held onto my fear of unintended pregnancy as shameful throughout my adolescence and young adulthood. It was a relief to not have to stay pregnant as a teenager if I didn't want to, and that my mom would fight with and for me. I knew I wouldn't be alone. But I didn't know if she'd respect my choice to carry a pregnancy to term, should that become a decision I was faced with.

I notice my mom and I were always alone whenever we talked about abortion. I am pretty sure that my dad, a Black man, would have been loudly and staunchly opposed to her telling his and their non-pregnant pre-teen daughter that abortion was ok – EVEN if he'd want me to stop being pregnant had I actually been pregnant. And honestly, I don't know his views as he never discussed them. His conservative religious views and behavior regarding the fear of or anger at young girl's and women's sexuality makes me think he would not have been cool or easygoing on this topic.

I wish my mom's message had been a clear statement that if ever I became pregnant, she would support me and help me with whatever decision was right for me – and also explicitly state all the ways abortion is good. Dismantle the shame instead of reinforcing it with the veiled threat my 12 year old ears heard: if you get pregnant, I'll get you an abortion whether you want one or not.

As I got older and became more involved in the work that would become my career, conversations about sexuality, including pregnancy and abortion, also happened more frequently. I learned about the ways my mom, a white woman, who came of age ten years before interracial marriage was legalized, and 20 years before abortion was legal in the United States, and she supported abortion access, love, and body autonomy. As I grew up, there were so many other lessons, conversations, and actions that helped paint a clearer and more nuanced picture for me as I explored my personal values. As I was exposed to more people, education, learning, more grown-up conversations, and experiences; my thinking about and exposure to abortion continued to evolve. I learned about friends' abortions when they began sharing their abortion stories with me. I recall a conversation with a friend – we were in high school, probably around 16 years old – and she pushed me to think about the complex ways abortion was a necessary, essential component of health care. My mom told me about taking her best friend's daughter to her abortion appointment because her friend had to work.

I have worked in sex education and the field of sexual and reproductive health care for my entire career. I learned about abortion care from providers in small non-profit organizations near the US Capital while abortion access was under attack. I learned about the tactics that anti-abortion and opposition groups use to restrict people's bodily autonomy and how to identify the violent, lie-filled rhetorical moves among the power-hungry, patriarchy-focused players. At another non-profit, my boss led the local abortion fund. Her stories helped me gain a deeper and humanized understanding of the real, lasting, unjust ways that abortion restrictions impact people's lives everyday.

These people – my mom, my friends, peers, my abortion provider colleague, my boss – are all white women. It is so interesting for me to reflect on the ways that a series of white women shaped my thinking about abortion rights, abortion access, and abortion care.

As I sought an even deeper understanding of abortion care, rights, and access, I did my own research – as a doctoral student in public health – and I did my own work, as a board member for the New York Abortion Access Fund (NYAAF). I had the opportunity to join the NYAAF board of directors – and did so, after I had experienced three miscarriages and was parenting the toddler that was born of the one pregnancy I carried to term. I was, to be completely vulnerable, worried that the trauma I was holding from my miscarriages might influence the commitment I held in my heart to funding abortions and directly and intentionally supporting others' access to abortion care. My worries swirled in my head because I didn't know what to expect or how my heart, my brain, and my body might find common ground on this important issue: *Would I have an emotional reaction to someone wanting to end their (presumably viable) pregnancy after all I went through?*

In anticipation of a potential (negative) reaction, and with a dire commitment to disaggregating my personal feelings and experiences from tainting the way I support others, I signed up for a workshop to explore my values around abortion. I also completed intake training with the abortion fund. I will always remember the cases I had during my first week taking calls from people who needed help paying for their abortions.

After a few calls, it was abundantly clear to me that their story was just that – their story. It had absolutely NOTHING to do with my own path or experience. Funding abortion affirmed my values to centering people, and believing in our shared humanity.

As a parent of a tween daughter today, I have made it a point to be careful and intentional about the words I use and messages I send about bodies, sex, gender identity, abortion, pleasure, etc. I try very hard to make sure these integral elements of our humanity are not mysterious or taboo by initiating conversations and explaining innuendos or euphemisms in song lyrics or on-screen dialogues. I answer her directly when she asks personal questions about anything from my age, weight, or the year I was born to what it was like to get my first period, and my experiences with multiple miscarriages. My hope is these small but powerful examples will help ensure that my kid is being raised without a sense of shame or stigma about sex, pregnancy, abortion, gender identity, or attraction. I hope she grows into a person who feels confident standing up for herself, others, and what she believes is right, and I hope she finds pleasure and has a fulfilling personal life – whatever that ends up looking like for her.

I answer her questions honestly when we talked about abortion. In 2021, when out with my family one weekend, we saw an anti-abortion protest march over the Brooklyn Bridge. My eight-year-old read the protestors' huge blue signs out loud and asked me what their messages meant. I proceeded to explain that those people were protesting people's right to have access to abortion. I explained that we don't agree with them – instead, our family believes in and values other people's right and ability to make decisions about their own bodies and lives, and that includes abortion.

I explained that an abortion is a procedure that a pregnant person can have if they don't want to be or stay pregnant. She asked how it worked and I explained that there are two ways: a pregnant person can end a pregnancy by taking pills that a doctor or nurse prescribe, or they can go into the doctor's office and have a procedure. She asked how long the procedure takes and if it hurt. I said some people might feel cramping or achiness, that the doctor can give medicine to help ease those symptoms, and sometimes the procedure lasted as little as ten minutes, and most times, folk can go home and rest, and be back to their usual self in a couple of days.

Her response was "Oh! Just ten minutes and back to your usual self in a couple days?! Sounds simple enough" and sipped her drink.

I asked my kid if it was ok with her to tell this story publicly before I drafted it. I want her not just to understand consent, but to experience it, and *expect* that her choices (for her body and her personhood) be heard and respected. By asking her consent to tell her story publicly first, I am building that expectation for her.

Title: Being Pro-abortion Is a Family Value

Writers Names: Bianca I. Laureano, Sara C. Flowers

Note to Educators

This lesson plan is about abortion. Be prepared to facilitate a conversation that challenges misinformation and myths about abortion. This must be facilitated from a pro-abortion and pro-abortion access perspective.

Learning Objectives/Instructional Goal

In this lesson plan, participants will discuss their knowledge and training on abortion as sexuality professionals.

Learning Outcomes

- List any gaps in their knowledge of abortion
- Identify trusted resources on abortion
- Create a script discussing abortion

Essential Questions

- Do I know of any gaps that exist in my knowledge and preparedness to discuss abortion as a sexuality professional?
- How do I find and identify trusted resources on abortion for the communities I serve?
- What would I say if a participant/client of mine ask about abortion?

CASEL Social Emotional Learning Competencies

Self-awareness: The ability to accurately recognize one's own emotions, thoughts, and values and how they influence behavior. The ability to accurately assess one's strengths and limitations, with a well-grounded sense of confidence, optimism, and a "growth mindset."

Social awareness: The ability to take the perspective of and empathize with others, including those from diverse backgrounds and cultures. The ability to understand social and ethical norms for behavior and to recognize family, school, and community resources and support systems.

Relationship skills: The ability to establish and maintain healthy and rewarding relationships with diverse individuals and groups. The ability to communicate clearly, listen well, cooperate with others, resist inappropriate social pressure, negotiate conflict constructively, and seek and offer help when needed.

Responsible decision-making: The ability to make constructive choices about personal behavior and social interactions based on ethical standards, safety concerns, and social norms. The realistic evaluation of consequences of various actions, and a consideration of the well-being of oneself and others.

Materials
- Review and consider printing/sharing/updating the resource list for participants
- Review and consider printing/sharing the two worksheets/handouts
- If meeting in person and wanting to maintain anonymity offer participants sticky notes to write their responses and put on the board or newsprint
- Newsprint to capture sticky notes

Preparation
Prepare by first offering the Media Literacy lesson plan and introduction. Review the hashtags offered for Activity 2 to become more familiar with what some of the content may be that they find.

There are three worksheets/handouts that may be used for this session which may be downloaded and printed or shared with participants. One is resources on abortion that are in support of body autonomy, the second is the Script by the author, and the third is the Script Worksheet. Both may be found at the end of the chapter.

Activity 1: Introduce Topic (five minutes estimated)

The goal of this activity is to understand what information participants need with regard to abortion. You may choose any format to receive this information based on your conversation and space. If you think it would be useful to have this conversation, be anonymous, decide how best to offer that option i.e. if virtual accept responses via direct message and read aloud, offer a virtual document that removes names for anonymous writing, and other options.

Invite participants to share what they want to know more about when it comes to a discussion about abortion and access to abortion care.

Share aloud the responses for all participants to understand. Share what this discussion will be a conversation about abortion where to find trustworthy resources online, trainings, and challenging myths. The goal is not to change people's ideas about abortion for themselves; instead, it is to help them identify when to offer powerful resources that meet the needs of their participants and clients.

Activity 2: Values Clarification (15 minutes minimum)

The goal of this activity is for participants to consider their thoughts and values on abortion topics.

Depending on the format that you are in for this course, consider how you want to do this activity that is accessible to all those present. For example, in a virtual platform, you may invite people to write in a chat box their ideas or use a reaction emoji or other offerings of the platform you are using. If there are mobility issues for in-person courses, please adapt the opportunities for all participants to be engaged. You are welcome to change these questions as you know your group the best. These are offered as a guide:

Instructions are to share with participants that you will be sharing a statement/idea and they are to consider what they think and share their position. If they wish to respond and share their ideas, they are welcome to do so in some capacity. You may decide if there is a Yes/Agree, No/Disagree, or Maybe/I Don't Know option

Questions/Statements

- My training in sexuality education prepared me to discuss abortion.
- I know how to answer value-based questions from students/clients about abortion.
- I know the state laws about abortion for the state I live in AND surrounding states.
- Finding trusted resources on abortion is something I am comfortable doing.

Invite a few volunteers to share why they chose the option they did after each question. Offer this question as a closing for this activity:

Why has abortion typically not been a core topic to understand when being trained/seeking training to become a sexuality professional?

Activity 3: Information Hunt (20 minutes estimated)
The goal of this activity is to encourage participants to examine resources online and share back what was discovered and what approaches they used to decide what is a trusted website or resource.

Begin by asking participants what are the ways they decide to trust an online resource, especially about a topic like abortion that has a lot of misinformation online. Be prepared to write what the participants share so there is a growing list of resources. Be mindful the language to use is either "pro-abortion" or "pro-choice" you know your audience best and what terms will resonate. If you have already discussed the Media Literacy section, remind participants of the five core questions of media literacy.

Next, place participants in small groups to investigate similar information and discuss together then decide on one person to report back to the larger group their findings. Offer participants the opportunity to engage with their devices, computer, phones, books, etc. that are available and do a search for information on abortion. One suggestion is to invite them to use their browser of choice and do a search for "abortion resources."

Another option is to offer the following hashtags for participants to investigate online and share back to the larger group. Offer some of these hashtags to investigate:

#AbortionRights

#ProChoiceIsProLife

#ReproductiveJustice

#RepoJ

#RoeVWade

Offer participants about ten minutes to investigate and discuss. Bring the small groups back to the larger group and invite participant leads to share what their group discovered by stating: their name, what they investigated, and what their findings include. Wrap up this activity with the following discussion questions:

1. What do we notice about information shared from each group? What are some themes?
2. Did this search answer any questions that we shared at the beginning of class?
3. How did your group decide what was a trustworthy resource?

Share some resources that are offered at the end of this lesson plan. You may create your own list and include some that are already offered. Please consider making your list relevant to the state participants are working within.

Activity 4: Scripts on Abortion (20 minutes minimum)

The goal of this activity is to discuss the reading by Dr. Flowers and how participants may note how race, racialization, and belief systems impact information about abortion for sexuality professionals.

Begin by offering the following discussion questions about the essay:

• What has stayed with you since reading the essay?
• How was race and racialization addressed in the essay?
• In what ways does the author make specific decisions about her professional development on abortion?

Dr. Flowers shares her confusion based on her white mother's response to "fixing pregnancy" that impacted her communication with her parents, her continued education on the subject, and the ways she communicates with her daughter. Below is the script you may read aloud or make a copy to distribute to participants to review.

> People were protesting people's right to have access to abortion. We don't agree with them – instead, our family believes in and values other people's right and ability to make decisions about their own bodies and lives, and that includes abortion. An abortion is a procedure that a pregnant person can have if they don't want to be or stay pregnant. There are two ways: a pregnant person can end a pregnancy by taking pills that a doctor or nurse prescribe, or they can go into the doctor's office and have a procedure. Some people might feel cramping or achiness. The doctor can give medicine to help ease those symptoms, and sometimes the procedure lasts as little as 10 minutes, and most times, folk can go home and rest, and be back to their usual self in a couple of days.

Invite participants to share thoughts about this script. Share some of these questions to facilitate discussion:

- What do you notice about the script she used to explain abortion to her child?
- When examining the word choice and language used what do you notice?
- How does the author explain the values their family holds?
- What do you think may be missing?

Next, offer participants about five minutes to write their own script for how they may respond to a similar scenario Dr. Flowers had with her eight-year-old child. There is a worksheet that may go along with this activity if useful. Once the five minutes end, partner participants together and invite them to share what they wrote to practice aloud talking about abortion.

Activity 5: Closing
Invite participants to respond to this closing question:
 I have identified my knowledge of abortion is ...

Glossary
Abortion Often discussed as one of three options for people who are pregnant. It is also the medical procedure for ectopic pregnancy and miscarriage.

Pro-Abortion and Pro-Choice Resources

Finding a Clinic or Healthcare Provider to Offer an Abortion
 Abortion Finder https://www.abortionfinder.org
 Has information on state laws and information about abortion, asks for age, address or zip code, and date of last menstrual cycle (i.e. number of weeks pregnant).
 National Abortion Federation https://prochoice.org
 A membership organization that offers some resources to clinics and providers in US states and globally and offers US state laws overview per state. Information debunking myths on abortion.
 I Need An A https://www.ineedana.com
 Website that asks for age, zip code, and date of last menstrual cycle (i.e. number of weeks pregnant).

Funding and Financial Support for Abortion
National Network of Abortion Funds https://abortionfunds.org
 Find your local/state, and national abortion funds.
 Guttmacher Institute State Funding on Abortion Under Medicaid https://www.guttmacher.org/state-policy/explore/state-funding-abortion-under-medicaid.

Spiritual Beliefs and Values Organizations
Religious Coalition for Reproductive Choice https://rcrc.org.
 Lists leaders and their responses from their faith-based practice on abortion.
 Faith Aloud https://www.faithaloud.org.

Access to religious and spiritual leaders that offer spiritual counseling and support.

Abortion Resolution Workbook: A Guide for those Seeking Emotional and Spiritual Resolution (free download) https://www.pregnancyoptions.info.

Pro-Abortion and Pro-Choice Resources

Legal Support for Abortion

If/When/How Repro Legal healthline https://www.reprolegalhelpline.org.

Offers information to those under 18 years old seeking abortion, information on self-managed abortion, and laws about abortion access.

Jane's Due Process https://janesdueprocess.org.

A Texas-based resource supporting teens who need information about abortion access and judicial bypass.

Continuing Education on Abortion

Cornerstone Doula Full Spectrum Training https://www.cornerstonedoulatrainings.com.

Offers training for those seeking to be doulas, midwives, or other support and care for pregnant people.

ANTE UP! Professional Development https://www.anteuppd.com.

Offers certification for sexuality professionals and features an abortion course that uses an intersectional, reproductive, economic, climate, and disability justice approach.

Script from Dr. Flowers Essay

Review the script that Dr. Flowers shared when answering her eight-year-old child's questions about abortion when witnessing an anti-abortion protest in her community.

> People were protesting people's right to have access to abortion. We don't agree with them – instead, our family believes in and values other people's right and ability to make decisions about their own bodies and lives, and that includes abortion. An abortion is a procedure that a pregnant person can have if they don't want to be or stay pregnant. There are two ways: a pregnant person can end a pregnancy by taking pills that a doctor or nurse prescribe, or they can go into the doctor's office and have a procedure. Some people might feel cramping or achiness. The doctor can give medicine to help ease those symptoms, and sometimes the procedure lasts as little as 10 minutes, and most times, folk can go home and rest, and be back to their usual self in a couple of days.

Script Worksheet

Instructions: Participants are to write down a script answering the questions: What is an abortion? and Does abortion hurt? You may respond for any age group that you work with at this time. You may notice different responses for different age groups and different access needs.

What is an Abortion?

_____

_____

_____

_____

_____

_____

Does an abortion hurt?

_____

_____

_____

_____

_____

_____

Note

1   I acknowledge this memory stigmatizes HIV status and welcome a discussion offered in the lesson plan about how our families and the values shared with us compare and compound sex, sexuality, and our experiences.

SECTION 3

ORAL NARRATIVES

Sharing our stories, lore, spells, and lessons is an essential part of transmitting culture. When we practice listening with our entire bodies, what new knowledge do we unfold? These interviews take many shapes. Some are exactly as our beloved reader may imagine with questions and responses, others are in narrative format as an essay. All of the oral narratives shared here are examples of how vulnerability and intentional relationship building offer pathways for connection and collaboration. There are no lesson plans offered for these stories and narratives, instead the invitation is to sit with the new knowledge and considerations found in this sharing. There are numerous oral storytelling and narrative curricula that exist and encourage the beloved reader to find them!

DOI: 10.4324/9781003181927-14

11

INTERSEX ACTIVISM, MOVEMENT, AND JOY

In Conversation with Sean Saifa Wall

Sean Saifa Wall and Bianca I. Laureano

Sean Saifa Wall and Bianca I. Laureano met on a zoom call in July of 2021. They begin by sharing a bit about their lives during COVID and discuss Saifa's work as an artist, activist, researcher, and collaborator for Black intersex liberation.

Bianca

Yeah. So my, the way my disability is set up, my immune system isn't working well so I had to.. my whole world just shrunk. Right, early last year, and I wasn't really seeing people and I'm over here in West Oakland and Saifa when I tell you, California really is the Wild West.

Saifa

yo, it's been a lot I've had two friends die within the year not because of the coronavirus but other thing is you know, when you can't engage in the rituals that you create it is hard. Other than that, things are okay,

DOI: 10.4324/9781003181927-15

because it's true at this point, I'll figure it out. That's how we're doing. This thing is so unfair, because folks, like yourself who are immunocompromised and given their power in the world like the UK and the United States, they're just totally throwing caution to the wind, and they're just like, Oh, we don't really care about the most vulnerable, we just want to do whatever and people should just go back to live their lives and these new variants are just like if you have the vaccine like you're fine you'll just have milder symptoms, blah blah blah. You know, I know I'm on my learning curve around Disability Justice but it's just like complete deficit. During this whole pandemic, it has literally been like we don't give a fuck mother fuckers can die.

Bianca

Right. And it's just like it's such a great reminder of the eugenics movement being alive and well as a global movement that people are like y'all are disposable, we don't care about disabled people anyway. A lot of medical doctors and other parts of the world who are publishing on the way that COVID impacts people's experiences in their bodyminds like long term but also "sexual dysfunction" and I'm like if we tell people that the way your body functions around pleasure and sex if affected –

Saifa

Listen!

Bianca

That can be a selling point to get a mask on and to get the vaccination but in this country, they are getting that data, so I'm literally reading stuff from doctors in India and doctors in Thailand. And it makes sense you know it's a respiratory thing but it affects a whole bunch of other systems.

Saifa

You know I have a colleague, and my homie here in Scotland has long COVID, both my homie here in Scotland, my homie colleague, and my colleague from my fellowship. Both have long COVID.

Bianca

Well, there're more disabled people that are being created, and, people are just now hoppin on the disability understanding because of Britney Spears, not because of COVID.

Saifa

Right. Right! Yeah, it's just so funny, right. I see like… it's so interesting the way disability is framed because it's seen as such an individual thing, right. Sort of like similar to intersex in that way. Right? Like your intersex variation is a particular medical thing. Right. um, and, you know, like how much more powerful, would it be if people had an awareness of what happens to me is not individual it's actually the systemic and the institutional forces that disable people.

I don't know, for me as someone who has recently come into an awareness of being disabled, I'm still working through shit. It's such a live conversation for me right now. I have to have an ergonomic setup like everywhere I go. Like I have to literally have my laptop stand and my keyboard with me everywhere I go, because literally, I will lose sensation in my hands. There have been times when it eases up but there are times when it's very chronic and I'm just in one of those times right now that's chronic, you know.

Bianca

What do you want people to know about Safia? Like who are your people?

Saifa

Oh, who are my people? Ooo that's such a big lovely generous kind of question, you know, I think what feels important for me is to share that I'm Black. I'm African American. I am queer. I'm intersex. I'm an activist. I'm a visual artist, and I'm a scholar. In this violent ass Academy. Violent! I'm a son. I'm a daughter. Both my parents are deceased. I've been an aunt. I'm an uncle. I feel like those things are important to name because I think they reflect my journey where I've been. And just like how I think it's taken me a long time to actually be comfortable with saying that, you know, I was an aunt. I'm an uncle. I'm also a son and a daughter. Those things are true because I think they comprise the whole story. I think there's something about integration and embracing all of who I am like my wholeness and not hiding anything anymore just really being like, this is the whole picture all the pieces fit together, as opposed to someone telling me who I am. I will tell you who I am and all of my complexity.

Bianca

Yes! Right before we started recording, we were talking about the grief that comes with being in this moment living on this planet. When the ocean is on fire. And I feel like I've experienced grief in a variety of different ways. There was that moment where, when my mom died, we knew it was coming. We just didn't know when. She was in a home in Puerto Rico being cared for, but waves of grief hit me and like my first relationship on the planet was gone. Right, so I'm learning a whole new bodymind, that layer of grief that comes. And you don't have to talk about your specific loss of your parents, hearing you speak and share it's like grief may be present so how's your grief?

Saifa

Hmm. You know, I think it was Satish Kumar, who talked about ongoing grief and ongoing love, you know, um, and I feel for me like grief was something that I ran away from when I was younger, because to feel it would be overwhelming; it would overwhelm my system, you know, um, and I feel like there're so many things for me to grieve, right? But what feels salient, and I think what comes to mind first there are three things. One is like grieving my body right? Grieving the body that I never got to have or to experience. The second grieving my father. And the third grieving my mother. I talk about those pieces, because I think those are pieces of me that through trauma, through experience get fractured. What does that mean? So I think the first grief that I experienced, that I could name, as an adult reflecting on it, the first grief was actually being separated, violently separated from my father. Because when I was ten years old, he was arrested, like I was with him when he got arrested by the NYPD, New York Police Department. And that was the last time I saw him alive.

I think that was like one of the starkest moments of experiencing trauma, because I think there had been previous traumas, but that was like etched in my memory. And I think I couldn't recognize it because at that time, this was like 1989 right? So my dad was a crack addict and my mom was on crack, this was like the height of the AIDS epidemic, the height of the crack epidemic. Growing up in the Bronx, as a child. There wasn't any space to process this grief, because it was literally like I have to survive and I didn't think about it consciously but looking back on it, it was like, I have to survive. I have to live. Right? And I think sometimes the body knows when it's safe to actually start the grief. But at the time, things weren't safe.

And I think the second grief is, my body changing because my mom didn't do any corrective surgery, so I had internal testes. I had, what's considered atypical genitals, I had a big ass clit, and I was like, I'm okay you know and I was starting to develop as male, and I didn't have a problem with it because testicles are meant to live in the scrotum, I was having hernia – I probably had hernias. I had a lot of growing pains. And because girls are not meant to have testes. I was castrated. And I think the most poignant grief that I have named, that written about, is literally watching my body change. Literally watching all the body here that I had grown, watching it fall out. Like, literally having muscle mass, feeling very strong and then, like literally, my body became fleshy, and I lost muscle. I saw these toned thighs that I had valued and cherished. Those thighs became abundant with cellulite. So, for me, it was like this, this body dysphoria that was not of my own doing. Like I was literally experimented on. I think only in recent years I've connected with that grief, especially last year when I saw a geneticist and basically, I asked him. I was like "Will I ever masculinize?" because I'm on testosterone and he was like at the age where I was castrated, the body produces a flood of hormones that are never replicated again they literally timed it. You know that literally, it's just so insidious, they literally timed that shit so that it changed the course of my body.

And I just feel like the death of my mother is so wound up with that grief, you know? Because it was like her grief, right, of having three intersex children. It was her grief of being a survivor of violent Jim Crow in the south. Being a survivor of sexual trauma, I carried her grief. And then in the end, she passed away, so she's free like her spirit is free and I think I'm left with the grief of her stories, her history, but also the ways in which she showed up for me and very profound ways in which she could not like really having a narcissist for a mother is a special kind of head fuck. [laughs] I think for me it's life. Because I'm 42 right now, life is just like this ongoing like learning and healing and grief.

Bianca

Absolutely. And, you know, you started by positioning yourself as an activist. Were there any particular moments where you're like, "Oh, this is going to lead me to action"? Was it an emotion? Was it an experience? What was your emergent moment or moments where you were like, "Oh, I gotta.. I gotta get active in a particular way"? What was it for you?

Saifa

Yeah, you ask great questions. Your questions are just fire, insightful, just just brilliant. The thing that moved me to action was the death of my father. He died in prison. And he died from AIDS in prison and I remember that. My mom was poking around in different funeral homes. No one would take his body. You know this was in 1993, no one would take his body. Hmm. And I think that's what motivated me around not activism but action because things were happening so fast. Things are moving so fast. I think sometimes if you grew up in a very traumatic dysfunctional environment things just happened so fast, right? It's just like someone got stabbed. Someone got this, you know, it's always one thing after another and that really motivated me to start volunteering at the Gay Men's Health Center in Chelsea. And my first volunteering position was with the Child Life program. And I remembered distinctly, it was for children who were infected and affected by HIV and AIDS and overwhelmingly they were like kids of color. Every year, I would raise money for the AIDS Walk. I would do the AIDS Walk. It's no wonder that I eventually went into public health. Although, to be honest, even though I have this long history of safe sex education and HIV awareness and blah blah blah, my ass don't use any kind of barriers, you know what I'm saying. I will just be out here. I mean, fortunately, I've been very, knock on wood, have not contracted any STIs because I do have conversations with my sexual partners; however, don't use barriers, all that education out the window. I think that's what set me on a path of really, you know, waking up to the world. Right and getting involved.

Bianca

Yeah you know as you're talking I'm thinking, we must have just missed each other in New York. I grew up in Maryland, but I spent like 17 years in New York, and I did a lot of the teaching in the public school systems to meet the NYC HIV mandate, where kids are supposed to receive × hours in real time throughout their school year about HIV education that's age appropriate but, the way that we are trained as educators to go and teach, or work with certain populations, We're almost given this idea that these are kids are HIV negative, or they don't come with any trauma or they've never experienced a pregnancy or anything else, It's like this imaginary audience.

And then when I get in there it's like, oh they know a lot more than I was trained to even offer them and so it's this immediately "Okay, I gotta reassess, and really meet them in a different way because people made up the story about who is going to be here when really nobody even asks them what their needs were." And so, it's also the HIV and AIDS complications is also a moment in time where I tell people or people don't think it's too popular but it's just a fact we talk a lot about the Americans with Disabilities Act being highly celebrated 30 last year. Great. But we knew in 1990 that people were dying of AIDS complications, people living HIV positive were not included under the ADA until a 2008 amendment. You know, hundreds of thousands of people in this country who died, right, couldn't get the care that they needed because they were discriminated against. Your father was, and those are the moments for me where I'm like, this is why Disability Justice is so important and the principles of it. Also, why it's so timely right now is because it's like we've seen some horrors that have existed while also acknowledging that like, there are some disabled people that are still alive today, because of the ADA and so it's this weird straddling of the both/and the multiplicities. The multiple facts. And that leads me to like the collaboration part of activism. What have you learned by working with other people? Whether it be a neutral learning or a positive or maybe even a negative. What are the lessons that you learned about working with other people around activism?

Saifa

I hate social influencers. [laughs] You know, and I say that because I feel like right now this is a heavy emphasis on the media. And influencers are not organizers, or they are organized in a digital space right which has its own value and merit. But I think it's just interesting how we create these like fandoms of social media influencers who have their own category of influence and privilege, which is strange. And I think it's even more strange when they come from the left, when they come from social justice movements. I love collaborating. I think it could be part of my codependence. I think we can go further together. And I think there's so much knowledge and wisdom to be shared. And I think it's the lie of capitalism that assumes that people just get there on their own through some special thing about them that they're just chosen because they're just so wonderful and ignoring all of the collaboration that went into supporting this individual. I just feel like I'm always down to collaborate and I think, sometimes the collaboration has been heartbreaking because I think I'm really committed to this particular cause like I'm committed to intersex liberation, Black liberation, queer liberation and I want justice and I think sometimes you collaborate with folks in, you know, organizations and institutions, and it can be frustrating! I think sometimes ego gets in the way. I do see the fruits of when you collaborate. I think it can be powerful, and especially I think, in these movements that are so small, like the intersex movement is so tiny. I think it'd behoove us to collaborate as much as possible. No, it doesn't erase, like the particular strengths that we bring, or the particular perspectives that we bring. However, I do feel like, you know, when we work together in a show of force. I think it really demands attention.

Bianca

Absolutely, I mean we need each other. And we talked immediately about how we're lonely. We're alone. It's hard, the lockdown. It's intense and in movement work, we forget that part sometimes. And I think that over the past, going on two years now, we're seeing how movement work doesn't stop, even during a pandemic where we can't touch each other necessarily. We use different strategies. So I hear you saying you know how to organize in a digital space, I also agree that influencers are not organizing. They are being asked to talk about their experience. That is not organizing. And I think immediately about how the digital space also can correct some of the things that get lost because of people's egos or people's misunderstandings or whatever people project onto organizing and movement work. I think a lot about when there was movement work with the hospital in Chicago last year. We're going to pause the surgeries that were being done on intersex infants. And I remember Pidgeon saying "it wasn't just me. It was Safia too." This anti-Black focus that erased your labor and collaboration. Talk with me about how it's not new. Like I followed your work for a while, what are the challenges of collaborating in a cross-racial way?

Saifa

I think people want an intersex narrative that is white, that is, you know, white Eurocentric and just specifically focused on intersex that is tragic, that's traumatic, that doesn't force, the United States and America to reckon with this treatment of Black and Indigenous folks, of people of color, of queer folks of, you know, marginalized identities and I've been consistent in my messaging since I've been vocal and public as an activist. I've been very consistent in my messaging that no one will tear me apart, in the sense of like, I'm Black and intersex, those things are happening at the same time.

And early on when we found out about the victory, I said to Pidgeon: you have to be very consistent in your messaging because I will tell you this victory they will ascribe it to Pidgeon period. They will make it seem like Pidgeon carried this whole thing by themselves. Pidgeon invented the organization. They will give all of the credit to Pidgeon. I said don't let them erase me, because they will do it. And sure enough they did! It was literally like swatting flies. Like it was literally chasing up every major media outlet: them, Teen Vogue, all of them who were consistent about erasing my contributions. And, you know, I think, even within a people of color organization anti-Blackness still operates. It always does whether you're in a predominantly white institution, anti-blackness is always there.

It wasn't until, towards the end of Pidgeon's departure, that we actually started to have very real conversations about anti-Blackness. I feel like, for me right now at the helm of the Intersex Justice Project (IJP), I think is very important for me to always remember it's not about me. For me, IJP. I want it to exist until it no longer needs to exist. And while it exists, I want it to center the work, and the contributions of Black intersex people as well as intersex people of color, period. Because I know that, whether intentionally or unintentionally, the intersex movement, which is globally overwhelmingly people of color, but what is represented is mostly white intersex folks, and I refuse to let Black intersex and people of color be erased, period. I refuse to be erased in this work. People may not want to acknowledge me. But God damn it, you will respect and acknowledge black people in this work.

Bianca

That colorism is always already present. And what I've noticed too in my collaboration work is that it's predictable; you know it was going to happen, and then it happens. We have this knowledge because white supremacy and all that bullshit is just so predictable. And listening to you talk about like your work and also the intersex justice movement being a global movement what does it take for this work, and the global scale of collective justice work, what do you think needs to happen besides pausing and acknowledging there's erasure and working to correct that? What do you think also needs to happen globally because like you said it's primarily Black people, primarily people of color at a global scale who are the leaders who are most impacted and we're talking about being led by those most impacted. What else do you think needs to happen for that collective work to actually meet its goals?

Saifa

You know, I think being here, I was having a conversation with my friend here, because you know the organization is really looking at their hiring practices specifically around people color and we had a really hard conversation about it. And the thing that feels true, to me, is it's like I'm tired of fucking talking. I'm tired of fucking talking, because we know what's happening as someone who does research, I think, whether it be white people in power, whether it be men in power, whether it be you know if it's country-specific, the ruling class, the elite, this is right now, for me what feels important to note, is that this is an issue of power and resources. People don't want to give that up. People want to have cyclical ass conversations about things like, "Oh, we need more Black people in leadership. Oh we need more people of color oh blah blah blah. We need more. Oh, let's have a process. Oh let's bring in a consultant. Oh let's …" You know, all of this fucking bullshit. Right? It's bullshit. I literally have been in the workplace for 20 years and I know and I can say that on God, that is bullshit, let's just acknowledge the fact that people in power, whoever they may be, wherever they're at, they don't want to give up power. You know, they only want to give a trickle of resources to keep people happy and to keep people feeling like they can buy the iPhone, like they can buy the iPad, like they can floss a little bit, and go on their nice fucking vacations. But mother fuckers don't want to actually shift institutional power and privilege, and that's on God. I'm just like, fuck a talk. Where're the money at? Where's the money at? Where's the checks being written? Where are the resources? When are the resources coming along? What are we actually going to do? I'm tired of talking. Like literally, it requires white women to feel uncomfortable, white men to feel uncomfortable, and men to feel uncomfortable. Anyone who's occupying positions of power, able-bodied people to feel uncomfortable, you know, like, heterosexual people. It requires all those people who occupy positions of power and influence to feel uncomfortable because when you feel uncomfortable, that should let you know that that's something that you actually need to follow up. I'm tired of having this conversation about privilege, trainings on this and that. No, Cut the check, run the check!

Bianca

Exactly/It's time for some action to quote Cypress Hill. And that to me is always what gets lost because people just want to talk and talk and talk and yeah that's a little bit of action but it's really not leading to any outcome, at the end of the day it's a paper trail, somebody's going to write something in a document. But then what? Then it gets lost. And then there's no, there's no action around it there's no movement. So as you talk about the research as a researcher. I love to segue into hearing a little bit about what you are doing? What are you doing with your PhD? What do you hope to do? What is your research looking like? And also this can be like a conjuring moment where you get to conjure what you want to have happen, and what your goals are with your research.

Saifa

So the European Commission sent out a bid for proposals of the sort of research they would fund in the social sciences. They funded ten research posts through the Marie Sklodowska-Curie fellowships that would look at different aspects of intersex rights and intersex experiences that aren't highlighted already in the research. So it was a very ambitious project. It was ten research posts in five different countries. What is radical about it is that out of ten research positions, five or six people are intersex.

Bianca

Oh Wow.

Saifa

So it's me, Adelieine, Daria, Steph, and Audra yeah six people are intersex, who are activists. Um, so that's radical and the reason why I applied is that I've been working in research, and I feel that if I am to change the course of research to actually have intersex-specific research, I think it requires me to have tools that will actually give me access. So, my specific project is looking at equality, diversity in policy making in the Republic of Ireland and England. Those are the two case studies. So basically, it's using action learning, however, because I'm extra. I wanted to do interviews with activists in both contexts, to get a sense of what the actual landscape is from an activist perspective and action learning sets are different from focus groups. They actually are about having this ambiguous problem, and where workers or colleagues solve it as opposed to an expert or a facilitator right. It was developed in England by a man named Reginald Revans. I tweaked it a little bit. Sort of like looking at how social work policy can actually address this issue of intersex of erasure that exists in social policy. So that's my focus because initially the project was supposed to be cross-sectoral and it needs to be focused and social workers work in different areas. Can we leverage one group to actually start change? Things are changing, especially in New York State. But it is disheartening, just to see how legislators are bought off by the American Medical Association, or the society of pediatric urology, who wants to continue the surgeries. It's disheartening. It's frustrating, it's maddening.

I feel like I want to do this work, because I really want to see structural change happen. Right. And I don't know if I want to be an academic, but I really want shit to change and I want the harm to stop and what can I do, from where I am at, to signal or help shift the power or bring about some change.

Bianca

Yeah, and I think, as we do that work, it's work that we've inherited that is part of our legacy of organizing with our families and our ancestors and I think a lot about how it might feel like the first time. Fresh. Trying something new and different and so, going in knowing it's not going to work the first time. Maybe it will, but also things will probably shift and change as you're in it, afterwards, years later.

Share with us a time where you've experienced the challenge or you've messed up. How do you imagine yourself responding to error or correction or it's July 2021? Things are evolving and changing from language to science or whatever to things that we just know and I'm witnessing people mess up and also not cope well with the correction or the requests from communities. Can you share with us a time where you messed up, or how you imagine that you would like to respond if that emerges for you either in your research, or in your life as you do this work?

Saifa

Yeah. Oh man, there're so many places I messed up. Jesus! You know, and I feel like if social media was around, there was Friendster and MySpace, but it wasn't this cancel culture that existed then. If social media was around the way it is now, I probably would have been canceled because I was a fucking fool, you know? Like I did some stupid shit right and I would not want anyone to judge me. I mean people can. People do. People will, right? But like what I was doing and how was moving at 25, 26?

Like, pre therapy, pre recovery, pre just life? Working on you, you know like, that's not how I'm moving at 42.

I remember one incident. I don't know why this came to me. But, I used to be a member organizer with this group called FIERCE. And it was, literally, the time after I graduated from college in 2001. I think I got involved with Fierce like late 2001. I left in 2003. We were children. We were babies. And I remember there were certain things I said like, like this song by 50 Cent song came out "I love you like a fat kid loves cake," I sang that song and you know I'm singing it around leftist folks would be like "ugh you're fatphobic" you know, and I feel like at this time, I didn't understand certain things. I literally didn't understand, I just graduated from college. I'm a nigga from the Bronx. Like the whole social justice shit was so new to me. Right, so I was making mistakes left, right, and center.

And I feel like right now with cancel culture, people are not allowed any grace, you know, it's so interesting that online culture is so black and white. Even near you here I'm like "Now, I know you niggas living with a lot complexity and some nuance offline." But it's something about online culture where people are just like, oh I'm a fucking saint. I don't use any slurs. I am 100%. And I am speaking from a very leftist position. I feel like people on the left just get so sanctimonious online, and I'm just like, I know y'all not living like that offline. People just don't have any space. People don't allow themselves space. People don't give each other space and you have to, it's almost like you have to perform. Right? Because people are like, if you don't perform, then you lose followers and people are like "oh that person is toxic." And, I'm not trying to say what people should be doing or not. Because I'm just in my little corner of social media minding my own business, right, trying to post about my dog and what I'm eating and the bullshit I be thinking about. But on some real shit like I feel like if I were to offend or hurt someone, I think I would want to give myself grace to be like, "Okay, how can you make amends?" But also, I would want to be in loving community, not necessarily with people online. I want to be in loving community with people who I know who I love and who I trust to actually be like "Safia come here. Let's have a conversation." For me, that has value. I am totally open to getting checked by people who I know and love and trust. If I don't know you, I don't want to talk to you. I think it's very interesting, this kind of false intimacy that exists online where a perfect stranger can be like, "oh you hurt me.

Oh, you... I'm disappointed in you." Hah! That is bizarre to me! And the thing is I can't address that. I can't fix that, but like, how can we, in offline spaces really just show each other some grace?

Bianca

Yeah. And like stop dehumanizing each other by pretending that we are supposed to be perfect in this white supremacist ideology, and you know and I too have messed up, you know, I think, as we're, we're both the same age and I think about, I've learned so many lessons and I've messed up publicly so much in my organizing too because I've acknowledged and welcomed in digital organizing and a variety of different ways. And I know that my public mess-ups make other people better.

So even though people wanted to critique me they learned, you learned from the way that I learned from the way that I responded. You also learned how my community showed up in a way that you don't have that community. So, where people will hold me accountable because of love and respect and care, not because of this idea I need to be right and I'm the only right one, and there's only way. And I think it is really really important and it reminds me of how much... like how much radical and revolutionary love surrounds us in so many different ways that for me now when I'm corrected, my immediate response I've trained myself to receive that it as a gift of love. And I say "thank you." And that really, you know, I feel like people really acknowledge that they're being heard and give me time to let me think about how I'm going to change my behavior and act differently, going forward, and that just brings me so much joy. And so my last question for you is what brings you joy? What brings you comfort? And again, this can be a conjuring situation too. You can conjure these things.

Saifa

Yeah, I mean, you know, as I'm sitting in my Airbnb in Scotland, looking out onto Arthor's Seat, which is like a mountain that people walk up. I think my friend's told me it's an inactive volcano or some shit and I think, for me, I find joy, comfort, and peace. I feel like the early part of my life was so chaotic, q\a lot of yelling, a lot of screaming, cops at the house, like domestic violence. And I feel there's something about the quiet, the slowness of my life. That feels comforting. I find joy in like good sex when it happens because you know people got the COVID people so like dating is yikes. Good sex when it happens, good food. I love good food. I love food that doesn't have to be nourishing. It can be just fucking a good combination of salty, fatty, and sweet.

Saifa

What brings me joy is talking to my homies. Like my homies who I'm building with, who I'm in loving community with, who bring me joy, you know, because I think being here it's a lot of solitude. And I sometimes think of solitude…I feel lonely. You know, and I think I've in the past, I don't know. I will say I started my recovery journey in 2007, so I feel like I've just had solitude. Especially between my relationships, I feel like in the last few years there has been a lot of solitude, which can be restorative but I think too much of anything is just not good for me. I think about the ways that I can balance solitude, but also really feeling loved and helped from my community. I think sometimes it's hard to feel that especially in these COVID times, you know.

Bianca

Yes. Here's to both of us finding all sorts of new joy as things are shifting and changing and opening up and closing and figuring it all out. I'm so thankful to finally have our worlds collide and connect.

This interview was transcribed by Chels Morgan, CSE.

12

MUSLIM SEXUALITY

Bina Bakhtiar

In the current polarized social justice landscapes, the use and overemphasis on identities within the United States is often hijacked from its significance and meaning. Currently, the use of identities has become politicized, often used as a weapon to "other" people and communities: hypervisibilization of one's marginalized identities while ignoring their privileged ones. Bringing attention to one's marginalized identity, generally speaking, identities can be a source and means to self-knowledge as well as a catalyst that brings people together, through shared values and meanings. Embedded in this is the aspiration to see each other, to connect, and to love. When harnessed, this can further create and allows for a deeper access to intimacy within ourselves and also with our collective. To illustrate this point, for some, language can serve as both a source and as means to harness deeper intimacy. As a bilingual speaker, I am naturally drawn to people who are able to converse in my native language. This mutuality of shared language (in this scenario) serves as a container and an entry point to experience a collective and cultural and social intimacy.

DOI: 10.4324/9781003181927-16

Practicing one's culture through language, in this example, is soothing as it offers a sense of familiarity and communicates a sense of belonging. As Audre Lorde reminds us that sharing of joy in any form is a bridge for sharers to experience joy and becomes the basis for what is common between them versus what is not. As a Muslim Pakistani American living in North America, I am encouraged to understand identities as more than mere labels and to know identities for the meanings they share and the stories they tell. When identities are tied and centered around human dignity, can encompass deeper understandings of hope, liberation, and connection to intimacy and pleasure.

As a Muslim American sex educator and a therapist, I am reminded of the varied lived experiences of many Muslims living in North America whose experiences of erotic marginalization are often lacking in articulation within Western and colonist theoretical frameworks. For Muslims, experiences of erotic marginalization are not limited to experiences of sexuality but extend to simple physical sensuality. I intend to use the word "identity" to note where they both have landed us as well as where they intend to take us and our erotic lives.

For Muslims living in North America, erotic marginalization combines Islamophobic stereotypes, racism, and both public religious identities and personal spirituality. One example from my own experiences in graduate school came from one of my white professors who declared that "Muslims are raised and live in patriarchal family systems." This sentiment was expressed when he was inquired about providing therapeutic interventions to clients who come from collectivist family systems and who are Muslim. Although this was not the first time that I heard a reductionist and simplified view of Muslims and Muslim families, it was opposite of my own upbringing being raised in a matriarchal family system. In *another class*, a professor commented "Islam is conservative [implying kink practices are deemed unapproving in Islam]." These remarks (*and attending conversations*) left an imprint of having been vicariously judged for my Muslim identity. This was one experience of many. What I was not prepared for was the repetition of these biases and stereotypes of Muslims in a myriad of spaces, especially in the academic and professional therapeutic circles (my expectation was that these spaces would be examining these narratives and instead Muslims were seen as homogenized). One of the direct impacts of these remarks was a conscious and unconscious decision on somewhat at the unconscious level to censor my relationship with God in public as I navigated these spaces. I became closeted by keeping my spiritual affinity hidden. This meant, among other things, refraining from saying Mashallah (praise to God) or Inshallah (God willing). This is me self-negating my connection to the spiritual and disconnecting from the deeper aspect of me that defines me.

Others have written about how psychology education is rooted in a Eurocentric frame of reference, devoid of concepts, theories, and inclusive experiences of BIPOC individuals. I have experienced this firsthand. What I find problematic across the board is the implicit view that Muslim experiences are not addressed in the mainstream western psychological thought due to the perception that Muslim individuals, families, and communities are unsophisticated and caught up in the chains of patriarchy and oppressive cultures.

As I embarked on the journey to become a sex therapist and a sexuality educator, I continued to find myself in academic spaces with boxed views and understandings of Muslims and their sexualities. Both the course work I was exposed to and the academic sexuality circles I was involved in appeared unwelcoming and uninterested in incorporating the intersections of religion, spirituality, and sexuality. As a Muslim, my understanding of pleasure, intimacy, and sexuality are deeply connected to my spirituality. Not only was this understanding lacking, but often Islam, Muslims, and sexuality are received with ridicule and mockery. The sum of these experiences and events highlighted a glaring gap in the existing sexuality field as well as the Western psychology concepts that leave no room for people or communities whose understandings of intimacy, pleasure, and sexuality are integrated with spirituality and religion. At the same time, I began noticing many Muslim clients' reluctance to seek care from white therapists.

The stereotypes in professional therapeutic healing spaces are a barrier for Muslims seeking sexual and/or mental health services because they prevent our needs from being understood, met, or prioritized. The experience of erotic marginalization alongside Islamophobia impacts the mind/body/heart/soul connection which informs as well as limit one's experiences. These experiences are often layered and nuanced, manifesting in ways that cannot be always articulated or described. The recurring theme around these experiences is the interplay and dynamic dance of one's attitude, holding more power, which leads to the other carrying out an act with less power.

In my professional role, what I have witnessed and observed is the impact of these biases among clients and community members. Many Muslims navigate a given context where they may reveal or disclose their identities and social location. As with many other marginalized groups, if the context is perceived as unsafe, they may reveal some parts of themselves while withholding other parts because it may be too dangerous to disclose, thus resulting in a forced censoring of self. For example, one client shared that she would remove her hijab before entering her white female therapist's office because she was worried to be perceived as "oppressed" Muslim girl and put the hijab back on once she would exit the therapist's office. She explained that disrobing and robing the hijab each time was exhausting, and she had misgivings about having to closet this part of herself and yet the idea of her Muslim identity interfering by creating misperception appeared less threatening to her.

In another example, one of my clients disclosed a past experience with a white therapist and was told "You are very outspoken for a Middle-Eastern woman." This client described the impact of this comment as multifaceted both on an unconscious and conscious level as she began to not share her opinion with others, fearing she was too much. This also prevented her from authentically sharing in therapy sessions even after she switched to a new therapist. This form of orientalist harm can deepen pre-existing wounds for these clients, especially those who are being told who, how, and what they should be. This is an example of many ways Muslims internalize the gaze of the Other by taking on attitudes by acting and reenacting these into behaviors and actions is often informed by dehumanizing framework.

Muslims in North America live in a social environment characterized by intense and persistent Islamophobia that influences one's sexual and erotic self and makes aspects of everyday existence, unsafe, unsure, and uncomfortable. Muslims find themselves consciously and/or unconsciously navigating this hostile culture throughout their life. Years of dealing with hostility, ignorance, and willful refusal to listen all inform and shape how we move through the world and engage with others. All too often the internalized dogma we inhibit and then ascribe and assign to others, without learning who they really are, strips others of their humanity and creates a perpetual feeling of lack of safety. The question I and other Muslims find ourselves having to regularly face is: how do I navigate my life around the dangers created by Islamophobia intersecting with various other isms? How do I handle having certain identities and certain ways of performing those identities weaponized? For myself, the answer depends on the day and the specific context I find myself in. One might wonder what makes the context unsafe. For someone who is navigating multiple identities at once and the attendant expectation to conform, the calculus of safety is complicated and cannot be distilled to a simple equation. Suffice it to say the repeated experience of others' refusal to extend genuine understanding rips away safety and creates a feeling of otherness that impacts intimacy and socializing. Identities ideally would not be utilized to ridicule or shame individuals yet so often those who identify as Muslim find their identity, spirituality, faith, experiences, and histories misunderstood and erased within both academia and broader society. There will not be an easy solution to the issue of Islamophobia and of Muslim voices being silenced or ridiculed in academia or broader society.

A good place to start would be to listen. Really listen. Refrain from assumptions about others' internal worlds and their erotic experiences and desires especially if you are speaking about experiences or groups outside your own experience. Be open to learning and prioritize learning from those with lived experiences. Going beyond listening is another move, which will involve moving back and acknowledging these identities as the culmination of a sophisticated mosaic. These are just a few steps one can take to make Muslim, and really all lives, easier, less fraught, and more erotically fulfilling.

Please Consider

- There are as many ways to be Muslim as there are Muslims. Muslim trans people exist. Muslim queer people exist. Muslim LGBTQIA + people exist. Muslims with marginalized identities have to learn to navigate both those things simultaneously in real life is hard enough without thinking about how to justify it to other people, too.
- It is not the responsibility of Muslim men and women to soothe anxieties of those around them who are threatened by how Muslim they look a.k.a. "Muslimyness."

- Not all Muslim families are Pro-Hijab. Some women have to go to great lengths and are met with resistance within their own families to wear the Hijab while also experiencing discrimination from the broader culture in the West.
- Assuming or having Muslims to defend their stance on polygamy is inherently rooted and guided by unexamined orientalism.
- For polyamory-aware practitioners, who have negative ideas towards polygamy, please evaluate if you hold a view of your version of love is better than those who are sympathetic to polygamy.

Another aspect of erotic marginalization, one even more under-studied than the first two, involves experiences of pleasure. Work in sexuality education allowed me to develop a view of pleasure as possible only through the alignment of many elements at once. Pleasure requires social intimacy, positive personal experiences of bodily autonomy, high levels of comfort and sensuality, and the mental and emotional freedom to experience both in relation to one's spirituality. Conceptualized in that way, pleasure is inaccessible to people who are marginalized.

13

THE F.A.C.E MODEL

Introduction to Using Fashion as a
Sexual Health Tool

Nhakia Outland

This is a portion of an interview between Nhakia Outland, MSW and Bianca I. Laureano.

My name is Nhakia Outland. My pronouns are she and her. I am a mother of three and I am a queer, Black, woman. I am a social worker, adjunct professor, sexuality educator, advocate, fashionista, and the Founder and Executive Director of Prevention Meets Fashion Inc, a 501c3 nonprofit that increases sexual health knowledge in people of color, Black, LGBTQ, and nonbinary communities through fashion, advocacy, community, and education (FACE).

My Connection to Fashion

For as long as I can remember, I have loved fashion but just how it would connect to my chosen profession was yet to be discovered. As a child, I was exposed to diverse fashion perspectives from my own culture and that of others. It has always interested me because I would listen to stories

DOI: 10.4324/9781003181927-17

from my mom about how people were allowed to dress being in the army to what she saw the local people wearing in whatever country she was stationed in. She would tell me about the strict clothing restrictions for women in the army and then tell me about men's shops that she saw and admired. It was no secret growing up that my mom loved menswear but what was a shock as I got older was why she never felt that she could wear menswear as a woman. She would tell me stories of these blue suede shoes that she wanted but the only issue was that they were in the men's store. Later, I found out that she never got the shoes out of fear. As you see, gender roles were strictly ingrained into her from my family to her relationships and past trauma with being looked at as a masculine woman. I held this story close to me as a child and now as an adult.

Another memory of mine is that of my grandmother. She would be so strict on us girls to wear dresses and skirts and the boys to wear suits. Basically, we had to look presentable at all times. At first, I thought it was because of my grandmother's religion but then I began to ask questions and found out how dressing like this was connected to not looking poor. It was about status. We had to get dressed to go to the store and into Center City. As I got older, I took a deeper look into this and found that this was connected to our Black history. I found that Black enslaved people were not given a choice of what they could wear. They were given two clothing options: work and church, which was often white clothes for church and some form of work clothes. Due to my grandmother's history, her clothing trauma was passed down to us.

Another memory that shaped my work today, is as a child growing up, I wore what my parents put me in. My parents never asked what I wanted to wear or what I was comfortable wearing. So, as a socialized girl, my mother dressed me in ruffles and lace from head to toe. Her ideal of what a little girl should look like. I literally looked like a pageant girl. I remember hating these outfits, while they were beautiful, I knew at an early age it did not feel right. It did not feel like me. I began to rebel and my dressing became extreme. I went from tight miniskirts to see-through clothing and later grew into what some may say is a tomboy and/or androgonous aesthetic. I began to wear oversized sweatpants, jeans, and basketball shorts. It wasn't to hide my body. It was to get the furthest away from what other girls were wearing. Eventually, I got called a "dyke" and my family had enough and I was put into modeling school. I would go on to model for 5 years. It wasn't that I totally loathed feminine things; it was that too much of it was anxiety-provoking for me. I began to mix the two and started wearing dresses with sneakers, wearing heels with sweatpants or blazers with sweatpants. This was before the social media craze, so I don't have pictures but I was definitely doing it before sneakers and dresses ever came down a Chanel runway. I didn't know it then but this was the beginning of me forming my "fashion identity" and my queerness. I realized that I had been using fashion as a tool my entire life to affirm my blackness and queerness.

Based on my own personal life experiences and that of my clients I learned that fashion was my way of comforting, communicating, and connecting to myself, my family, my community, and my clients but also a place of safety at times. All of these experiences led me to found Prevention Meets Fashion Inc and create our programs, services and eventually our FACE model to use fashion in a more intentional way to work with Black and LGBTQ+ people. We used this model to primarily look at sexual and reproductive health issues but it has since evolved to look into other issues, including clothing insecurity, self-esteem, environmental, and gender justice to name a few.

Bianca: Tell Us about How You Created and Evolved the FACE Model?

As a social worker and sexuality educator, I did not like how existing models such as the medical and behavioral models led with risks, especially when discussing sexual health and wellness. I wanted to create a model that for whoever used it, saw the person first, not their risks. Risk implies stigma and stigma can have negative effects on the client and influence perception of risk. Having seen how this can have adverse effects on clients led me to create the FACE model. The FACE model uses a fashion-based approach that I have created to engage clients around sexual and reproductive health. Fashion is known to be a good engagement tool. The model uses basic social work skills to more technical skills and strategies and is taught in the context of seeing the client first not the client risks. Social workers practice skills such as engagement, assessment, empathy, authenticity, conversational style interviewing as well as motivational interviewing.

FACE is an acronym for the four stages of the model: Fashion, Advocacy, Community, and Education. It is not a linear model but fashion is the initial stage or engagement stage. This is where the social worker engages with the client, which for many social workers is the hardest step. The FACE model is very simple yet, it is not for every provider, social worker, case manager, therapist, or community organization. Using the FACE model takes authenticity, empathy, and an understanding of intersectionality.

The FACE model is comprised of four parts:

- Fashion – We use fashion to engage, assess and intervene with the client. Clients may contact us because of a clothing need. The clothing need could be because of a financial hardship, needing affirming fashion, fleeing a domestic violence situation, or any other clothing need. Providers are urged not to rush through this part because you can also begin to do an assessment of other needs here and eventually provide intervention strategies.
- Advocacy – We provide education and guide the client to be self-advocates for themselves.
- Community – We engage with the individual to connect with the community as a part of their healing process. These can be PMF support groups.
- Education – We provide education designed to increase the knowledge and understanding of prevention, sexual health and wellness, and reproductive health through webinars, internships, volunteer opportunities, leadership, and training opportunities.

The model has evolved from individuals to being used for community participation and community engagement.

- Fashion – We use fashion as the platform to promote sexual health and wellness (mind, body, and spirit).
- Advocacy – We provide education, encouragement, and actionable steps to engage in advocacy that will lead to policy change, community change, and individual change.
- Community – We engage with the community to provide programs for folks who want to learn about or who are already working at the intersection of fashion and sexual health.

- Education – We provide education designed to increase the knowledge and understanding of prevention, sexual health and wellness, and reproductive health through webinars, internships, volunteer opportunities, leadership, and training opportunities.

Much like art therapy, fashion can be used in a therapeutic manner. But, because of the image that fashion is frivolous, we overlook the value and importance that fashion has played in our history, especially for Black and queer folks. When you move fashion beyond the superficialness; you can begin to see how fashion has used us, connected us, divided us, and reunited us.

Bianca How Is Fashion Therapeutic? What Are the Ways That You See a Therapeutic Element beyond What You've Shared around Fashion and Doing This Work That You've Been Doing for So Long?

When I think about this question, I always think about fashion therapy but this is not what we are discussing. Fashion therapy is temporary and does not get to the root of the person's problem.

Using fashion as a therapeutic modality on the other hand can be done. People don't look at fashion in a healing way. However, we remind people that fashion can be very healing and or part of the healing process. Fashion is a tool and can be used in therapy and wellness. Just like assigning a person journaling as part of CBT, you can assign a person to look in their closet and edit their clothing choices as part of the FACE model. Have them think about questions, such as what do I want to see myself wearing? Do I currently have these items in my wardrobe? What items do I need to feel safe or affirmed? I think the way that we look at fashion as being therapeutic is that we affirm that it's okay to wear whatever makes you feel safe and we can also work towards you wearing what you want again. For example, let's say, someone was sexually assaulted for wearing something tight, if their ultimate goal, is to be able to wear something tight again someday then we work with the client to develop actionable steps to get them to their goal. We do not dismiss that one of their goals is clothing, we use it. In many therapy spaces, these conversations are noted but often ignored. Trauma around clothing is very hard to deal with and many people experience it but have nowhere to discuss it, and through PMF's FACE model and our trauma and fashion support group, we provide that space.

14

BJ

Bianca and Juan in Conversation

Juan Fernández and Bianca I. Laureano

Bianca and Juan met to discuss queerness, Chicano experiences on the west coast, and various forms of ephemera and media.

B: Tell me where you struggle is with words like Gay? Why is queer a better fit?

J: Queer is easy for me to hold on to as an identity, because for me, it is integrated in the politics of of the identity. It is not the blanket LGBTQI+ go-to word, but also the political history and impact. When I started using queer as an iden-tity, at least for me, I had already been exposed to a world of AIDS and HIV, not only as the community, as a country and globally, and I think that we would be remiss to not acknowledge all of the political work that those folks did for us. I think its clear for me because that's how I came into my own identity as a queer person is because we grew up with all of these politics, our identity wrought with all of

DOI: 10.4324/9781003181927-18

these politics. And so I think I would be lying if I said those things didn't affect me, and how you can either go one way or the other. I think as a Latinx person of color it's impossible for me to go any other way also have academic work starting to be popularized within the 80s and 90s. And so I'm attached to a lot of that work.

And for Chicano, it's complicated. The history it's raw with misogyny, racism, and homophobia but it's also a part of what we grew up on, and so I can't ignore that those things are a part of me, and that I don't struggle with those things and that I don't slip into those from time to time and have to correct myself. So using Chicano initially when typing it I use an 'o' at the end. Also, because you and I have had these conversations before about what we think about the use of the 'x'? How are we using the 'x'? To be a catch all? Is that where you get rooted? I don't know enough about it, I haven't taken a dive too deep into the conversation to understand or even speak on it. Culturally, I carry whatever Mexican ideology my parents came to the United States with in the 70s and that's as Mexican as I get. Which again goes back to these ideas from my childhood. If you go to Mexico now, it's super queer, politically evolving, and feminist, and not in that the government is feminist, but that the people are and the people make it known if you walk into any public place there's enough messaging on the walls on the street to know that women and queer folk are taking charge of their bodies, whereas here people are still scared to go out into the streets that way. I don't want to be scared. It's almost as if we don't know how yet. I think the spelling of Chicano with the C.H. and the 'x'. At the end is probably the most effective for me at this point in my life and I can change; for now, I think this is where I am, only because I don't want to take up space using an identity that I'm not fully informed on nor am attached to. Queer suits me much better.

B: You grew up in Los Angeles, CA, were you born and raised in LA? Tell me a little bit about how your family got to California?

J: Home is in L.A. My parents migrated slowly. So they were in Guadalajara, my dad was on a little rancho called Trojes, while my mom was in a Pueblo outside the city proper in Tonala. When they married, my grandfather had already migrated to the US with an artist visa. My family were Mariachi performers. So my grandfather, his entire life's career was in Mariachi. He and his brothers, my uncle, were all performers and they basically attempted to train their children to work in the trade. So that was part of what played a big role in my family's migration. My family slowly came, because once my grandfather got his green card, he was able to start bringing over his children. Meanwhile my parents migrated from where they were in Jalisco to Tijuana, my father was a leather tool maker, he handmade leather goods that he would sell at the border crossing and other spaces. So he started doing leather tooling. I think they did a short stint in the fields too but I only know what my sister has told me because I wasn't born yet. Eventually they got this tiny apartment in Northridge, CA which back in the day, there was a little community in Northridge that was basically on the outskirts of the projects, but it was still low rental apartments. People from a very specific community in Tijuana who were all migrating ended up in these buildings and and so there's a history there – it even had the nickname of "Tijuanita" or Little TJ. I was born in Northridge, CA in the San Fernando Valley. My parents were able to buy a home in Pacoima, which is another Latinx enclave in the valley. People recognize it because of the movie La Bamba about Richie Valens. If you watch the movie, it's supposed to take place in Pacoima which is where I actually grew up. From that point on, I grew up, and as a teen I met other queer folks and I started partying and clubbing. Being queer is home I made my way into the city of Los Angeles. It forced me to leave home. I was always trying to leave. It was limiting and I couldn't be myself there.

B: You come from a family of artists, musicians, and creatives. Talk to me a little bit about growing up, because I, too, grew up with a father who is an artist and a musician, and that definitely impacted the way that I view media and the way that I view the world. I have a pretty vast, inclusive definition of media. I'd love to hear your definition: how do you understand and define media?

J: I think of media as a form of communication and story-telling. I think the second an idea or message becomes translated, processed or understood it becomes media. It doesn't have to be tangible, obviously. But I think once someone is communicating an emotion it becomes a form of media. That's the most simple way to describe it. But, my father was creating media when he did his leather tooling. He was creating stories through the flowers and designs he carved on to little purses, or belts etc. If you ask him those things mean something, they're not just flowers. They represent something to him so I think anytime you're trying to communicate something. An idea being written, spoken, visually readable and that idea or concept is exchanged between 2 people or more then they become media.

B: What are some of the real types of media that you grow up around? You shared your family are Mariachis, and your dad did leather work. What were some other forms of media that you were surrounded by?

J: Oh, it's always music. Because it was the one thing that balanced everyone out at home. Music can be empowering. We weren't all enjoying or listening to the same things, but there was always music playing, and we tolerated it. I would say music and later film and television from the 80s. It formed how I view the world outside of my home. Those 80s teen movies helped shape the insecurities and weird things that I still feel about my body, all of those things are definitely rooted in the media I consumed.

B: I feel growing up on the east coast the things that I remember are very different from what people on the West Coast recall. We just had a very different life, even though we're on the planet at the same time in the same country, we still had a very different reception of the media that was supposed to target us. I think of Care Bears and Strawberry ShortCake. Then I get out of the era of Cartoons and into

MTV and watching music videos. What were some of the 80s shows that you recall?

J: It was a combination of North American and Mexican television. That was really interesting. I think, in terms of American television, obviously you said, with cartoons. That media didn't have a huge impact on me, and I think it's because it didn't fit anything. The Muppets stand out because everyone was inherently different, everyone was able to be chaotic, and bring their whole self to whatever adventure was happening. And no one was giving a shit about it they were all fucking up and figuring it out. The muppets are really joyful and kind of spiritual.

Novellas definitely had a huge impact on how I experienced my mother. And how her sense of longing for something else, I did not fully understand her but I think those characters definitely impacted how she perceived herself. Why, I wasn't enough or the world that we were in wasn't enough and I understand it now. As a kid you're watching how rap hypnotized these worlds, that was impactful for me. And then, on the other hand, the differences between sexuality in Latin American television and American television where in Latin American television generally, there's almost a rule to strip the women to near nudity. The false sense of reality in North American television was impactful too: you have functional families eating at the table, and that was not my life. It got to a point where I even tried to recreate that for myself, and it didn't work, because those were not the tools that I had and so setting the table, it's not going to look or be experienced the way it was on TV because those are not the tools that we had – down to the food.

B: My parents came from Puerto Rico to the States. And I remember this assimilation approach in the media. I think a lot of those representations also don't take into consideration immigrant parents who are exhausted by the end of the day, not just because their parents or they were working, but because of all the other things that happened in their lives throughout the day.

J: Yeah, my mom, who was a housekeeper and cleaned 3
        families' homes, no way she facilitate this weird 5 course
        pancakes, cornflakes, eggs, fresh juice, breakfast everyone
        seems to be having on TV, we're gonna grab a doughnut
        on the way to drop her off at work. And then that became
        the ritual. Morning donuts while dropping off my mom at
        work with my dad. The reality was that I'm still with my par-
        ents, I'm still eating processed sugary food, and I'm still
        safe. I think being able to accept that is powerful. Especially
        because at the moment, there was a part of me that resented
        them for not overfeeding me every morning. You were talking
        about not really knowing what our parents are going through
        at the time and now I can reflect back and think about my
        mom, every time she would start a new job it was always a
        risk, because it was all under the table, and there were sev-
        eral times where she didn't get paid, they would withhold pay
        even though she did the job because they could. Same with
        my father. He had finally landed the job that he thought was
        a great job and then he got injured, and then he wasn't able
        to work again. Meanwhile, I'm letting TV tell me they're not
        doing enough. It was a confusing time.

B: There's a lot of layers to it. and when I think about what I
        grew up knowing about California, and LA it was definitely
        dictated by the media, and it was definitely things like 90210
        and those were very white normative bodies. Those people
        are still famous today. Still get work in the media today, and
        it completely erased a large chunk of communities that live
        there. And so I remember the only representation in the
        media of Chicanos was very stereotypical and one dimen-
        sional. *Blood In Blood Out*, and *Stand and Deliver*. Puerto
        Ricans we had *West Side Story*, Maria on *Sesame Street*, but
        that was pretty much it. Were you witnessing people make
        fun of them in media and art? What was it like in LA at the
        time when Baywatch was the cool thing on television that
        didn't represent you at all?

J: Well, it's interesting because even now, as an adult, that
        city does something to people. I grew up in the valley so I
        wasn't really exposed to too much, although I will say that

my local junior high became one of the sites for a magnet program, and it was a theater magnet program, and it was actually one of the better ones in LA for a while. Celebrities attended my school, people that were on TV like Christine Applegate were a part of our program and she had already been on television. I will say that LA itself is a city a lot of the time. It feels like a movie set, because it changes every time it almost feels too easy. I won't go to the city for 6 months and then I'll go out and it's a completely new town, and it's almost like they're shooting a new movie. It's also interesting growing up there as a young adult, because every other third person you meet or friend, you have worked in the industry somehow and so you're always connected to it in one way or another. My high school job that I did with another friend was extra work. We were doing extra work and every other teenager was too. You get paid 50 bucks a day, and they overfeed you, and that was our high school job. Now when I watch movies it's really hard for me to suspend my disbelief, because it's almost surreal to think about it and look back at it. Now I'm like what were we doing? What was happening? One thing we witnessed was this humanizing of these white feelings and these white young people that were fairly well off and wealthy and didn't really have much to worry about and so could really focus on their feelings or recreate this drama in their life because there was no one else that existed. It's interesting because I think about high school for example, I somehow found myself in this mix of white and brown folk. And it was interesting when I would hang out with my white friends, and how different their lives were! It still wasn't so much that it was TV, but there was a level of boldness and the level of taking up space that I still don't find, if I felt uncomfortable doing. And there's almost a I flare for it there's this it doesn't matter idea it's let's go to this concert it's $25. It's fine and it's me saying "Look, I don't have $25". Everything felt possible and then I'd go home and I'd get laughed at saying I need 25 bucks for a concert.

B: Yeah, exactly. It totally makes sense because it's a different level of body autonomy. It's a different level of self-determination that isn't something to say that we didn't have at the same age, we did. It just looked different. We could play with it differently and that still felt liberatory for us and then, seeing it acted out in a completely different way I don't understand what it means to have parents who can support you with a loan for your first home. I don't know what that means as an adult. Now that's a very adult example, but I also don't understand what it means to not have to interview for a job or have this disposable income for the things that I want to do on a whim and not worry about transportation and food and gas. How am I gonna get there? Who's gonna drive me? Who's gonna pick me up? I think other things that show up for me, too, around just being mobile.

J: Yeah, mobile is a big deal. I didn't drive in LA. I don't drive as a person who grew up in LA, and it was alien. My mother was taking me to work with her, and she rode the buses. And she taught me how and it became easy, and I didn't have to worry about the same things. My friends are worrying about their cars and I'll be there if you want to pick me up that's cool but otherwise I'll figure it out. Mobility is a big one still I just think about for queer folks and for people of color and LGBT community sometimes just getting there is the hardest part, showing up getting there.

B: I want to ask what is your understanding or your definition of sexually explicit? That's the first part of the question. And then how is that connected to any type of art that you grew up with or that you love today by queer Latinos or Chicanos?

J: I might go on a little too long although I don't have a definition. I have an understanding, I haven't thought about it this way, but, culturally speaking, it is dependent on where you are in the world. It seems that most things labeled queer at least in this country have been considered explicit. It can change as well, if you are able to change your understanding of sexuality then things seem less explicit. My ideas and fear of sexually explicit content comes from my Mexican American Catholic upbringing. And so, showing skin, even in the most innocent ways, can be especially threatening. These Victorian puritanical approaches have infiltrated our psyches and I think my experience at home and what I learned became my understanding of sexually. Let's say it was basically access to seeing sex on film and media or pornography. Images of people being public or at least open with their expression of desire. I think any public display of desire can translate to explicit content. I grew up with immigrant parents and Mexican film in the 70s and 80s became really raunchy: full frontal for women was mandatory, you had these actors, like Lyn May. And she's the first person that comes to mind; she's a Chinese Mexican performer. She was in many films that live in my memory and she was almost exclusively naked or close to nude in films, and always in service to these really unattractive, really gross, usually drunk comedian type actors. I remember being taken to the Mexican movie theaters on a family night for a double feature, and it was porn with some jokes thrown in. The hypocrisy of my parents saying "Don't look at this" yet here, look at this on a big screen or when I go to my dad's side of the bed and there's stacks and stacks of pornography. I remember when my mother realized that I had found it, and that I was exploring it. It became a cleansing ritual, she threw it all away in this big dramatic scene. There was just a lot of tension, and I got spanked, and it was this whole embarrassing thing for me to experience that ultimately made me just more curious.

I think we longed for those visuals for a very long time in terms of the masculine form in Mexican media, for example, or at least what I was exposed to and also considering that I'm the child of immigrants, so I'm looking at this through this other lens, and men always showed off; they weren't so much being sexualized as they were being postured as the epitome of masculinity. And that was what sexualized them. There's really good artwork out there that reflects what we wanted to see or what we weren't able to see. There're illustrators who are prolific in using the style of erotic jail or prison art. Where it's usually big-breasted women with big hair, some artists are doing it to all men and bodies that we were never really meant to see. Even down to growing up thinking that your foreskin is gross, it really fucks with you. To this day I tend to not choose lovers that are white and not for any other reason than I don't want to explain my body. I don't want to explain my body to anyone. This is how I look. This is how I smell. This is how I'm shaped and I don't want to explain that to you this is my body. It's much easier to fully enjoy an experience when you're not explaining yourself outside of safety protocols and consent. You're really able to let someone enjoy who you are. It was a big part of my early sexual experience. I was always explaining myself.

B: Yeah, absolutely. And I think also for me, we were just so groomed by television to eroticize white men in a really particular way, and also find white women in a very narrow representation, attractive. But white men had a little bit of a more diverse representation. I remember my parents wouldn't get mad at me for watching, *Like Water For Chocolate*, for example, or something similar where the people were not racialized as white they had a particular cultural connection and we're expressing desire and sex but when it came to watching Madonna, I can't remember what her tour was in the early 90s and she's performing like she's masturbating

J: Blonde Ambition tour

B: Yes! My mom would say "don't watch this" it wasn't just that it was Madonna a white woman. It was also their definition of what I wasn't allowed to watch that was definitely connected to the media that told us these people are engaging in something that's really explicit. When we do it in our communities it doesn't look like this, it could look like dancing in a particular way, or as a deep passionate kiss. We can watch that! There's a contradiction that I also grew up with around the media. They made it really clear how the whiteness was different. And when I do a lot of my classes and trainings, the sexually explicit and pornographic material people have very rigid ideas of what that is for them, and a lot of what we watch I think it's very sexually explicit yet others think this isn't actually explicit at all. I think culture really helps us understand what sexually explicit means, and it's so different. To so many different people.

J: Yeah, I got really excited because you mentioned the Blonde Ambition tour, that was a huge part of my life, and it's really funny because Madonna is so so polarizing and she's this white woman who appropriated hella cultures and still does. I never found her music to be amazing, you won't catch me listening to it on a regular basis. Well that's not true. I listen to Madonna but I just remember discovering this show, this tour that was broadcast on HBO when we were 12, maybe 10 years old. Yeah, I was 12, because I remember coming home from my aunt's house with my parents and my sister was watching it, and it was the cone bra version and I just remember, as soon as we got home it sucked me in and then they re-aired it when I was a little older, probably 13 and I recorded it, it wasn't the music I was into at that time, and even really attuned to what that was but it was a performance. It was the expression the sexuality, the fact that all her dancers were Black and Latino, Dominican and Puerto Rican, and Asian, and the fact that she learned from them. Appropriation or not, she chose these folks to teach her how to do some stuff and then gave them a big platform. Obviously, I've been thinking about that all the time, but I wasn't turned on by it, I was mostly thinking "Oh, there's this other way to be to feel desire and that can express joy, that can express confusion" and all of these things, and It was a very big moment for me when I discovered it, and I used to watch it over and over and over. I can count the steps. If we watch together, I can tell you exactly what is next. And I get a lot of shit for liking Madonna, but without that growing up with something visually to show me a template of something that I didn't understand at the time I don't think I would have been able to get here.

B: I totally totally agree. It's this wild idea of the entry point into understanding other ways that people expressed desire definitely drew this white woman who's still alive. Who's still doing it this is her pattern, it works for her, and it's still working for her for 40 years. So you'd mentioned briefly when we first started this connection to this reaction to the term machismo, and I ask it, because when I first heard this word, it was when I was going into college, and I remember thinking what is this word? What does it mean? And then, when I read the definition, thinking it is not my reality. I don't have men in my life who are violent or engaging in sexual violence. If anything I had people in my life, men in my life who had experienced that and we're choosing not to engage in such a way. So, I'm pretty much this proponent of asking Latino people what they think about machismo. Don't let the research tell you what they think it is because that's an outsider perspective. I don't think people understand that this was an outsider perspective on Mexican men in their communities. and an outsider watching them and trying to come up with this idea of this is why they're so different from us. So talk to me a little bit about what it means, how it shows up how you see it maybe how you queer It In the ways that other people do.

J: Yeah I agree and I don't see it any different than I would media interpretation of masculinity in general. I think that you brought up the definition and I just looked it up. And it's an inherently violent definition. It's just a strong aggressive masculine person. I always thought of it as a silly word, cartoon, it's mighty mouse, and it's not as interesting because this is a form of masculine aggression rooted in colonialism. They found another word for the same thing that they do to put on brown folks essentially, or Latinx folks, and then branded that so that it can be used against us in this way. It's no different than the violence that is so eurocentric, It's more a perception of what certain folks imagine a Latinx man to be versus the reality. And when you think about the reality of somebody being aggressive, it's to protect themselves, what are they protecting themselves for? Emiliano Zapata, he was fighting colonialism. He was standing up against a eurocentric ideology protecting his wife and now you're calling him these other things and of course, he postured. It was a very masculine way. He had to and that doesn't make him any different than George Washington, who's being brave he was a found father. Emiliano. I'm using him as an example but that's it. He was doing the same thing, protecting his people, but he's put into this violent expression of aggression, masculine aggression, which is essentially replicating and mimicking what you're already doing.

B: And I'm thinking about the archive that you've investigated an examined throughout your career, and through your studies of queerness and Chicano identity. Why do you think it's important to have an archive, beyond the agency beyond pictures. Tell me a little bit about what you think makes it a good archive?

J: I think it's important. Folks get really caught up in these ideas of nostalgia and I think archives are different than that. I don't think that archives do the same work as a piece of nostalgic ephemera. I think that's superficial and it doesn't really speak to actual life experiences. And I think the importance of an archive for me is to reflect on life, how people did things or why people did things, or even how we looked or existed, or what our resources looked like at the time. Whether we were using multiple cameras or digital cameras That's all really important. And it helps draw a line back and forth. I think folk can easily get caught up in nostalgia, and that's masturbating. And hey, I'm a sucker for nostalgia. I can sit here and reminisce all day but it doesn't serve me any good. I think outside of entertainment and pleasure, maintaining our archives for our community is important because it helps set a template for people who are lost in their current lives.

For example, at a personal level, I think archives can serve in that sense, people struggling with their own identities and not seeing themselves. I think if you can look back at an old photo book or AIDS activism, the way people found each other the networks that were created that way. I think, for the queer community, the one thing that has kept us together and growing is the way that we network and connect and communicate. We can do it better, we can reflect on and think of your purpose again. There are other forms of queerness. I listen to this podcast and they speak about LA in the 90s and 80s in the most beautiful way, because there is a reverence for it but they also just let it go. This is what it was and this is how he did it. This is the origin of this building, what it used to be. It's not that anymore. So let it go but have fun.

B: I grew up with Walter Mercado in our home. And that Netflix film *Con Mucho Mucho Amor* came out a few years ago. And it is another example of how he looks different. How it shapeshifts, but also, Walter's queerness was never questioned it was accepted in a way that maybe compare him to Liberace. It was more than what Liberace was doing. It was a whole lifestyle, it wasn't just for performance. It was 24/7. This is how I'm moving in a particular way and watching that documentary and hearing other men say this is what he meant to me and to my family shifts and complicates the narrow understanding of machismo. And to hear these people say that Walter Mercado and his bedazzled capes are queer. What does that mean? Walter Mercado was in my house, and then hearing that Walter Mercado was everywhere spanish-speaking families homes; did you also see or did you have Walter Mercado in your home?

J: oh, yeah, yeah, absolutely. And he came on when I got home from school. So he was usually on around 3, 330. I think the one thing that we can say about Walter Mercado is he was a healer and if we think about his indigenous practice, and within the Latinx community as well I think South American indigeneity. I know growing up, my aunt had a house boy who was the most flamboyant person. He scared me. I was young, I was 6 or 7 and I'd never seen anything like it. He was in full possession of femininity. He was not the other men that I was surrounded by and he really made a huge impact on me, and, I said, I was scared of him. But I was fascinated by him, and the way he was in the world, in 1985, with long black hair and tight shirts with the buttons open in this little provincial town. There are folks out there within all queer space we cannot hide our power. I think Walter Mercado was one of them. Our family culturally speaking, globally speaking, we've been assigned this one way to come out to the family: the formula is to sit folks down, tell them your gay. And well, no I don't necessarily need to sit my family down and tell them for them to know I'm queer. They don't need to know about my sexuality, because when you're coming out you're essentially putting your sexuality out on the table and some Latinx scholars argue that families already know, and not all cultures believe in coming out the same way. And the way that mainstream culture frames coming out is actually really damaging.

Are you familiar with Juan Gabriel? He passed away in 2016. We were living in New York when he passed away, and we had just seen him at the [Madison Square] Garden the year before. He has also always been one of the figures that were unabashedly always present but with more flare. And people couldn't challenge him because he was Mexico's best songwriter. For many years, he wrote some of the most beautiful songs that to this day you play at funerals at weddings. He's almost every Mexican mother's favorite singer. My mother saw him in concert many times. My mother loves him and so I remember thinking when I was a kid as well, if she loved him, and he's this, and I'm this, then she'll eventually come around to me because Juan Gabriel and I are the same and she loves him. And I had an encounter with him when I was in my 20s. That's a whole other story for another day. But it affirmed a lot of things for me about him, and it just made me love him more. Like Walter Mercado, he just existed and wasn't part of anything he's just undeniably himself. And he happens to be writing the most beautiful lyrics ever to come out of Mexico. As he got older and then later died all of these secrets of his sex life with all of these men, and all of these guys trying to write tell-all's and it's just as if nobody knew a shocking secret girl. We know it's fine.

B: Yeah, there is definitely love that my mom had for Juan Gabriel, excited to see him in concert when he would come to the DC area, but it was also a different love where she was, Oh, my God, I love his songs! I feel serenaded too, I feel he's speaking to the life that I'm living. But then, when it came to Luis, that was different. She said it was a different desire that came out of wanting to see him. And so for me, understanding how music manifests in my mom is what love can look like in various ways when it comes to music and representation. Because in my mind you're pining for this man who's maybe I don't know 20 years younger and then to see that happen with Ricky Martin later on. I have a very Caribbean Puerto Rican centric understanding of queerness which make sense to me. Here's what it looks like in this Mariachi example. Here's what looks in this lowrider culture or whatever else it is because that's not what we have. We have a carnival. These performances are not performances. It was really people showing up. Bringing their full selves into this long-term musical legendary archive that they're offering us, and I feel like that's what I've seen. So when I look back at pictures of Menudo and Ricky Martin I'm seeing he was totally queer then, too. The relief to be in a space where, Ricky Martin, a fifty-something, gay dad can now take, pictures in BDSM attire and leather. I don't know if you saw that spread.

J: No, but i'm about to look it up.

B: This being an aesthetic of BDSM kink attire that is now being incorporated into a more mainstream public which is really interesting. It's become a fashion thing on the red carpet.

J: Well, one thing I wanted to say as we were talking, I remember when I worked in New York, and I worked at a Latinx specific organization LGB because the Director was not trying to work with the trans community. But It was a really toxic place, and it was predominantly Black folks who worked there and were predominantly Caribbean identified. And what struck me and made me feel like an outsider is the drag of machismo. It is drag to the point of surgery and these ideas that were thought to be feminine were flipped; where back in the day, before plastic surgery, machismo was translated as I'm not gonna take a shower that's for girls I'm a man and I smell like a man! Ranchero! Machismo of my people. It was about trying not to appear too manicured or to clean, because that meant that you were partaking in beauty care. And now it's this thing where men go and get surgery to implant big muscles and big chests and big butts, and then we wear super tight clothes. Yeah, that's the gayest shit of everything, that deep voice that you're fighting to maintain and fashion with different men. Truly it's tight clothing. And then at a bathhouse there was this guy dressing up, getting ready to go out in the locker room. I had always wondered How did you guys get on such tight clothes? It's so tight it looks so uncomfortable. but it's the fashion and this guy started putting on a basically a griddle, I with the buckles and everything, and you're in this space that's hyper masculine supposed to be for men, and space where gay and heterosexual men might go to hideout and see desire and pleasure, and he goes out into his daily life wearing a girdle, that has always been assigned to women. It's interesting how these things get sort of lost, we're not talking about machismo standards now, it's just a beauty standard, it's not real. I think culturally now, the shift has been. is that achievement of the concept is more of a performance.

B: Yeah, then it used to be that it was meant to be exciting, and make you desirable versus back in the day, where it's supposed to make you intimidating. I think the Ricky Martin spread it's just such a great representation of machismo as performance. He has this chest plate made of silver or titanium, whatever it is. but that's chiseled. And yeah, maybe he does have a body but it also is just it's this performance that is playful. It's definitely queering but it's also fashion, and I appreciate this because then his queerness isn't the accessory. His kids aren't the accessory that's really who he is, and the accessories and the adornment of his body become these other pieces, and he chooses to engage in a particular narrative, a particular type of storytelling. And in 1987, would Ricky Martin have thought this was possible? Those are interesting representations to be a part of and to witness that happening actively really shifts the perspectives of what it means. What are important reminders that you would like to note for readers or are there any reminders?

J: I don't know if it's an important reminder, but it's just some things that I either thought about or questioned myself. I feel the pandemic, for example, starting in 2020 until now, has been an uptake on social media. Instagram and people expected sexuality. I don't think people were doing it as much as I've seen it rise to the point where you have people looking to have a good time and Twitter accounts really showing off not only through words, but visually what they desire, or what their longings are. I think that separation from that gap in socialization really puts people in this place where desire and longing to be desired and understanding your own body, all of that I think was impacted when we were forced to sit with ourselves. And so I think that moment of reflection really opened that up for a lot of people. And I don't know where that would fit in here and I definitely have to unpack that a little more. But I have been really nosy lately. When 50 Shades of Gray came out, for example, you had these clusters of women who were becoming more open sexually, or talking about their sexuality more in ways that have never been experienced. I think it was because they were exposed to it in a way that was not violent or was not as they were, not a victim to something. And so I think that that level of empowerment really helped.

On apps, for example, the disparities how gay men are so quick to attach themselves and their identity to a sexual position. How that's someone's preferred sexual position, for example, bottom or top, how that is at the forefront of how people make decisions. I worked in sex shops from when I was 18 until I was 23 so I'm familiar with those who are either uncomfortable or proud or indifferent about how some approach their sexuality. I think now from what I'm seeing on social media and the trends that I'm seeing there's this all out submission for more straight men who are willing to bottom that's now an option for a lot of straight men!

B: A lot of my friends in LA who are femme share there are no more tops in LA and I think first of all that's just not true and I hear what you're saying is more or y'all are noticing that you want to be cared for that you want to be taking care of and held.

J: I remember my first real boyfriend when I was 14. He was 18, and he asked me "are you a top or a bottom?" I had no idea what it meant, but in my imagination at the time, my uninformed imagination I said Bottom, not because I wanted him to fuck me, but because I wanted to be held. That's how I translated it. And it makes sense to me that more people need this holding in a particular way at the point in the world that we're in. So it makes a lot of sense for real.

LIST OF CONTRIBUTORS

Jessica Jolie Badonsky, MSN, FNP-BC is a board-certified Family Nurse Practitioner with 18 years of experience in the wellness space. For over ten years, her focus has been on sex, menopause transition, and mind-expanding healing modalities. Jessica is a parent of three amazing children, partner of a US military veteran, and constant student of emotional intelligence, sex, sexuality, intimacy, science, wellness, consciousness, psychedelics, and erotic wisdom.

Bina Bakhtiar is a Muslim sex therapist, educator, and an activist, working with communities of color, immigrants, and bicultural/multicultural communities. She considers her therapist and educator role as a form of activism – by honoring the experiences and voices of others, bearing witness to their journeys and their healing, and empowering them to shape/reshape their narratives to living a value-based life.

Karen B. K. Chan is an award-winning sex and emotional literacy educator in Toronto, Canada, with 25+ years of experience. BK is dedicated to having difficult conversations that are real, transformative, and kind. She integrates curriculum content into stories, and theory into practice. BK works with individuals, groups, and organizations, and trains professionals across disciplines. Her YouTube video *Jam* is used as a teaching resource internationally, and her chapter on the importance of creative play was part of the AASECT 2014 Book of the Year. BK's work has also appeared in Toronto Book Award finalist *Any Other Way* (Coach House 2017), Sexology International, the Tete-a-Tete, and Action Canada's national education manual. BK's favorite ways to learn and teach are through stories, metaphors, and things that make people laugh.

Juan Fernández analyzes the various ways digital social media is used by contemporary Chicana/o/x artists and cultural producers. His thesis focused on the performance of ethnicity, gender, cultural citizenship, and sexuality within social networking apps like Instagram and the effects of the digital identity on the reflected community. Juan earned his MA in Media Studies + Social Change at Queens College, CUNY. He is also a graduate of UCLA holding a BA in Chicana/o Studies & LGBTQ Studies. His previous work as a scholar/activist has focused on gay Chicano fiction and storytelling, performance, and archiving Queer Chicana/o/x cultural productions. This includes archiving the work of the Maricón Collective for the UCLA Chicano Studies Resource Center. He also created and produced the Movida Storytelling Project in collaboration with the Bronx Academy of Arts and Dance.

Kalash Magenta Fire, CMT, MSW is an east coast native with a BA in Psychology and a Master's in Social Work and Sociology. Kalash (pronounced: kaa-lish) is Certified Massage Therapist, Reiki II Practitioner, empathic life coach and Doula dedicated to helping others obtain their optimum physical, mental, and emotional balance. Kalash enjoys the study of anatomy, neuromuscular therapy, theta healing, and yoga with authentic movement, with a special interest/experience in working with diverse bodies, cultures, and experiences. Kalash is an agender femme Intersex extraterrestrial unicorn dragon with firm pronouns of they / them. Kalash is neither female nor male.

Sara C. Flowers, DrPH, is the Vice President of Education & Training at Planned Parenthood Federation of America. Planned Parenthood is the nation's largest provider of sex education, providing expert information, resources, and guidance to parents, caregivers, and young people, both online and in communities across the country.

Dr. Flowers' passion for sex education began as a high school student, when she led the Annual AIDS Awareness Day for her peers at Spring Valley Senior High School in the late 1990s. Since then, she has written, implemented, and evaluated sex education programs and curricula for Boys and Girls Clubs of Greater Washington, The George Washington University Student Health Service, the Association of Reproductive Health Professionals, and Cornell University Cooperative Extension – New York City.

Prior to joining PPFA, Dr. Flowers was Director of Youth Initiatives for Love Heals Center for Youth & Families at GMHC. In this role, she expanded existing and launched new programs as well as oversaw sex education and leadership program curriculum development and revision. She also coordinated quantitative and qualitative program evaluation and reporting; cultivated and maintained community partnerships; and hired, trained, and managed staff and a freelance health education team. Concurrently, Dr. Flowers was an adjunct assistant professor for York College, CUNY while serving as a Post-Doctoral Research Fellow for the college's Collaborative Research Group on Health Policy & Promotion + the UrbanHealth Lab.

Dr. Flowers previously served as a member of the Boards of Directors of both the New York Abortion Access Fund (NYAAF) and SIECUS: Sex Ed for Social Change. She is a member of Women of Color Sexual Health Network (WOCSHN), a trainer on emotional intelligence with Equilibrium Dynamics in San Francisco, and a published author. Her most recent publications are "Sisterhood Unexpected: "I Met My Best Friend in LEAP!" and Other Narratives by LEAP for Girls Alumnae New York City, 2006–2016" (2022), and "Enacting Our Multidimensional Power: Black Women Sex Educators Demonstrate the Value of an Intersectional Sexuality Education Framework" (2018).

Dr. Flowers holds a Doctorate in Public Health from The Graduate School and University Center, CUNY, as well as a BA in Psychology and a Master of Public Health degree, both from The George Washington University.

Elliott Fukui lives in California and has been an organizer, trainer, and facilitator for 20 years across different movements, working with organizations, collectives, friends, and family. He came to community organizing through his own lived experiences of violence and oppression, having spent much of his adolescence being forcibly shuffled in and out of psychiatric facilities, day treatment programs, and special education classrooms due to his psycho-social disabilities. He comes to this work as a survivor of childhood sexual abuse and hate violence. At 16 years old, he went non-med compliant and began the long journey of learning how to survive as a mad queer and trans-low-income survivor of color in a deeply misaligned and oppressive world. In his early 20s, and about to reach a breaking point, he reached out to comrades and chosen family and asked if they would be his wellness and safety team, so that he wouldn't have to go back onto the wards or back on medication. It's been over ten years since they began that experiment together, and he has not been back to a facility or back on medication since. His website, the resources, and facilitation and training are imperfect, ever-evolving offerings for anyone who has experienced an emotional crisis or loved someone in an emotional crisis.

Melina Gaze is a sexuality educator and performer based in Chicago. Melina is the co-Founder and Director of Vulgar.mx, a Spanish language sexuality education group focused on pleasure and social justice. In 2021, Melina started a PhD program in the Department of Comparative Human Development at the University of Chicago, where they are researching emerging trends in sexuality education. In addition to their education work, they create and perform original cabaret and have played a bunch of DIY spaces internationally, including the National Feminist Conference of Mexico and Gay Pride Amsterdam.

Serina Payan Hazelwood, CSES (she/her) is a queer, Indigenous-Chicana, scholar, and somatic community collaborator. She is a certified Holistic Sexuality Educator and yoga teacher dedicated to liberatory praxis through Indigenous Knowledges. Her work is rooted in the cosmologies of the land. Reclamation, Ritual, and Renewal are the guiding value systems that inform the human experience of her work. Serina is transdisciplinary and her work is influenced by the Nahui Ollin Mexican Indigenous Epistemology (Way of Knowing). The anti and decolonial, queer, and feminist of-color methodologies support the andro-heutagogy (self-determined) and Indigenous pedagogies that create collaborative and sustainable learning spaces.

Serina established a Sustainability in Justice Policy and a Boundary Statement for White Participants that facilitates dialog and the potential for systemic changes within predominantly and historically white institutions (PHWI). She co-authored the published article, Reimagining U.S. Federal Land Management through Decolonization and Indigenous Value Systems in 2021. Serina is in the final stages of a Master's program that will lead to a Doctorate in Sustainability in Education from Prescott College.

Serina is a 48-year-old daughter, mother, sister, partner, friend, and Pisces with a Gemini rising. Serina was born and raised on the Hohokam, Tohono O'odham, and Akimel O'odham sacred lands (Phoenix, Arizona). Her matriarchal ancestors descend from New Mexico, Chihuahua, Mexico, and colonizing Spain. Her patriarchal ancestors are settler-colonists from England, Scotland, and Ireland. Serina regenerates from the systems of white supremacy by finding radical joy in gardening, rollerskating, reading, cooking, and dancing (solo and with the community).

Bianca I. Laureano, PhD, MA[2], CSE, CSES, is an award-winning educator, curriculum writer, and sexologist. She is a co-foundress of the Women of Color Sexual Health Network (WOCSHN) and The LatiNegrxs Project. Her most recent project is ANTE UP! a virtual freedom school offering professional development and courses we need for the world we have inherited. Bianca has spent her entire adult life working on topics of sexuality, racialization, justice, and gender. She has earned a BA from the University of Maryland, College Park in Latino Women's Health (2000), a master of arts degree from NYU in Human Sexuality Education (2002), and a master of arts degree from the University of Maryland, College Park in Women's Studies (2006) with a focus on race and racialization where she was a CrISP Scholar trained in intersectional and feminist theories and supported the creation of the Intersectional Research Database. In 2020 she was awarded an honorary doctorate by the California Institute for Integral Studies for her work in expanding the US sexuality field. She has written several curricula that focus on communities of color: *What's the REAL DEAL about Love and Solidarity?* (2015) and *Communication MixTape: Speak On It Vol 1.* (2017) and wrote the sexual and reproductive justice discussion guide for the NYC Department of Health and Mental Hygiene published in 2018. She has written curricula and led the curriculum development for the award-winning Netflix film Crip Camp and PBS documentary I Didn't See You There, both guided by disability justice principles. Bianca has been on the board of CLAGS, the LGBTQ Center at CUNY, and The Black Girl Project and SisterSong. She is an AASECT-certified sexuality educator and supervisor. Find out more about Bianca at her website BiancaLaureano.com and AnteUpPD.com.

Nhakia Outland (she, her, hers) is a queer, Black woman and mother of three children. She is a social worker, sexuality educator, social work field instructor, adjunct professor, and consultant with more than 15 years' experience working primarily with people of color, Black, Latinx, and LGBTQ+ communities in different capacities. Nhakia has worked in diverse clinical, community, private sectors, non-profit, and healthcare settings throughout her career. Currently, she is building Prevention Meets Fashion Inc (PMF), a 501c3 non-profit that she founded in 2018 after being frustrated with the way many Black and Black LGBTQ people were being treated when coming in to access sexual and reproductive health services. She knew that there could be other ways to provide historically excluded communities with the much-needed information about comprehensive sex education and have a space to discuss these crucial topics in a non-judgmental, non-risk-based manner.

On the academic front, Nhakia received her Bachelor's degree from Chestnut Hill College in Human Service and Women Studies in Philadelphia, PA before earning her Master's in Social Work (MSW) degree in Community and Policy with a focus on Children, Youth and Families from Temple University in Philadelphia, PA and post-graduate certificate in Sex Therapy from Council For Relationships. She also has a host of other certificates and certifications.

To keep in contact, email Nhakia at preventionmeetsfashion@gmail.com, follow PMF on Instagram and LinkedIn @preventionmeetsfashion, and visit our website www.preventionmeetsfashion.org

Francisco Ramírez, MPH, holds a Master of Public Health (concentration in sexuality and health) from Columbia University's Mailman School of Public Health where he was named a Rosenfield Scholar in Sexual and Reproductive Health. For 20 years, Francisco has dedicated his career to responding to the sexual health and public health needs of diverse communities worldwide. He has led multi-lingual training, education, and research efforts for organizations including: the United Nations (UNICEF, UNAIDS, UNFPA, UN Department of Peacekeeping Operations), MTV, Planned Parenthood, Durex, Hetrick-Martin Institute, Albert Einstein College of Medicine, New York Academy of Medicine, and the NAACP. He is a frequent speaker on sexuality education, sexual violence, and diversity and inclusion. He is co-founder of the newly released sex education app OkaySo and sits on the advisory board of Circle of 6, a sexual assault prevention app with users in 36 countries. Since 2008, Francisco has offered #FreeSexAdvice, free advice on relationships, sex, and dating to passersby in New York City parks. Francisco also serves as a prominent voice in the media on sexual health issues. He is a regular host and producer at MTV as well as other television networks. His contributions include overseeing production of content for the award-winning MTV Staying Alive campaign and serving as a Global Correspondent for MTV Voices. Francisco is also sought out to create dynamic multimedia content for health education organizations. In addition, Francisco has been featured in: The New York Times, The Wall Street Journal, National Public Radio, and the Savage LoveCast with Dan Savage.

Jadelynn St Dre (she/her) is a facilitator, trauma therapist, organizer, and interdisciplinary performance artist, based out of Durham, NC and the Bay Area, CA. As a queer, biracial, Latinx, cis femme, Jadelynn entered into the practice of psychotherapy intent on contributing to the eradication of oppressive systems within the field. After obtaining her MA, Jadelynn worked within nonprofit antiviolence agencies and shelters providing clinical services, consultation, and program development. Currently, Jadelynn is a Licensed Marriage and Family Therapist and AASECT Certified Sex Therapist, specializing in sexual and intimate partner assault, intergenerational trauma, and sex therapy, primarily with LGBTQIA2S+ individuals and relationships. In addition, she offers consultation and facilitation around accountability and trauma-informed care and provides support to emerging practitioners. Jadelynn is a core facilitator with Ante Up! Professional Development and is adjunct faculty at Lesley University (Massachusetts).

Jadelynn's original and collaborative artistic work has been shown nationally, internationally, and in print. Her multidisciplinary artistic project, Choreographies of Disclosure: What the Mind Forgets will be written about as chapters in two upcoming publications.

Through the above, Jadelynn has rooted her heart in community organizing, having worked within the antiviolence movement for over a decade. She was the co-founder and artistic director of DISCLOSE, a queer collective of artists and educators committed to organizing arts-based community engagement in the eradication of sexual violence. Nationally, she organized as part of the Leadership Team of The Monument Quilt, a crowd-sourced collection of thousands of stories from survivors of rape and abuse, displayed on the National Mall in 2019. She is honored to be a queer mother to a magical little one, whom she lovingly tends with her brilliant partner. Together, they are the source of her most profound joy.

Christina Tesoro, LMSW, is a writer, sex educator, and pleasure-focused somatic trauma therapist from Queens, NY. They are also the author of *Death to Whorephobia: A Guide to Sex Worker Affirming Care*, an adaptation of her graduate thesis studying sex workers' experiences of sex work stigma from mental health care providers. Christina writes about sex and gender from a qariwarmi and non-binary, reconnecting indigenous, and ancestral veneration perspective. In their therapeutic practice, they celebrate queer alternatives and adaptations to oppressive colonial systems and the harms of nuclear family model and supports work queer folks of all relationship styles in creating relationships based on care, reciprocity, and a dynamic balance of autonomy and interdependence.

Sucia Urrea (they/them) is a disabled, nonbinary Colombian educator and researcher based in Mexico City. Sucia is co-founder and director of Vulgar, a sex ed collective in Mexico. They have over ten years of experience in program development, facilitation, and anthropological research, and they are passionate about alternative pedagogies for individual and collective liberation. They also love writing poetry, making jewelry, salsa dancing, and perreo. Sucia is a PhD candidate in Sociocultural Anthropology at the University of Illinois at Urbana Champaign.

Sean Saifa Wall is a Black intersex and transgender activist known as the co-founder of Intersex Justice Project. The organization's #EndIntersexSurgery campaign pressured Lurie Children's Hospital of Chicago to become the first medical institution in the United States to denounce and further investigate intersex genital surgeries on infants. The Google/Stink Films documentary Stonewall Forever documents the campaign. A seasoned community activist, Saifa made history by confronting the surgeon who performed his non-consensual surgeries on ABC News Nightline. His features include the *Huffington Post*, NBC, Afropunk: Solutions Sessions, *Gender Outlaws:The Next Generation*, *Trans Bodies, Trans Selves*, *Narrative Inquiry in Bioethics*, *The Washington Blade*, *The Guardian*, and *The Remedy: Queer and Trans Voices on Health and Healthcare*, and his TEDx talk "36 Revolutions of Change."

Saifa is the former Board President of interACT: Advocates for Intersex Youth and a former advisor to the Astraea Intersex Fund for Human Rights. Born and raised in the Bronx, Saifa attended Williams College and has since lived and worked in New York City, the San Francisco Bay Area, and Atlanta. He is currently pursuing a PhD with the INIA Project in England with his dog, Justice.

INDEX

9781032021126